Adaptation in Bulgaria:

Three Bulgarian Productions of American Plays

ALSO BY KEN MOSKOWITZ

Greater Washington Area Bicycle Atlas

Cover photo: Ivan Vazov National Theatre of Bulgaria production of *Angels in America*, premiered on October 26, 2010. With Snezhina Petrova, Vladimir Karamazov, Vladimir Penev, and Zahari Baharov. Photograph by Atanas Kunchev.

Adaptation in Bulgaria:

Three Bulgarian Productions of American Plays

Ken Moskowitz

Penny-a-Page Press
Washington, D.C.

Penny-a-Page Press
Washington, D.C.

Copyright © 2015 by Ken Moskowitz
All Rights Reserved

Published by Penny-a-Page Press, Washington, D.C.
http://pennyapagepress.blogspot.com

10 9 8 7 6 5 4 3 2 1

Library of Congress Cataloging-in-Publication Data is available.

ISBN: 0692384871
ISBN-13: 978-0692384879

This book is dedicated to Dr. Iskra Nikolova, Professor of Theatre at the National Academy of Theatre and Film Arts (NATFA) in Sofia, Bulgaria. Dr. Nikolva, an inspiration to her students and the supervisor of the doctoral dissertation on which this book is based, passed away on November 12, 2012, after a long struggle with cancer.

The author wishes to thank Dr. Yoko Shoji, who designed the tables and bar graphs in the appendix.

TABLE OF CONTENTS

Introduction:		1
Chapter ONE:	The Bulgarian Dramatic Theatre	7
Chapter TWO:	Literature Review, Audiences, and Methodology	17
	The Literature of Adaptation and Audience Reception: A Review	
	Audiences and Reception: The Ivan Vazov National Theatre Case	
	Methodology or Research Design	
Chapter THREE:	The Three Productions: One Flew Over the Cuckoo's Nest, Angels in America, and The Goat, or Who is Sylvia?	63
	Public Reception: Thematic Controversy and Awards	
	Translation and Language: Obscenity and Humor	
	The Gay World in U.S. and Bulgarian Theatre and Society	
Chapter FOUR:	One Flew Over the Cuckoo's Nest: A Free Adaptation	77
	History of the Play's Productions	
	The Ivan Vazov National Theatre Production	
	The Critical Reactions	
	The Public Reception: Results of the Audience Questionnaires	
Chapter FIVE:	Angels in America: A Faithful Adaptation of Political Message	131

	History of the Play's Productions	
	The Ivan Vazov National Theatre Production	
	The Critical Reaction	
	The Public Reception: Results of the Audience Questionnaires	
Chapter SIX:	The Goat, or Who is Sylvia?: A Faithful Adaptation	165
	History of the Play's Productions	
	The Ivan Vazov National Theatre Production	
	The Critical Reactions	
	The Public Reception: Results of the Audience Questionnaires	
Chapter SEVEN:	Conclusions	199
	Audiences, Equivalences, and Free Adaptation	
	Audiences and Success	
	Mamet on Adaptation and Success	
	Answering the Research Questions	
Bibliography		221
	Articles and Books	221
	Reviews	235
Appendices		245
A.1	Table of Reviews of One Flew Over the Cuckoo's Nest in New York and Chicago	245
A.2	Table of Reviews of One Flew Over the Cuckoo's Nest at the Ivan Vazov National Theatre	247
A.3	Table of Reviews of Angels in America in New York City	249
A.4	Table of Reviews of Angels in America	252

	at the Ivan Vazov National Theatre	
A.5	Table of Reviews of The Goat in New York City	256
A.6	Table of Reviews of The Goat at the Ivan Vazov National Theatre	259
A.7	Questionnaire for One Flew Over the Cuckoo's Nest	262
A.8	Questionnaire for One Flew Over the Cuckoo's Nest, Bulgarian language version	265
A.9	Table of Bulgarians' Results for Cuckoo's Nest (44)	269
A.10	Table of Americans' Results for Cuckoo's Nest (8)	273
A.11	Questionnaire for Angels in America	277
A.12	Questionnaire for Angels in America, Bulgarian language version	280
A.13	Table of Bulgarians' Results for Angels in America (36)	283
A.14	Questionnaire for The Goat	287
A.15	Questionnaire for The Goat, Bulgarian language version	290
A.16	Table of Bulgarians' Results for The Goat	293
A.17	Table of Americans' Results for The Goat	298
A.18	List of Interviewees and Dates of Interviews	299
A.19	National Theatre Flyer for The Goat	301
A.20	Positive Reviews at the National Theatre, Sofia	302
A.21	Comparative Success of the Plays in Sofia	303
Index		305

INTRODUCTION

What the audience wants is so different from what a serious playwright wants. – Edward Albee in an interview with Steven Drukman, *New York* magazine

When plays from one culture and language are translated and adapted to different languages and culture, there inevitably will be ramifications in the interpretation, understanding, and audience reception. This study looks at three successful plays from the American stage and compares them to the Bulgarian translations and adaptations of the plays.

This work on the adaptation and reception of the plays is the result of good timing in several ways. Thanks to the America for Bulgaria Foundation, the Ivan Vazov National Theatre in Sofia recently featured three American plays, which have won acclaim in their native productions. They are *One Flew Over the Cuckoo's Nest* (Broadway premier, 1963), by Dale Wasserman; *Angels in America* (1992), by Tony Kushner; and *The Goat, or Who is Sylvia?* (2002), by Edward Albee. The Kushner and Albee plays were originally written as dramas, but *Cuckoo's Nest* was based on the eponymous novel by Ken Kesey. *The Goat* opened in Sofia in the fall of 2009, and the other two were part of the Theatre's American Season of 2010-11. *Cuckoo's Nest* and *The Goat* were hits that were still running at the Theatre in June, 2012.

The American Season also included adaptations of Arthur Miller's *Death of a Salesman* (1949) and Tracy Letts's *August*

Osage County (2007). I chose to study the first three plays, however, because of their range of styles, subjects, and diverse challenges for adaptation, as we shall see later. Also, because they are all roughly contemporary American works: though *Cuckoo's Nest* opened in New York fifty years ago, I was able to interview the producer of the first successful production of the play, and even saw this production. For similar reasons, I chose the other two plays because I have seen other works by their authors, and also because I had opportunities to interview the playwrights for this study.

Since I was also residing in Sofia from July, 2009 to July, 2012, I was fortunate to have the opportunity to see each productions multiple times, and to talk at length to the creative teams behind them, while also bringing my experience of play-going in the United States. This is not to claim a unique status, but just to say that this personal situation aided me in this cross-cultural study. There might not be many scholars with so fortunate a background, and to have this advantage in making the effort to understand how the Bulgarian practitioners made their creative choices and went about their productions.

This study is composed of three major sections: a review of the literature of cultural adaptation of theatre, and of audience reception; an examination of the critical and professional reviewers' reception of the three plays both in the U.S. and in Bulgaria; and an empirical study of the audience reception of the plays at the Ivan Vazov Theatre based on audience questionnaires that I developed and distributed. Of course I do not have survey results from the audiences in New York, but then most of these questions probe how well the plays were adapted in Sofia, and tie this to demographic data, which are not within my subject of study. I do have some comparative audience demographic data based on others' surveys in my conclusion, chapter seven.

The most basic question I am trying to answer is: Are these current Bulgarian productions successful based on the terms the directors, dramaturges, and their creative colleagues have set for themselves? In other words, have they achieved what they set out to do? I analyze and measure with reference not only to the questionnaires, which tell me if the audiences understand or appreciate the plays in the ways that the creative teams do, but also relative to what the original playwrights and directors in the U.S. have said about them—when they have said anything definitive or clear at all.

These questions are important for theatre producers and directors who face three challenges when they adapt plays: commercial and critical success, of course, but also bringing the impact of a foreign work to a domestic audience. Any follower of the Anglo-American theatre can see how difficult this is, in that even Broadway or London hits often fail to translate well across the ocean. The challenge is much greater when language and broader cultural differences are involved.

This goal of understanding success, a term to be explored later, necessarily encompasses a study of two broad topics, i.e., both the

American and Bulgarian productions, and the audience reception, but confined to that in Bulgaria.

My methodology, as noted above, will be cross-cultural, with a comparative perspective, and inter-disciplinary, in that it encompasses both theatre studies and the empirical or sociological element of the audience surveys.

Concretely, my three research questions are the following:

1. What transformations did the Bulgarian "adapters"—the dramaturges, directors, and translators—of the three American plays make in the adaptation? What if anything was "untranslatable" and how did they handle that?

2. What lessons or messages does the reaction of the Bulgarian theatre audience and the Bulgarian theatre critics to the three plays have for the creative teams?

3. What do these three adaptations tell us about the problems of theatrical adaptation in general? How do these lessons diverge from current thinking or the literature on adaptation?

The structure of this study is as follows: Chapter one introduces the contemporary Bulgarian theatre scene, and the unique place of the Ivan Vazov National Theatre in it. This may help to clarify some of the artistic choices as well as the audience's social or cultural attitudes which may incline them to react to the dramas in certain ways.

In chapter two, I review the literature of cultural adaptation. I attempt to familiarize the reader with critical terms and findings to better conceptualize the research questions, and to critique the literature of adaptation and audience reception. I find that much has been written about cultural adaptation, by practitioners as well as by scholars and theorists, but much less about audience reception, and of that, not all of it is written with precision and objectivity. In this chapter, I also explain my research design and the choices I made regarding content and objectives.

Chapter three provides an overview of the three plays under study, and chapters four, five, and six look at each play in turn. I do this first analytically, but then also in regard to the two methodologies of the study, that is, by contrasting reviews and criticism of the plays in the U.S. and Bulgaria, and then by analyzing the audience questionnaires mentioned above.

Chapter seven provides my general conclusions, and discusses these findings, and asks to what degree I have accomplished my goals.

I also provide appendices containing the questionnaires themselves, spreadsheets summarizing the critical reviews in both countries, two tables of results, and two bibliographies.

CHAPTER ONE: The Bulgarian Dramatic Theatre

It is in observing the current Bulgarian theatre scene that I am most conscious of my role as an outsider. Whereas Bulgarians talk with pride of an artistic tradition that has sustained its most gifted and skilled performance artists, as well as masters of written Bulgarian, I see two major trends that may influence critical and popular reception of play productions. One is the unique role of theatre in contributing to national identity in Eastern Europe and the Balkans. The second is the legacy of the socialist state's support for the arts. I would hesitate to mention these, except that these influences are particularly pronounced at the Ivan Vazov National Theatre because of its leading and indeed unique role in Bulgaria.

Regarding national identity, one can observe a wave of romantic national revival that swept across Europe from West to East starting with the Enlightenment. This has been celebrated as the Renaissance or Vazrazhdane (възраждане) in Bulgarian history. The core elements of identity were (and to a degree still are) the mythic landscape, the vernacular or national language, and the native music, from modest folk melodies up to the classics. One chief result of this nationalist wave, in addition to national museums, was the construction of national theatres, the sanctums of the sacred languages. The process is documented well in Ivan T. Berend's *History Derailed*, in which he quotes the Bulgarian romantic nationalist Ljuben Karavelov: "Every nation should take pride in its language…[and] purify it of foreign garbage—namely Turkish, Greek, Russian and Church Slavonic words" (Berend, 2003: 51).

This historical phase is also noted by the French actor, poet, director, translator, and theatre manager Antoine Vitez, whose formula is that the theatre is, "the place where a people comes to hear its language." He has said that, "the construction through subscriptions of the National Czech Theatre in the Germanicized Prague of the Austro-Hungarian Empire: It was an explicit political declaration" (Pavis, 1996:127). Vitez adds, tellingly, "The stage is the laboratory of the language and actions of the nation. Society knows more or less clearly that in these edifices we call theatres people work for hours on end in order to increase, purify and transform the actions and intonations of everyday life" (ibid.).

A central part of the nationalist wave was the national drama, usually an epic or tragedy. Enter Ivan Vazov, often cited as the Patriarch of Bulgarian literature. Along with Dobri Vojnikov, the name of Vazov and, in turn the national theatre named in his honor, cannot be detached from this tradition. This singular honor was granted to one who produced, according to the Hungarian-American Berend, "mostly second-rate" work (2003:72), though the legacy of Vazov, and his anti-Ottoman masterpiece, *Under the Yoke* (*Pod Igoto*, "Под игото") (1889-90) have been a matter of heated debate among scholars of Bulgarian literature. "A great many national cultural heroes who had a tremendous impact on the development of their countries did not represent the highest standards of contemporary art and literature" (Berend, 2003:58).

However, a number of contemporary literary critics, such as Milena Tsaneva (2000) and Svetlozar Igov (2010), have defended the artistic value of Vazov's work, arguing that Vazov's poetry was a true event in the history of Bulgarian literature that opened new creative horizons for the nation's poetic tradition, while Vazov's prose is no less significant, since he is the founder of the Bulgarian novel tradition and the first Bulgarian master of short stories.

It seems that when audiences today enter the hallowed halls of the Ivan Vazov National Theatre, they are *inclined* to like what they watch. They are observing not any theatrical effort, but a national cause, as it were. Appreciation for such national productions is an expression of national pride and solidarity. With too many bright Bulgarians comprising a debilitating brain drain to the West, the national poets, playwrights, and actors, tethered to their unique national language, remain. This is one region where perhaps emigration has had very little effect. We should keep this in mind when we observe critical and public reception later (in particular my remarks in chapter two below on audience expectations and reaction).

The role of the socialist government's support for the arts is better known and documented, as both a boon for some artists, but also a Faustian bargain that demanded self-censorship and fealty to corrupt ideals. Officially sanctioned dramatic optimism was coupled with the creation of new theatres and troupes, as well as the National Academy of Theatre and Film Arts (NATFA). Theatrical careers benefited from membership in the state-controlled Actors Union.

In this era, the National Theatre was official, accepted, strong, and somewhat staid, according to Nikola Vandov, theatre historian and dramaturge at the Satiric Theatre in Sofia (all references from him are from a personal interview, 18 May 2012). It attracted talented directors and actors, and served those in power, including as a venue to entertain distinguished foreign guests, mostly for productions of Bulgarian classic plays.

Lest we decry this period as a unique totalitarian aberration, it's helpful to quote poet and revolutionary hero Hristo Botev from the earlier period, that of the nation-building nineteenth century: "Science, as well as literature, poetry, and journalism…should have the character of national propaganda" (Berend, 2003:58). In that national spirit, the Salza i Smyah (Tear and Laughter, or Сълза и смях) professional troupe was founded in 1892, and the Ivan Vazov National Theatre was built in 1904. (Today the National Theatre has absorbed the Tear and Laughter, now housed in a smaller, nearby theatre of its own.)

The present National Theatre building, built according to an Austrian architectural design, was inaugurated on 3 January 1907. Its posh interior and lavish façade justify its inclusion on the list of Bulgarian architectural monuments. It has undergone many reconstructions and renovations, at great expense, the most recent being just several years ago.

The Theatre's three halls host about four new productions each year. The American adaptations are hardly rare: in recent years, the Theatre has hosted productions from France, Russia, Ireland,

Germany, and Japan, and it is currently (2012) featuring a Russian theatre season. Many Bulgarians express pride in the National Theatre, even though of late subsidies from foreign sources have meant that it features more plays of foreign origin that the other commercial theatres in Sofia, according to Vandov and other specialists. The permanent staff of 111 and in-house troupe of 41 actors are modest by Western national theatre scales, but outsized in the domestic theatrical world.

As touched on earlier, the National Theatre is fully subsidized and is in some sense a child of the Government of Bulgaria. Its budget is provided by the Ministry of Culture, but it is the Ministry of Finance which keeps a tight rein on its revenues and expenses.

According to the National Theatre's publicity materials, there were 77,910 spectators (presumably both paid and complimentary) in the year 2008 in the halls, and seat capacity that year was 79% of the total. This largely confirms Theatre managing director Pavel Vasev's (2012) claim that the halls are mostly full (Apostolova, 2011:17), which has been the case at every production I have seen.

The pride of the National Theatre's management is evident also in these assertions from its publicity materials:

> The best Bulgarian playwrights, directors and actors have proved themselves on the stage of the National Theatre "Ivan Vazov." At present the theatre has a leading role in the cultural life of the country, defending the high goals of artistry and popularity, and stands as a valorous member of the Thespian community in Europe.

We will see later that though it is not always possible to combine both "artistry and popularity," surveys below show that the National Theatre does a good job on this account. The Theatre's pride is reflected also in the creative momentum that it enjoyed several years after the fall of the Berlin Wall, according to Vandov. Vasil Stefanov, the new managing director in 1990, changed the status quo, and brought in new young directors and actors, though the talented, famous actors he fired still bear him a grudge. The 1990s were a painful period, with many experiments, and some awful shows, but this was needed for the transition, Vandov says.

Stefanov recruited and helped launch the careers of some of Bulgaria's most talented directors, including Alexander Morfov, Galin Stoev, Ivan Dobchev and Margarita Mladenova. Though no longer blessed by the authorities, the National Theatre maintained its prestige. More broadly, Bulgarian theatres jettisoned the propaganda, and in fact rushed to mount formerly banned works, as they enjoyed the freedom of the end of censorship, as well as spectacles, traditional Bulgarian plays, and avant-garde productions (Kortenska, 2000:11). There was also more entertainment, as theatres strove to earn revenue from ticket sales since their subsides were withdrawn by the new government. They provided more immediate thrills, but "were less interesting than the theatre in the parliament and in the public square, and they needed to entertain to compete," Vandov says.

The contention for the diminishing spoils of state or municipal subsidies has become fiercer during the current economic downturn.

Despite this, the Ivan Vazov Theatre and its branch, the Salza i Smyah, have an enviable position as theatres generously funded by the national government (along with the National Opera and Ballet). Whether they mount a national classic or an American import, they can do it in relatively lavish fashion. And this is in addition to the occasional, healthy infusions of grants from foundations or others.

In the case of the plays under consideration, the America for Bulgaria Foundation (ABF) was the benefactor. All three of them received generous sponsorship from this bi-national NGO, a legacy of the Bulgarian office of Bulgarian-American Enterprise Fund. This in turn was created by the U.S. Agency for International Development (USAID), a U.S. Government entity that both funds humanitarian relief and promotes Western values such as civil society. ABF does not deliberately aim to promote outré or racy theatre or other arts, but does openly aim to promote a European or American model of an open, democratic society. According to its website (http://www.americaforbulgaria.org/page/home, accessed 3 April 2011), "As part of the ABF mission, an effort will also be made to bring quality American art and artists to Bulgaria." So the Foundation's choice or approval of American theatre plays of a provocative flavor seems to reflect the wishes of its Board of Directors or Sofia-based staff. The two later plays are edgy even for the United States, and perhaps even more for Bulgaria today. The Foundation directors must have realized that even though *Cuckoo's Nest* and Albee have been popular in Bulgaria, this did not insure the success of the new productions.

One Flew Over the Cuckoo's Nest and *Angels in America* were supported by a grant to the National Theatre as part of an American theatre season, mentioned above. The ABF granted the National Theatre 140,000 Bulgarian leva, about US$100,000 (at an exchange rate of one US dollar to one lev in October, 2011), which covered the purchase of the staging rights and set costs. For *The Goat*, the ABF simply paid the costs of the visit of Edward Albee when he visited Sofia from New York City for about two weeks in 2009 to supervise the rehearsals and premiere, according to Nadia S. Zaharieva, Director, Programs for Art and Culture at the ABF (phone interview, October, 2011).

Given its custody by the Ministry of Culture, the National Theatre's budget is less of a concern than for other theatres and theatre companies, including those in the United States. Almost all Bulgarian actors and theatre people have confirmed that the Ivan Vazov National Theatre is the place to work for prestige, artistic merit, and job security.

I will return to the question of the position of the National Theatre and its dependence on state subsidies in the chapter below on *Angels in America*.

CHAPTER TWO: Literature Review, Audiences, and Methodology

What counted was what came over to the audience, no excuses and no mercy to be expected...The audience was an enemy that had to be overwhelmed and dominated like a woman, and only then loved.
− Elia Kazan's view of theatrical success, in Arthur Miller's *Timebends: A Life (*1987:272-3)

The Literature of Adaptation and Audience Reception: A Review

I will consider the literature of adaptation and audience reception separately below. My survey encompasses both scholarly analyses and the views of outspoken practitioners and playwrights, especially regarding adaptation.

ADAPTATION

According to Iskra Nikolova, "Broadly speaking, adaptation involves interchange between different sign systems, arts, genres, media and cultures. It spans a vast and varied territory bordering on translation, on the one hand, and on the intertextual and intercultural collage, on the other hand. It is often a collaborative process, in which the transition from page to stage or screen requires not only conceptual, semiotic and intermedial transformations but also adaptation to specific target audiences, horizons of expectation and modes of reception" (Nikolova, 2009:4).

In more general terms, the problem of adaptation is often framed as one of maintaining the spirit or intention of the original work, yet making appropriate changes so that it becomes understandable, fresh, or attractive, as much as possible, to a new or foreign audience. In

Bulgaria, Dr. Nikolova has said, "adaptation" means only a rewrite or translation; "cultural adaptation" more accurately refers to the process involved in bringing the three American plays to Bulgaria, i.e., both literal translations of the play texts and certain changes in the texts' references and the staging to make the works more understandable and appealing to the domestic audiences.

In one of the articles collected by Patrice Pavis, Marvin Carlson describes the works of intercultural directors Peter Brook and Ariane Mnouchkine as basically that of a hybrid that doesn't claim authenticity or any ethnological character. An intercultural adaptation like those of these directors is an effort to transform a non-Western, often classic original source into a meaningful Western theatrical product. The dilemma for such performances remains whether to favor the source or target culture (Pavis, 1996:80).

Carlson even goes so far as to introduce a system to assign numbers designating the "seven steps or possible stages of relationship between" the "culturally familiar and the culturally foreign" (Pavis, 1996:82). Though this work will take a more empirical route, I accept what seems to be one of Carlson's main points, when he quotes Javanese theatre expert Roger Long on Brook's production of the *Mahabharata*: Long says that no work of cultural adaptation can retain the essence of *both* the source and target culture (Pavis, 1996:83).

The literature commonly posits two schools of cultural adaptation. One is described as the "ethnocentric translation," or the type of translation that assimilates the original for one's target audience. Such cultural translators find equivalents of the original language, but risk distortion or loss of fidelity. The other and opposite method is to keep close to the original and produce an "exotic" or faithful translation, one perhaps more literary than immediately accessible, and which risks not being well understood by the new audience. This is more daunting in the case of the theatre than, say, for novels, since the text must be performed as well as read, which brings additional complexities.

Alexander Shurbanov, poet, literary critic, and Bulgaria's noted translator of Chaucer and John Milton, is sensitive to this problem of translating for readers versus translating for theatrical audiences (remarks from an interview in December, 2010). In both cases, the goal is to keep in mind your audience while not betraying your original writer. Interestingly, he is sympathetic to the growing number of Shakespeare experts who say his plays were written to be read and not only performed, given the great length, e.g., of *Hamlet*. This might be said with equal justification about *Angels in America*, which is not only considerably longer than *Hamlet*, but has similar ambitions given its lyrical or elevated language (to be discussed in chapter five).

Shurbanov makes the further claim that, in the case of poetry, for example, the text must be completely re-written, not translated, presumably to convey the meter and verbal tone of the original. In effect, he says, the translator thereby becomes a co-author.

This sort of radical adaptation has been applied to plays dating back well before our contemporaries, however, and has been done even by Goethe and Schiller. Pavis writes that Goethe

> did not place much importance on mediating the plays deriving from foreign cultures as they appeared in their original textual form. He was far more eager that the contemporary audience feel the full effect directly. To that end he was prepared to make far-reaching alterations and changes and he was vigorously and energetically supported in this by Schiller. (Pavis, quoted, 1996:29)

In his case, Schiller cut an "obscene" porter scene from *Macbeth* in order not to offend his conservative Weimar audience. Also, Pavis reports, Goethe cut *Romeo and Juliet* to such a degree that a later Shakespeare scholar called it an "amazing travesty" (1996:29). Despite the horror and indignation of this Shakespearean scholar, neither Schiller nor Goethe *added* their own dialogue: Compare this to what Aimé Césaire did to Shakespeare's *Tempest*, page 48, below. The most commonly heard justification for such liberal adaptations is that it makes the characters, events or situations more accessible to modern audiences. As Anne Neuschaefer writes about Vitez's updates of *Electra*: "The familiar gestures of the actors – lighting a cigarette, having a drink or gathering around the radio – are signs that the ancient drama does not happen outside the actual world in an abstract space, but that it takes place in our midst" ("Antoine Vitez: The Script and the Spoken Word," Pavis, 1996:137).

Here then, is where "adapters," as they are sometimes called, encounter the displeasure of authors such as Albee. From his playwright's perspective, he bluntly says about adaptation, "I don't like it." (All otherwise unsourced quotes and paraphrases are from my telephone interview with Albee on 4 October 2011.) Albee thinks that the task of the creative theatrical team should be to render a "literal translation" of the playwright's text onto the stage, and above all, respect the author's intention. He is seconded by the Austrian playwright, poet, and novelist, Franz Werfel, who asked the theatre and film director, Elia Kazan, why his play, *Jacobowsky and the Colonel* (1944), was being adapted. "What was wrong with presenting a simple, straightforward translation of his work? Who here was a better writer than himself?" Kazan told him that, "it was a matter of the American theatre audience," to which the enraged Werfel attacked "America's theatre, its films, its culture, and above all, the American character. 'Savages!' he yelled. 'You are savages here!'" (Kazan, 1989:241). Such are the perils of precipitous theatrical adaptations.

What particularly riles Albee is what he sees too often and labels "free adaptation," that is, an appropriation of the text to make it applicable to the country where it is being performed. An example would be that of Jean-Claude Carriere, whose 1986 adaptation of *Mahabharata* for Peter Brook included his "entirely rewritten scenes while keeping the proper names and tonality of the epic poem" (Pavis, 1982:194).

This is the school in which the adapter is considered a co-creator opposed to or unbound from the original source. This can happen even in an original production, prior to translation and production abroad, when an *"auteur"* director is in charge. This returns us to the adapter, Elia Kazan, about whom John Lahr has written that

> In the theatre, Kazan had sometimes been accused of a kind of imperialism—of overpowering the playwright's vision with his own energy. In time, he pleaded guilty to this: he came to see his growing impatience with the theatre as symptomatic of a need to express himself, instead of playing handmaiden to playwrights (2010:93).

In Bulgaria too, a number of theatre directors seem to challenge the playwright's intention or vision with their own artistic goals. Teddy Moskov and Alexander Morfov, the director of *One Flew Over the Cuckoo's Nest* in Sofia, both have reputations for taking a free hand in translation and adaptation of the plays they work with. This approach is not necessarily true to the spirit of the original, and such adapters do not wish to get closer to the original text or spirit. To them, this faithful or respectful adaptation is pedantic, and not worthy of their theatre work.

Albee and the American master Arthur Miller usually agree on the subject of adaptations of their play—but not always. Albee told me that he does not see any particular need to make changes to his work. Such a resulting foreign-looking work calls to mind the point raised by Carlson that intercultural productions are hybrids without authenticity in any culture. As a spectator of such a play produced overseas, I would want to know where the adapted story is taking place, in the source or target culture? Also, is it about American characters or, in the current case, Bulgarians? Although Carlson creates a scaling system to place such hybrids, in which he assigns values to elements of language and staging, one might find something in the middle range uncomfortable, neither fish nor fowl, and lacking the essence or impact of a secure grounding in one culture or the other.

Addressing this issue, Albee says about his plays, wherever they might be staged, "My characters are American and should be seen as such." Miller, on the other hand, when he traveled to China to see a local staging of *Death of a Salesman*, asked the Chinese actors not to appear Western, with wigs and makeup, but rather to be a Chinese *Salesman* family. "They were shocked at first by this departure form the traditional conventions," he writes (Miller, 1987:431). This seems to me, at least, perfectly natural. That is, if the emotions explored in the play are universal, they should as meaningful in a Chinese family as in an American one.

In general, the artistic changes peculiar to adaptation, in Albee's view, are made by theatre directors, "who think they have a right to violate the copyright of the playwright." He adds these thoughts: "Adaptation is like a distortion. Cultural distortion is worse, but directors are fond of it. It leads to free adaptation." Albee is particularly critical of this free adaptation, and notes that, "I don't want to see *Hamlet* in Brooklyn." (I.e., even if he goes to the Brooklyn Academy of Music, a notable performing arts center, he would not like to see an adaptation of the character of Hamlet as a New Yorker.)

Instances of playwrights' rebellions are not unknown. When New York's Wooster Group theatre appropriated and rewrote Miller's *The Crucible* as *L.S.D. (Just the High Points)* in 1984, and American Repertory Theatres put Samuel Beckett's *Endgame* in an abandoned subway station with black New York characters (1984), the productions resulted in lawsuits from the outraged authors. Mark Fortier wrote that these reactions were "little informed by an understanding of contemporary critical theory" (1997:92).

Tony Kushner for one is surely aware of such current thinking, and has a more moderate view of creative adaptation. He said (personal phone interview, 21 May, 2012) that the Wooster Group production was "a stunning homage to Miller," and that his *Crucible* was used as, "a conduit to a current crisis" of McCarthyism that inspired Miller. But I understand Miller's viewpoint: He set *The Crucible* in Salem, Massachusetts, during the historic witch trials as a metaphor for the fear and injustice of contemporary McCarthyism. He did not appreciate the appropriators making his allegory concrete, not did he like their adding much extraneous and, to his mind, irrelevant material about LSD and the Beat poets.

Kushner, though, focused more on the "shattering performances" that were part of "a great work of art…I can't imagine being provoked enough to close it. It was a mistake to fight with the lawsuit," he said, and, changes are "the name of the game. The vagaries of performance are infinite. It's a mistake to try to control them."

Regarding adaptations of his own plays, Kushner says he went to many European productions of *Angels in America* in the late 90s (Germany, France, Italy, Poland), and had a "fascinating experience." He seemed resigned to the changes, and said he did not have a lot of control because he did not speak the languages. "The German translator asked many questions so I assume it was precise," he added. Only when "great liberties" are taken with the text, it "bothers me," or when a lot of text is removed. "But I can't do anything, the play is there," he said.

This concern for one's written text is what one might more generally regard as the playwright's position. Miller holds the extreme position: "The very idea of someone editing a play of mine or so much as changing a word was enough to make my skin crawl, and to actually submit pages to a producer who became the owner of what one wrote the moment one wrote it—this was unconscionable" (1987:231).

Miller provides clear examples of why playwrights share Albee's horror and outrage. In one case, a 1965 Soviet production of *View from the Bridge,* Eddie Carbone betrays his niece's lover as an illegal immigrant (who could then be deported) because he loves her and wishes to dispose of a rival, which makes his love clear in emotional terms. But the Soviet theatre added a Carbone line, "I love her" to his wife, making the love for his niece explicit. Thus the director spelled out the human relationship verbally and dismissed Miller's complaint by saying, "We are not interested in all the psychology." Miller in retrospect sounded an Albee note in saying that this amounted, "to a contempt for an author's right to his own work" (Miller, 1987:570).

Even worse, for Miller, was when Soviet doctrine intervened. The bourgeois characters in *Death of a Salesman* were distorted in conformity with the communist ideology. Willy the salesman was caricatured as a total fool, and the successful Charley, who offers financial help, "was rewritten and acted as a clownish idiot, since as a businessman he could not possibly be even slightly altruistic or have a shred of sincerity" (Miller, 1987:570).

When pressed, however, Albee, at least, relaxes his guard. Regarding, for example, the work of Shakespeare or Molière, there is no longer any copyright issues, he said, so legally directors can do what they want, and they are free to update the plays. "There is some virtue in this [because] it shows the sturdiness of the plays," he told me. This then would exonerate the creative adaptations of Vitez, Goethe, and Schiller, cited above, who worked with Sophocles, Shakespeare, and similar playwrights who preceded them by two centuries or more. He might not approve, however, of Vitez's adaptation of *Electra,* that added discordant or unpleasant boat sirens and ambulance horns to suggest the tense contemporary Greek atmosphere under the military dictatorship (1986), and thus rendered "Electra's lament more sincere, more objective," according to Neuschaefer (in Pavis, 1999:138). With this accretion, Vitez is commenting on contemporary Greek life, which is entirely extraneous to Sophocles's play.

According to Neuschaefer, however, Vitez has taken a far bolder step than mere commentary. She claims that the 1980s French audience at the Theatre National de Chaillot, where he was director, *could not understand* ("hardly demonstrable to a modern audience") the chorus's role in *Electra*, which was to point out the rupture between Electra and the other characters, or that Electra cannot achieve a compromise with the status quo (the murderous events in her family). Thus he transfers the story to "its proper dimension and renders Electra's extraordinary position intelligible to his audience" (Pavis, 1999:139). In short, this adaptation is necessary not just because it adds an interesting but non-essential political dimension to *Electra*, but because the modern audience would otherwise not understand Sophocles's classic.

The writer, playwright, and adapter Laura Eason, like Vitez, has had similar experiences with living and deceased playwrights. Her adaptation of Mark Twain's *Adventures of Huckleberry Finn* was difficult, she writes, because of her reverence for the author, and as a result she produced a first-draft adaptation that, "lacks enough of my own voice and perspective" (Eason, 2009:146). Once she overcame the reverence, as for example, with Jules Verne, she abandoned what she felt was his voice, and made an adaptation "very much my own" (Eason, 2009:165).

Eason's situation of course is different from that in the Ivan Vazov Theatre because her theatrical adaptations were from different media (novels by Twain and Verne, and stories by Chicago writer Stuart Dybek), which entailed more than bridging national, cultural and language divides. Curiously, though, one of her works was supervised by the original story writer—just as Albee supervised the production of *The Goat* at the National Theatre. In her case, she felt that her first draft

> stayed too true to the source material. The tendency to make a first draft very close to the original text was amplified in this process by Stuart Dybek having power of approval over the adaptation. Knowing Stuart would review the final draft of the material and sign off on it—or not—made it scary to step away from the original text and invent as much as I needed to invent to make the story work in a theatrical context (Eason, 2009:170-71).

If one substitutes the final words above with "in a Bulgarian context," we would have a parallel case of what Albee and Miller have decried. In fact, they would applaud Stuart for being in the theatre and terrorizing an adapter who would think the theatrical production needs "her own voice."

To be sure, modern theatre allows a wide berth to creative adaptation; Albee has attested to that, and scorned it. Throughout the late twentieth century, experimental theatre put Shakespeare in all sorts of modern settings (*Richard III*, the 1995 film with Ian McKellen, in fascist 1930's Britain), musicals (*Kiss Me, Kate,* 1953, based on *The Taming of the Shrew; West Side Story*, 1961, based on *Romeo and Juliet*), Japanese approaches (Kurosawa's film, *Throne of Blood,* 1957, based on *Macbeth*), etc. A recent hit *avant-garde* production, "a magical romp inspired by" *A Midsummer Night's Dream,* called *The Donkey Show,* in New York City and Boston, allows the audience to "party on the dance floor as the show unfolds around them." (See the website, accessed 22 September 2012, of the American Repertory Theatre's Oberon Theater in Boston: http://www.americanrepertorytheater.org/events/show/donkey-show).

This generated a lot of fun and hoopla, but is not likely to have the same impact that Shakespeare intended. I think these adaptations really use the original plot, and some of the thematic material, to create in effect new works of art, such that Kazan would want.

It seems that updating and fun are often part of the theatrical adapters' agenda—and not always to the detriment of the original. Even Albee spoke with admiration of an adaptation in Prague of his 1975 hit, *Seascape,* in which the Czech creative team had the human characters speak normal Czech and the lizard-like sea creatures speak Czech with Russian accents (personal interview).

The curmudgeonly Miller also softened up his hostility to "artistic adaptation," in this case for a *View from the Bridge* in Britain. After he concluded that there was no way for the cast to learn a deep Sicilian-American accent in Britain, they "worked out among themselves an accent never heard on earth before, but…it convinced British audiences that they were hearing Brooklynese." He adds that, "this newly minted language along with the mode of acting created a wholly fictional world, but one that was internally consistent and entirely persuasive even if its resemblance to the

Brooklyn waterfront was remote or nonexistent. *View* came over under [Peter] Brook's direction as a heroic play of great emotional force" (Miller, 1987:431). This is a rare instance of an artist accepting Carlson's "hybrid" work of art, but only as a necessity. What won Miller over was the essential internal consistency.

On the theoretical side, Pavis seems to evince a cavalier disregard for Albee's and Miller's insistence that directors adhere to their creative intent:

> *Mise en scene* does not have to be faithful to a dramatic text. The notion of faithfulness, a cliché of critical discourse, is pointless and stems in fact from confusion. Faithfulness to what?...faithfulness to the 'ideas' of the 'author'...the very illusive faithfulness of the performance to what the text has already clearly stated. If producing a faithful *mise en scene* means repeating, or believing one can repeat, by theatrical means what the text has already said, what would be the point of *mise en scene*? (1992:26-27).

Pavis's idea is that the playwright's job is over and his concerns should end with publication of the play, which is when the theatre's creative team should assume full artistic control. He is very clear that the team then has the right to pick and choose what they like from the play's text.

> The actors do not have to carry out the instructions of the text and the stage directions as if these had the illocutionary force of a 'cake recipe' in order to produce a stage performance...*Mise en scene* [sic; he means the creative team]...is not obliged to carry out stage direction to the letter, reconstructing a situation of utterance identical in every aspect to the one prescribed...Although one should not forget that they

form part of authorial speech, it should be remembered that the director has the choice of either using them or not, as in the case of Gordon Craig who considered stage directions an insult to his freedom (1992:28-29).

On the other side of the barricade, there is another practitioner even more contrarian and hard-line than Albee or Miller, the playwright, screenwriter, and director, David Mamet:

> Consider the…phenomenon of a director's setting the existing play in nontraditional form: *Hamlet* in space, *Othello* in a convent, any number of Chekhov plays in modern dress, et cetera, as if changing the costumes changed the play. These "good ideas" differ in extent, but not in intent, from those of the ideologues full stop: to usurp power from the text and impose upon the audience a view more advanced than that of the author (Mamet, 2010:66n).

Mamet's rationale for his blunt attack on creative adaptation is grounded in his belief that the essence of a play is not intent or "ideas," per Pavis above, but *plot* (ibid.:19). *Mise en scene* and costumes for him are non-essential. Text and actors are essential to carry the story forward, and audiences, which come to the theatre to be "delighted," must be driven to ask what will happen next (ibid.:136). Mamet cites as evidence the radio play, which, he claims, can produce as much pleasure as a staged play with an elaborate set.

Also relevant for this study is the consequence of Mamet's thesis for language adaptation. He writes: "we are not actually moved by…the presence of poetry. We appreciate plays in translation, and what do we know of the Russian of Chekhov? And we have argued for four hundred years about the 'meaning' of *Hamlet*...Poetry is insufficient; beauty in language itself...is nonessential" (ibid.:19).

The reductionist nature of Mamet's approach is evinced in his comment on *Hamlet*. What he implies, I think, is that we enjoy the revenge story even if we don't know what it means, and even if we watch it performed in, say, Bulgarian. The 'arguments' over the ideas of Shakespeare and other classics involve the (non-essential) critical human facilities, but for the audience at a successful play, it must be moved at a "preverbal level," and is not involved in the ideas of the drama, "but rather experiences the thrill of the communal hunt" (ibid.). As for the presentation of ideas, this according to Mamet, is not a play but a "lecture" (ibid.:18).

Since we have now struck a sort of foundation, I believe, of contrary ideas about adaptation, let us move on to audience reception. I will return to consider ideas about adaptation after studying what the Bulgarian adaptations tell us.

AUDIENCE RECEPTION

In my survey of the academic literature on theatre, I have found no generally accepted definition of *audience reception*. There is however, a substantial literature on various theories of reception or response that was dominant in the post-structuralist era of literary criticism through the 1990s:

1. *Audience reception theory*, particularly a theory developed by Stuart Hall. This theory assumes a "reader" or audience as

the primary subject of study, rather than the author or playwright. Hall describes three possible readings of a media text: preferred or dominant (the director's or creator's way of reading), oppositional (rejecting the dominant view, the audience's created reading), and negotiated (the compromise reading). This was a dominant view in the 1980s (Bennett, 1990:168).

2. The *reader-response theory* or *reader-reception theory*. Developed at the Constance School in Germany in the 1960s as hermeneutics, the theory started with the assumption that there are no facts, only interpretations (or, as Nietzsche is usually translated, opinions). The theories of Wolfgang Iser and Hans Robert Jauss led to a larger role for the reader or audience for texts and artistic works. Iser in particular described a reader's repeated interactions with a text as an interactive dialog or dynamic, not a one-way street. This trend has also supported the work of theatre audience studies.

3. *Identity-based (feminist, race, ethnic, queer) and post-colonial theories*. These theories followed audience reception theory, and seem to have been in vogue at least into the 1990s (discussed in Bennett, 1990:168), but also prevalent in the articles in Geis and Kruger, 1997).

Pavis wrote an influential study of intercultural theatre, *Theatre at the Crossroads of Culture* (1992), in which he follows the thread of the citation (page 22, above) about why creative teams need not be faithful to the playwright's text. Pavis argues that "faithfulness" to the text is meaningless because this assumes that there is an ideal and fixed meaning in it, whereas in fact, based on what he knows about reception theory, each spectator brings a different personality and personal experiences to the theatre and draws a different meaning from it (1992:36). Since texts themselves are unclear, every text must be interpreted, "textual literalness does not exist [and] there are as many literal readings as there are readers" (ibid.:45). Carlson agrees that local conditions determine each performance, and that since performances have manifold meanings, no two playgoers see exactly the same play, and even performances change each night (Fortier, 1997:91).

In his *The Intercultural Performance Reader* (1996), Pavis provides space for European as well as Third World theatre scholars and practitioners to voice their theories and enthusiasms, but it mostly contains concerns, critiques and even denunciations of the famous works of intercultural theatre, all adaptations of various sorts, and those performed mostly in France.

Pavis is actually more concerned with how Western theatre people use foreign or non-Western traditions, stories, and other elements to create successful productions. He has in mind the works of contemporary directors and writers such as Brook and Mnouchkine. (e.g., *Mahabharata* and *L'Indiade*, respectively). He asks important questions such as whether these artists are somehow preserving the intent or essence of the foreign elements, or somehow distorting or appropriating them, and he is sensitive to the often pejorative tone of these loaded terms. He acknowledges, for example, that there is always some transformation or re-elaboration of the source (foreign) material, which marks the truly intercultural representation (1996:12). He constructs an hourglass metaphor to depict how a source (non-Western) culture's product is filtered through the waist of the hourglass because of norms dictated by the target (Western) culture, so that the resultant "universal" product is really a construction of the dominant, capitalist West (1996:17). The ideology, he believes, emerges in some form or other on the stage.

Pavis's anthology contributors take many perspectives on how the theatre practitioners try to meld or assemble the elements of two cultures into their productions. They raise and discuss questions of what is native and what is foreign in these works, and pay particular attention to the unequal economic and power relations of the source and target cultures. There is much effort by the practitioners at overcoming cultural barriers, and about striving for cross-cultural understanding. Yet the preponderance of experts still decries these works' putative exploitation.

The tone of the volume is captured by Clive Barker, who condemns these intercultural works for "the appropriation of cultural devices for exoticism or spurious novelty" ("The Possibilities and Politics of Intercultural Penetration and Exchange," 1996:246). He shares with the other contributors their hostility to what he perceives as one-sided or "uni-directional exchanges," and has recourse to the most severe vocabulary: this is not only the "tourist approach" of misguided intercultural theatre at certain festivals, but plays which become for him a "zoo" (1996:252). The most extreme view of such appropriation is perhaps that of Rastom Bharucha, who warns intercultural directors not to exploit source cultures like 'cunning western vampires' (1984, cited in Pavis, 1992:179).

On theatre audience reception, Pavis articulated his theoretical views in a 1983 article, which he then summarizes later as follows: "the production of performance presupposes a theory of the reception situation, and the reception of performance takes on meaning in relation to the Social Context of that reception and the continual revaluation of signifiers and signifieds, as a result of the continual change in the Social Context " (cited in Pavis, 1992:89). In layman's terms, Pavis seems to say that one cannot produce a serious play without analyzing the shifting social situation, and that the audience will receive or understand the play as a function of its semiotics or signs, composed of elements like words, gestures, and scenery, and their literal and connotative meanings.

Oddly enough, in his introduction to *The Intercultural Performance Reader*, when Pavis refers to "reception" and reception theory, he sometimes means reception of the foreign culture by the creative theatre people, not by the audience, as in the present study. The volume addresses audience reception, and how best to adapt a play to a foreign audience, only marginally. So though there are parallels in his study, terms, and theories to my study, his focus is actually quite different. Indeed, his later work is more sweeping and more challenging, since my paper does not go beyond Western culture, and does not study theatrical works based on borrowed or combined Western and non-Western elements.

The second central text on spectatorship is *Theatre Audiences* by Susan Bennett (1997). Bennett chooses her study as a result, she writes, of the post-1960s theatrical trend to "speak for dominated and generally marginalized peoples." These emergent theatres have "sought the centrality of the spectator as subject of the drama" who "can think and act." This "productive and emancipated spectator is my subject," she writes (Bennett, 1997:1).

In other words, since the creative teams of recent theatre productions have made explicit references to their audiences, Bennett decides it is important to study these audiences, which are non-traditional or "generally marginalized." Her object is both theatrical practices and theories "which have suggested the centrality of the spectator's role" (ibid.:1).

Bennett's study of theoretical practices takes in Bertolt Brecht, Mnouchkine, Brook, and others in the *avant-garde*, radical, or intercultural theatrical world. This study offers the occasional interesting observation. Her study of theories of the spectator's role leads her to a new theory of "the audience experience of theatre" relying on "two frames": an outer frame: theatre as a cultural construct through the theatrical event, the selection of material for production, and the audience definition and expectations of a performance; and the inner frame: the event itself, and, in particular, the spectator's experience of a fictional stage world (ibid.:1-2). "It is the intersection of these two frames which forms the spectator's cultural understanding and experience of theatre" (ibid.:2).

Bennett directs the reader to her third chapter—"the site of my own theorizing"—which is an 80-page exploration and critique of the social positions of theatre audiences (income, gender, education), theatres' various financial and societal positions around the world, of their selection of plays, and various unconventional theatrical productions from *Hamlet* to Ibsen and to the radical 1997 Nobel Laureate in Literature, Dario Fo. We learn that, "we lack any detailed picture of the theatre audience, and in particular, their role(s) in the production-reception relationship" (ibid.:86). Also, "the relation between production and reception, positioned within and against cultural values, remains largely uninvestigated" (ibid.). Missing, however, is any development of the "two frames" theory. There is only one passing reference to this theory, restating what we read earlier (ibid.:156).

Another problem of Bennett's theories of drama and audience response theory is that they ask many questions, but provide few answers, and seem to carry ideological assumptions. Her work also makes undisciplined use of post-modernist jargon (foregrounding, coding and overcoding, liminalities, etc.) without defining or clarifying these terms. The term "codes," for example, often assumes something implanted deliberately in works of art by the creator, especially when the work is critiqued for its political ideology. But most great art cannot be predominantly deliberate or conscious because no single artist, such as Shakespeare or Molière, could conceivably have intended or encoded all that centuries of critics and interpreters have found in their works. This error is one of the chief targets of Susan Sontag's insightful book, *Against Interpretation*. She is "against"... "a conscious act of the mind which illustrates a certain code, certain 'rules' of interpretation" (1961:5).

In the 80s and 90s, Umberto Eco and others made important contributions to critical thinking on interpretation of texts. In *Interpretation and Overinterpretation* (1992), Eco argued against this endless, indefinite interpretation of texts. His view was that there are "bedrock facts" in any story that limit interpretations. "No reader-oriented theory can avoid such a constraint." For Eco, overinterpretation starts with the fallacy that though everything can be conceptually linked to everything else in the universe, it is a mark of sanity to be able to distinguish relevant, significant similarities from illusory ones. He argues that the limits we place on any interpretation cannot be linked to the intentions of the author (like Shakespeare), but rather to the text's intention—the bedrock facts (Dutton, 1992:online).

So how does the text's intention differ from the author's intention? Eco may be arguing that the text introduces certain subject matter, so the interpretation has to be about that material, and not about something entirely different, but embedded in a coded way. The author's intention, if not stated in the text, is much more difficult. Miller can say that *The Crucible* (1952) is really about McCarthyism—but it does not mention McCarthy. It might be fairer as interpreters to say that the play is only about the Salem witch trials, but that we can see the parallels between that era and ours, and draw conclusions not about what Miller "intended," but about how the play exposes a social situation like that of the 1950s in the U.S., or even suggests how universal such persecution is.

Yet another problem is that Bennett continually (chapter 1) assumes that the theatre audience is "passive," which is undefined, and is not used in a persuasive way. A completely passive audience is a sleeping or somnolent one. Brecht especially acknowledged a critical, feisty audience, such as one finds in New York. For him, the active spectator will appreciate art and sincerity and reject pretension, nonsense, and failure. A more sympathetic interpretation of Bennett is that audiences in traditional theatre enter into a social contract in which spectators agree to be physically passive but open, eager and active in their acceptance and decoding of the signs presented to them (Fortier, 1997:91). This may be what Bennett means, but her work needs further inquiry or analysis

Concretely, there is nothing groundbreaking in the current "interactive" play, such as *The Donkey Show* (see page 29, above). I recall seeing in the late 1980s in Budapest a performance of *Cats*, the 1981 hit musical by Andrew Lloyd Webber, in which the felines crossed the proscenium and deposited themselves in spectators' laps. These were both commercial productions, not revolutionary endeavors, and they did not require the "change in structure in the performance" that Bennett calls for (quoting Bernard Dort, 1990:18). Her urgent but vague call for "performance theatre" seems to respond to a narrow, perhaps outdated ideology of challenge to what she thinks are established theatrical norms.

For example, the march of time seems to have dealt a blow to a contemporary theatre of performance in Japan that raises questions about nuclear power in the wake of the Fukushima disaster. The company, Akira Takayama's Port B, "is known for departing from the stage with interactive works in which his 'cast' consists of non-actors whose experiences provide the 'text' of pieces that explore people's relationship to their community, environment, and history" (Grunebaum, 2011:11). In this late, post-Brechtian era, Takayama has had to admit that, "We have to adjust our expectations to reflect current audiences' desire of a less confrontational approach than theater in the '60s and '70s…Overtly political works will simply be ignored" (ibid.).

Parenthetically, I note that Bennett also writes, "Dramatic practice, unlike theory, has always been concerned …with the involvement of the audience" (1990:18). If so, what is the need for the new "liberated theatre"? Is it that the audience is really passive, and needs to be awakened from its bourgeois slumbers? She cites the example of the practice of playwrights rewriting and directors making changes during preview runs (ibid.). This seems like an unfortunate example to me, since the audience involvement in this case is not the result of audience initiative, but rather one in which the spectators are a sort of laboratory guinea pig for the creative team. What seems to be new in liberated theatre is the agitprop or politics, not the audience involvement in any concrete sense.

41

Steeped in leftist and semiotic thinking, Bennett calls for the emancipation of the "oppressed" spectator, which she finds in non-traditional and often marginalized theatre practices (Fortier, 1997:91). Here her lack of precision and definition of "passive" carries over to "oppressed."

Bennett is surely aware of the work of thinkers such as Paulo Freire, who called for dialectical pedagogy in which the "oppressed" students teach the "so-called" teachers. That is, students should not be passive, but active. So too, for Freire, Aristotelian theatre is a "form of political indoctrination, intimidation and coercion, whereby an ideological acceptance of the status quo and fear of change is instilled in a passive and oppressed audience." For Brecht and Augusto Boal, the radical Brazilian theatre director, "the oppressive ideology and passivity of theatre are highly complicitous [sic]… [this] means the audience is not allowed to think for itself, and the audience's passive position as spectators means it is not allowed to act for itself" (Fortier, 1997:140). Bennett seems to be arguing for an active audience because, if it is not active in this political sense, it will be "oppressed" by the playwright and creative team.

Bennett therefore provides me little theoretical nourishment for my inquiry on cultural adaptation. Her other topics, such as radical identity theatre and theatrical multiculturalism (how certain exotic shows like Brook's *Mahabharata* blithely eradicate cultural differences, or how a dominant culture's cosmopolitan products are exploited for profit), do not help indicate meaningful answers to my research questions.

I should mention that most of the academic contributors to Pavis's collection (1990) are driven by their leftist politics drive to focus only on the theatre of protest, also called variously "problem plays" or "message plays," though these terms generally designate something a bit different. Robert Brustein, the creator of eleven theatrical adaptations, does the same thing in his study of eight modern "playwrights of rebellion," *Theatre of Revolt* (1964). Brustein clearly articulates this type of drama in contradistinction to the "theater of communion." In the latter, the plays reinforce the beliefs of the audience or society, while in the "theater of revolt" the plays attack social values and the audience's beliefs. Since the former can degenerate into agitprop, which might serve a worthy social or political goal, but not artistic truth, our standard of artistic success should be guided by intrinsic dramatic value.

Finally, it is helpful to cite again the sharply contrarian voice of David Mamet:

> Champions of so-called theory, whether feminist, Marxist, multiculturalist, or other, in an attempt (supposedly) to cleanse expression of bias, are involved in a postmodern rendition of book burning. For the question of art is neither "How does it serve the state?" (Stalinist) nor its wily modification into "How does it serve humanity?" but 'How does it serve the audience?'" (2010:66)

This lonely, iconoclastic view is not only a clear rejection of "theory" in favor of something like another theory, art for art's sake, but also something to keep in mind when I turn to my methodology in chapter two, below.

Audiences and Reception: The Ivan Vazov National Theatre Case

CONDITIONING THE BULGARIAN AUDIENCE

There is a great deal of interesting literature on how certain theatrical venues or situations condition audience reception, such as Carlson cited above, or what Bennett called the "outer frame" (see p. 33). This literature sheds light on the audience reaction in the National Theatre. For example, Josette Feral writes that theatre festivals such as the Festival of the Americas in Montreal attracts special, highly interested audiences that cannot be equated with a typical theatre audience. (Pavis describes this argument as one close to Eugenio Barba's, which "privileges the professional identity of theatre groups," Pavis, 1996:51). As I argued in chapter one above, spectators at the National Theatre seem to fall into what Pavis calls, "an aesthetic or ethic of festivals...(whose audiences...comprise festival-goers rather than some 'real' population)." In particular, he continues, the special financial backing (as at the Ivan Vazov Theatre), "alters the activity, inducing a cultural attitude which has little to do with original roots and audiences" (ibid.).

Similarly, Carlson concluded that audiences attending the celebrated intercultural plays of Mnouchkine and Brook tended to receive them in a certain way—that is, as expressions of the creative activity of the directors and their companies rather than as fusions of cultural material—precisely because they were "knowledgeable in theatre matters (and such audiences clearly make up a far larger percentage of those attending a Brook or Mnouchkine production than of those attending more conventional dramatic fare)" (Carlson, "Brook and Mnouchkine: Passages to India?," in Pavis, 1996:84). Carlson concludes that these knowledgeable French audiences clearly received these productions differently from the Indian reviewers, who picked up on or emphasized the elements that were "highly evocative of India." Carlson judiciously declines to say which reaction is right.

Carlson makes one further argument relevant to audience reception of productions at the Ivan Vazov National Theatre. He writes that "the considerable international reputation of both Brook and Mnouchkine," along with their inevitable publicity, condition the reception by reinforcing a "focus on the producing organization" rather than on the Indian source material (ibid.). Given the National Theatre's singular reputation for artistic excellence, this would tend to produce positive reactions to the American plays, and to give this "producing organization" the credit for the success. In addition, I think the Bulgarian public's admiring view of Kesey, Kushner, and Albee, given their stellar international reputations, condition them to like what they see. Carlson calls the "pilgrimage" to highly publicized theatre festivals "international events," which, I would argue, is something like what happened with the fanfare around the premiers of these shows at the National Theatre.

Regarding the fanfare, the advance publicity generated, for example, by the two-week stay of Albee himself at the National Theatre working with the director Yavor Gardev, and his creative team, created a vibe akin to what Carlson describes as attendant on the work of the intercultural directors: "the reputation of Brook and Mnouchkine, the inevitable advance publicity stressing the importance of these artists over the material itself...worked to encourage in audiences an expectation of a major cultural event" (Carlson in Pavis, 1996:87).

This phenomenon carried over also, literally, in the National Theatre's publicity. The flyers that the Theatre distributed (see appendix A.19) have the name "Edward Albee" in large black typeface at the top, and in smaller red letters, the actual title, "*Козата, или коя е Силвия?*" In the case of *One Flew Over the Cuckoo's Nest*, however, since the play is publicly viewed as a sort of watershed or symbol of liberation, the title itself gets top billing in the publicity.

FROM BROADWAY TO THE IVAN VAZOV NATIONAL THEATRE

It is my conviction, after living in Japan for ten years, that Tokyo today bears a closer resemblance, in many respects, to New York today than to Tokyo in the postwar period. Of course language and deep cultural norms persist over time, but the fast-paced modern culture of international commerce, video games, social media, as well as international concerns including environmental degradation, greater tolerance of racial minorities, work patterns and international travel have made the global village a smaller place, where cross-cultural understanding is not the insurmountable barrier it was for our provincial ancestors. Young Japanese play the same video games, watch the same Hollywood movies, and text incessantly on the same smart phones as Americans or Bulgarians, and thereby willy-nilly imbibe the same values and norms.

What this means practically for this study is that the task of adapting *Angels in America* or *The Goat* in Bulgaria today is a far sight easier than adapting *King Lear* in Stratford, England today. Modern British may understand Shakespeare's King James's English—more or less penetrable without a dictionary—but the Elizabethan values of royalty, class, personal honor and chivalry are largely fading historical memories, deep in the cultural heritage of native-born British, granted, but of little consequence in today's multicultural Great Britain.

This mindset drives me to ask what, apart from the English language, is uniquely or peculiarly American in our subject plays that requires cultural adaptation in order to reach Bulgarian audience understanding? Social attitudes toward homosexuality (all three plays), the Absurdist examination of the failure of language and the "quiet desperation" of the educated upper middle-class (*The Goat*), the antihero McMurphy or his Freud-fueled attack on an oppressive and complacent "Establishment" (in *One Flew Over the Cuckoo's Nest*), and the angst and anger of the gay AIDS generation on Reagan's America—these seem to be the core social and political phenomena.

The problem with adaptations based on the theoretical musings of Bennett, Pavis, Vitez, et al., is that they do not help explain how adapters might bridge these cultural, geographical, or time differences, but rather, only provide justification for how to politicize the original works. For example, the playwright Laura Eason asks how to update and adapt Jules Verne's novel, *Around the World in Eighty Days* (1873) to make it "relevant to a modern audience." But in practice what she did was mostly add language criticizing American and British colonialism and imperialism (Eason, 2009:147, 159), and observe political correctness by substituting the American Indians who attack Phileas Fogg's train with racially neutral "bandits" (ibid.:160). In other words, the goal is not to help the new audience enjoy or appreciate the original author's work, but to apply the adapter's political agenda, which is extraneous to the original, and possibly antithetical to it.

In a more radical example, Aimé Césaire turned Shakespeare's *The Tempest* into *Une Tempête* (1969), a post-colonial adaptation, so the romance of reconciliation becomes a story purely of imperialism, domination, and struggle. Caliban, the resentful island native, no longer says, "You taught me your language," but snarls a political screed: "You didn't teach me a thing! Except to jabber in your own language so that I could understand your order—chop the wood, wash the dishes, fish for food, plant vegetables, all because you're too lazy to do it yourself" (Fortier, 1997:134). We can presume that this played well to Césaire's constituency audience in her political circle. I would call this a political adaptation, not one geared to a more general public audience. Its goal is polemical, not artistic.

This is, however, where the literature leads. I will return to these issues of political versus artistic adaptation in my conclusion.

Methodology or Research Design

One may strive to serve the audience and apply concrete tests to determine if one has succeeded. (Did they laugh, cry, tell their friends?) – David Mamet, 2010:67

As I said in my introduction above, my methodology and research are grounded more in empirical research (questionnaires at the theatre) and in comparing newspaper and popular magazine theatre reviews than in probing the literature of audience reception. This is partly due to the paucity of such literature relative to the richness of popular articles on the dramatic texts and performances themselves, and because I intend this to be a practical study of the success of the plays in Bulgaria. The two leading scholars of audience reception, Pavis and Bennett, both discussed above, helped me to define and delimit the project.

As noted in my introduction, I chose the three plays for timing (during my stay in Sofia and during the National Theatre's American Season), variety, and success on Broadway. I discussed the plays' themes, content, and production challenges with the directors, translators, and other members of the creative teams. My aim was to learn as much about the creative projects as I could, and especially how their view of the plays and their creative approaches and goals differed from that of the American playwrights and directors.

With this arsenal of information, my methodology fell into three parts:

1. A look at the background to each play, its performance history, and an analysis of its peculiar difficulties in cross-cultural adaptation in language, taboos, Americanisms, political and social issues, etc.;

2. A discussion of the lessons learned from a comparison of the play's reviews and critical reaction in the United States and at the Ivan Vazov National Theatre; and

3. An empirical study of the audience reception at the National Theatre based on audience questionnaires.

THE CRITICAL RECEPTION: THE SURVEY OF REVIEWS

For the critical reaction, I read through the popular newspaper and magazine reviews of the plays, both in the U.S. as a standard of comparison, and at the Ivan Vazov National Theatre.

This survey of the success or failure of the plays looks only at *reviews*. A "review" for my purposes means a critical article that, *inter alia*, rates or judges the effectiveness or success of a particular production, and in effect makes a recommendation to the reader. These reviews can appear in a daily newspaper, an arts or culture magazine, or even online or in a scholarly journal. I do not include articles that merely repeat or report what other critics have written. Nor finally do articles that critique the play text (as opposed to a production or performance) qualify as a review, whether they are positive or negative.

My methodology here was to collect these reviews in tables (see appendices A.1 to A.6) and study the composite success as judged by these critics. In the case of the Bulgarian adaptations, choosing the reviews was pretty straightforward: The National Theatre provided me an electronic collection of the reviews of the three plays. I augmented this with a fair number of online reviews I found myself, as well as a website with a table like mine that carried reviews of these same plays. All of the reviews were of the productions at the National Theatre.

In the case of the multiple productions of the plays in English, however, I had to set some parameters. To be true to my goal of contrasting the American audience and critical reaction to that of the Bulgarians, I included only American productions, although one might wish to include the highly professional productions in London or Canada in front of native English-speaking audiences and critics. Nor did I include reviews of the American productions by Canadian or British critics, though one could argue that this restriction was academic or purist. I did however study reviews of any reputable American production, though for comparison I focused on only one Broadway version. In the case of *One Flew Over the Cuckoo's Nest*, however, I used the 2001 Broadway revival, for reasons I will address below. For the other two American plays, I focused on the original Broadway run. As expected, the percent of favorable reviews at regional playhouses fell off a tad from the gold standard on the Great White Way.

The final product of this process is the six tables, two for each play (American and Bulgarian), that contain data on favorable, neutral, and unfavorable reviews, with some "favorable-neutral" and "neutral-unfavorable" reviews for those whose judgments are hard to categorize. The tables also provide information on what the reviewer wrote about the plays' themes, and some language or summary of comments on the plays' humor and unclear or perhaps misunderstood elements, labeled "mystery" in my table headings. My assumption is that a puzzled critic is generally (not always) an unhappy one, which indicates that the creative team has failed to convey a clear message, thought, feeling, or mood. The tables in the end provide me hard numbers on the percentage of favorable or unfavorable reviews, or on the critical success of the plays, so that the relative success of each play in the U.S. and Bulgaria by this measure can be compared.

I must note here the need to decide what was a review and what was puffery. That is, newspaper articles in both countries were often really reports from backstage, or interviews with the star actors or director, and these are almost always flattering. No articles are included that carry the "buzz" or hype-filled reporting on a show's previews, or copy from publicists, though these articles are useful and informative for other purposes. I did not take them seriously as critical reviews, and did not include them in my tables.

The assumption above, about the purpose of a play or drama, is of course a matter of endless debate across the centuries. But in addition to Aristotle's classic formulation of the catharsis of pity and fear, the late Christopher Hitchens, for example, in *Vanity Fair*, wrote that the stage is "supposed" to "entertain or instruct, synthesize some tragic element in the life of humanity" (1993:72). In studying laughter, for example, I tried to capture the entertainment, but the instruction is harder to be sure of. It is clear however that all three playwrights have spoken at one time or another of their mission as attempting to instruct or provide a political or social "message" to their audiences, though not in the heavy-handed, post-colonial style of Césaire.

I have created a separate bibliography for the play reviews, since many are very short, and hold no particular insight for scholars apart from the empirical data noted here. In fact, I could agree with Arthur Miller decrying the lack of content in the reviews of his movie, *The Misfits*, which focused on the scandal of his wife Marilyn Monroe's trouble on the set, not the play, "with barely a mention of any theme, dramatic intention, or style" (Miller, 1987:534). Veteran critic David Cote echoes this complaint about the shallowness of most American theatre criticism (2011:30). This in large part is what I found.

If an article did have analytical or other information worthy of quoting or including in the text of this paper, it merited inclusion in the bibliography. But there is sufficient information in the tables themselves for interested readers to locate the reviews.

Further observation about reviews vs. criticism: In the *reviews*, mostly from newspapers and mass-circulation magazines, the comments focus primarily on the acting. This is because the actors are often celebrities or stars, and readers turn to the reviews to follow their favorites as much as to know if the show is a hit. In the *criticism*, which is mostly in scholarly journals, the bulk of the commentary is about the meaning, themes, and social and political significance of the drama. These judgments or insights are gleaned primarily from the *texts* of the works. This is because, I believe, most of the writers are English literature scholars, and approach dramatic productions from that perspective.

I hope here to move a step beyond these two types, and will focus neither on the acting, nor the text, but rather on the audience and the audience's reception, which has been far less examined in the popular literature.

Take, for example, *Approaching the Millennium: Essays on "Angels in America,"* edited by Deborah R. Geis and Steven F. Kruger (1997). Of the seventeen contributing writers (not counting an interview), five work in theatre or drama departments, two are listed with expertise in both theatre and literature, four are in gay-lesbian studies, education, or arts departments, and seven are professors of English. This is not merely an academic distinction. Those professionals trained in the visual arts will naturally approach a production visually, focusing on set design, costumes, blocking, and acting. Those with backgrounds in music will pick up nuances of voice and sound. The connoisseurs of language will see special significance in the words.

Equally important, the Geis and Kruger essays do not look at a particular theatrical production until the last part, "Theater of the

Fabulous: *Angels* in Performance Contexts." Even this part contains an interview with Robert Altman on his ideas about how to film the play (which he never did—the Emmy Award-winning HBO movie was directed instead by Mike Nichols). Even when the scholars tackle the actual production, one of them, Art Borreca, admits that he did not even see the second part of the play, *Perestroika*, though, but only read reviews of it (Geis, 1997:260, note 15).

Otherwise, the scholars in the Geis volume examine Kushner's text as literature, and mine it for insights and lessons about American racial attitudes (bigoted), politics (oppressive), and, above all, the LGBT (Lesbian, Gay, Bisexual, and transsexual) cause. There is very little variance from this one-sided refrain, however justified by Kushner's left-wing politics.

The most insightful writings, it seems to me, are by those in the major arts magazines for the educated layman, such as *New York* and *The New Yorker* magazines, where gifted critics have spent a lifetime in the theatre, spoken to all members of the creative teams, and have an erudite mastery of ancillary fields in the arts and humanities. They too may carry political and other ideological biases, but these seem to be submerged beneath their obvious appreciation for the art form.

THE AUDIENCE RECEPTION: THE QUESTIONNAIRES

My questionnaires to audiences at performances of the plays at the National Theatre (see appendices A.7, A.10, and A.12) were designed to elicit information to answer one of my fundamental questions: Has the Theatre's creative team accomplished its stated goals? If they call the play a comedy—and all of the American productions produced robust laughter—I simply asked the spectators if they thought the show was funny. If the play was described as a tragedy or melodrama, I asked if they understood it or were emotionally moved. I also attended each play at least twice and observed if the audience was laughing, since, as Mamet has written, "the wise dramatist will watch them [the audience] and learn form their spontaneous, visceral reactions" (ibid.:107).

What I have not done is probe for literary, social, political, or symbolic meanings, or write about possible interpretations (e.g., Kornelia Slavova, 2009, et al.). My purpose was only to learn what critics and audiences understand or feel, and to compare the audience reactions, including reviewers and critics, in the U.S. and Bulgaria. For example, I did not ask if audiences were "astonished" in Brecht's sense, but only if they had empathy with the characters of *Angels in America*, as in Aristotle's sense, though this is according to the play's interpretation by Slavova based on Walter Benjamin's reading of Brecht (Slavova, 2009:140). Kushner of course acknowledged Walter Benjamin as a source of inspiration, but my focus is on what the audience gets out of the production, and the sources only so much as they help us understand that. The questionnaires could perhaps find out if Slavova is right, but this would not tell me if the creative team was successful.

In other words, my assumption is that the success of plays is how they communicate to audiences in the theatre, not to scholars in the academy. This belief is shared by Elia Kazan, cited in my epigraph above, that success is finally measured by the audience, that is, the box office receipts. Arthur Miller describes how Kazan differed from director Harold Clurman, whose "mind implicitly appealed to some high court of culture at whose feet he lay his offering of artistry; if he failed in the real theatre, he could find solace in a transcendent judgment of his work's high, if mundanely unappreciated, value" (Miller, 1987:272).

My reading of the many works of Albee confirms that he shared Clurman's snobbism, especially during his difficult period in the 1980s, when his plays were scorned as obscure by critics and the public, and he countered that their meanings were apparent. My decision to employ audience questionnaires rather than academic literary judgments was inspired partly by Kazan, one of America's greatest theatre and film directors. One practical decision on this score is that though a number of professional theatre people filled out the audience questionnaires, I have cited their opinions, when included, by name and title, and not anonymously, since they carry added professional authority.

My audience questionnaires provide another empirical measure of the success or failure of the productions. They ask the playgoers straightforward questions about whether they like and understood the productions, whether they were funny or amusing, and whether they were moved by them. The other questions probe how much they actually understand of the play's theme, in order to determine if the playwrights' stated or generally accepted themes were those perceived at the National Theatre.

I also ask the spectators if they think the characters are American or Bulgarian, in order to indirectly measure to what degree the play was adapted, or fitted to an easily assimilated Bulgarian context. This is parallel to Carlson's system of assigning numerical values to cross-cultural adaptations (see p. 17), but my goal is to first determine whether the National Theatre adaptations favor the source or target culture, and then to determine which strategy worked best.

My last question about the plays is whether the spectators' views were changed on the political or social issues taken up by them. This is because all three playwrights have said, in different fashions, that a cause is at least partly an issue in their work. This wish is consistent with the leftist history of American drama, despite the many experts' near consensus of criticism that capitalist society's commercial theatres have destroyed genuine political or *engagé* drama. The Theatre of Action and The Group Theatre performing the agitprop of such plays as Clifford Odets's *Awake and Sing!* (1935) to revolutionize downtrodden workers under orders from Communist cell leaders, is told in detail by Elia Kazan in his autobiography (1988:127-33). The "movement's" message is clear: "The theatre is a weapon. A play must teach a lesson" (1988:132). The ongoing interest in feminist, queer, post-colonial and similar plays is part of this lineage.

This theatrical tradition was recently reviewed by the mainstream *American Theatre* magazine. The American history of activism, wrote executive director Teresa Eyring:

> is inexorably intertwined with our legacy in the arts. From the Living Newspapers of the Federal Theatre Project in the '30s, to the Free Southern Theatre bringing 'art and social awareness' to the Deep South in the '60s, to the long-haul commitment of such activist troupes as the venerable Bread and Puppet Theater, the San Francisco Mime Troupe and Cornerstone Theater Company, theatre artists have long been at the center of social change (2012:8).

The American leftist theatre was naturally in synch with European leftists, notably Brecht, the great theoretician of the didactic play, the *Lehrstück* (see Esslin, 1982:236-37). In this spirit, Wasserman, though ignored by Morfov, has said that his *Cuckoo's Nest*, "may be a sentimental account, but I regard theatre—all theatre—as a form of propaganda and propaganda is not a bad word" (Horwitz, 2001:21). This is consistent with Kesey's novel, which has been interpreted partly as social criticism, and one that obviously critiques the practice of locking psychiatric patients up in a hospital ward, which he considered the very opposite of therapeutic. It has also been viewed as a metaphor for the repressive American society of the early 1960s (Lehmann-Haupt, 2001:47).

Kushner, for his part, was less straightforward about his political goal. Yet *Angels in America* is also part of the activist gay community's crusade to change Federal law that began with the

Stonewall Riots in 1969, and culminated in Moisés Kaufmann's *The Laramie Project: Ten Years Later*, which helped bring about the Mathew Shepard Act to protect victims of crimes motivated by gender, sexual orientation, or disability (Eyring, 2012:8). A scholarly assessment found that the play lacks clear themes, so can't really "preach" (Fortier, 1997:86-7), though that could still mean that Kushner wished to change minds and educate. Kushner's own view of his apparent polemic is this: *"Angels in America* aims to subvert the distinction between the personal and the political, to refuse to be closeted, to undermine the category of the 'normal,' and to question the fixedness and stability of every sexual identity" (quoted in Fortier, 1997:86). He made it clear to me (personal interview, 21 May 2012) that the play does not articulate any specific political message, but his sympathy for his left-wing characters surely generates support for their struggles and convictions.

I think that Albee, much like Kushner, but at a lower volume, also wishes to convey social or political ideas, though not in any narrow sense of championing a topical cause or leading a crusade. "I don't like to leave people where they were at the beginning of the play. They should emerge different from who they were when they went in. They should grow—or diminish" (Albee's remarks in a personal interview with me, October 4, 2011). In a similar vein, Kushner has said that theatre, "asks people to engage collectively in a relationship with an event... and be transformed by the degree of your engagement with it (Feldman, 2010:online)."

Since Albee has been an activist in his personal life outside the theatre, he has been asked if his political concerns come through in his playwriting, and he has replied that, "all plays are political, way deep down underneath" (Albee, 2005:286). The difference between Albee and Wasserman, I believe, is that a "propaganda" play of Wasserman – though this is too strong a word for his actual work – would be deliberate and open in its polemic, or even didactic. Albee's plays have a political dimension; the spectator should grow, but not in any pre-approved, correct manner. So we can see clearly that all three playwrights have a political purpose to some degree.

Finally, the questionnaires ask the viewers to provide basic demographic information such as their age, education, frequency of theatre attendance, and nationality. It is my hope that these responses will help me generalize about segments of the Bulgarian audience, and their theatre tastes and preferences.

CHAPTER THREE: The Three Productions: *One Flew Over the Cuckoo's Nest, Angels in America,* and *The Goat, or Who is Sylvia?*

Public Reception: Thematic Controversy and Awards

In introducing these three American plays, one can point to obvious themes and subject matter in common, but the most striking similarity is extraneous to their stories, and that is the controversies that greeted their premiers. In fact, they all probably caused the biggest theatrical controversies of the year: *One Flew Over the Cuckoo's Nest* for its early attack on the 1960s establishment (even though the story was well known from Kesey's book); *Angels in America* for its stark depiction of AIDS victims, its coarse language, and its graphic depiction of gay sex on stage; and *The Goat* for its discussion of, of all things, bestiality, and its sympathetic portrayal of its practitioner.

I should note that this societal reception is not the same as the audience reception. The playgoers had their own political views that may well have influenced how much they liked or understood the plays, but the public reaction described here is that in the broader media and political establishment, often by people who never saw the plays. They merely heard about them, and that alone was enough to cause concern, generate applause, or provoke protest. This public reception certainly generated interest in the plays among potential playgoers, and probably inclined them to like or at least be more receptive to challenges or new ideas in them. (See an example in east Texas in chapter five, below.)

In addition to these similar public reactions, all the plays are in some way are about sickness: mental illness, AIDS, sexual perversion. All have homosexual characters, and two are by gay authors. All are very much about that ancient and universal taboo, sexuality, and all try to push the envelope in their discussion of it. Indeed, Albee has almost made his theatrical career by teasing American society's hang-ups and hesitation about addressing issues of sexuality. For example, the Pulitzer Prize committee for the Best Play in 1963 recommended Albee's *Who's Afraid of Virginia Woolf*, but the Pulitzer board, with sole discretion in awarding the prize, rejected the recommendation due to the play's perceived vulgarity.

Another curious similarity of the plays, perhaps due to their controversial reception, is their success, both among the public, and in the awards sweepstakes. There is one exception to this in that the original Broadway 1963 run of *One Flew Over the Cuckoo's Nest* cannot be considered a success, for reasons I will discuss below. But the 1971 off-Broadway New York revival was a commercial success, and the 2001 Broadway revival won the Tony Award that year for Best Play Revival. *Angels in America* collected eight major domestic awards, including the Pulitzer Prize for Drama and the Tony Award for Best Drama, both in 1993. The play is also the last item in prominent critic Harold Bloom's controversial list of the most important works of literature, *The Western Canon* (1994). As for *The Goat*, it earned Albee his second Tony Award in 2002, among other lesser prizes.

Translation and Language: Obscenity and Humor

Since this study asks what the Bulgarian audience understands or fails to understand about the American plays, I wish to look at elements in the original texts that might cause difficulty. I will study particular elements of the plays in the respective chapters about them that follow, but for now a few comments about their common problems are in order.

All of the plays owe their success and reputations for controversy to some degree to language that is colorful or lyrical, obscene, or comic. All of these elements pose difficulties to the translator. Culturally embedded jokes, as well as the puns and wordplay of Albee, are naturally tricky to convey.

Valeria Tasca, writing about her translations of the plays of the Italian Noble Prize laureate Dario Fo into French, calls the work "truly a diabolical undertaking." In particular, she cites his unusual words, "gems of wordplay," musical devices, and insults (Tasca, "Dario Fo from One Language to Another," in Pavis, 1996:116). This may sound closest to Albee, but there are similarities to all our playwrights, as I will show in later chapters.

In her description of "bad words," however, Tasca offered some insight that I found most helpful in understanding the Bulgarian adaptation of *Angels in America*. She points out the difference in the French and Italian preferences for scatology and sex, respectively.

"Fo's obscenities are carefully constructed and meaningful," but he is "very restrained in his handling of sexual terminology" (Pavis, 1996, pp. 117-118). Similarly revealing their own personal preferences, we shall see that Kushner shows little restraint in his description of sex or use of profanity—which particularly offended the conservative religious and government establishment—whereas Albee uses relatively less profanity (he wants it to sting when the character do swear) but bombards us with sexual language in *The Goat*.

Tasca also notes the differences in translating written and spoken language, including, for example, oral language's "syntactical chaos and extremes of vulgarity" (Pavis, 1996:118). This is something that Haralampi (Harry) Anichkin, the Bulgarian translator of *The Goat* and hundreds of other English plays and movies, has pointed out (personal interview, November 11, 2010). Speech always carries its own rhythms, and the translation calls for precision as well as timing, in order to maintain the pace of the original production. As Tasca writes, "It is always said that translating for the theatre is a matter of rhythm" (Pavis, 1996:119).

Tasca makes one last telling comment that bears on this work: "One translates for the theatre by ear as much as and even more than for meaning. But everyone has a different rhythm. The same translation spoken by two different actors, as I have recently experienced, can sound bland coming from one and vibrant form the other" (Pavis, 1996:119-120). The upshot then is that the translation has little value by itself if it is meant for performance. Only in actual performance will the translator know if he has the right meaning and rhythm, since that will depend on the actors' voices and skills.

Several of the theatre people I interviewed in Sofia also made a point that Bulgarian actors tend to play up the humor in the drama. The director Stefan "Teddy" Moskov was insistent that his actors tone it down so that the balance is not lost. Kushner expressed to me the same concern that humor can undercut the drama. Laughs and hamming are hard to avoid, he said, because actors know that laughter is "the most direct communication with the audience." While there are also gasps and crying, "they are softer and more atomized. All actors crave laughs, because it shows the audience is with you, which is important to the theatrical experience," he said. On Broadway, he added, "I have to police productions or actors will expand the laugh moments, which are not necessarily my best friend."

These observations introduce a note of caution that though we can credit the creative teams for generating laughs in almost every play genre, and I note that in the questionnaires, in the end there is still a matter of balance, and that laughter should come at the right times.

The Gay World in U.S. and Bulgarian Society

Each of the plays has either a gay character or, in the case of *The Goat*, both a gay character and someone whose behavior is even more outrageous to traditional society. In *Angels in America*, most of the lead characters are gay, and they include a Mormon, a Jew, a WASP (white, Anglo-Saxon Protestant), and an African-American. Only in *One Flew Over the Cuckoo's Nest* does sexual orientation seem to be a secondary theme—though the sexual repression of the hospital management and the emotional imbalances it causes are key to Kesey's story. For example, the mental patient Dale Harding is a repressed homosexual who can't satisfy his voluptuous wife, while the adult Billy Bibbit is still tied to his dominant mother's apron strings. These fragile patients fall victim to Nurse Ratched's emotionally destructive group therapies, apparently designed to control them by destroying their self-esteem.

If we are to understand the American and Bulgarian audience's and society's reception of these plays, we will need to look at the climate for Lesbian, Gay, Bisexual, and Transgender (LGBT) people in the U.S. and Bulgaria, since public attitudes surely influence how the plays are be understood and received. According to a Pew Global Attitudes poll conducted in 2002, 50-59% of Americans said that homosexuality should be accepted by society, while only 30-39% of Bulgarians did. A more recent poll by the European Union showed that only 15% of Bulgarians support same-sex marriage. By contrast, in 2010, 44% of Americans believed that marriages between same-sex couples should be recognized by law. More significantly perhaps, a 2010 Gallup Poll showed that over half of Americans now believe that gay and lesbian relations are morally acceptable (http://www.gallup.com/poll/135764/Americans-Acceptance-Gay-Relations-Crosses-Threshold.aspx, 2 April 2011), which has historically been a indicator of the lagging acceptance of gay civil union or marriage.

The Gallup organization concludes:

> There is a gradual cultural shift under way in Americans' views toward gay individuals and gay rights. While public attitudes haven't moved consistently in gays' and lesbians' favor every year, the general trend is clearly in that direction. This year, the shift is apparent in a record-high level of the public seeing gay and lesbian relations as morally acceptable. Meanwhile, support for legalizing gay marriage, and for the legality of gay and lesbian relations more generally, is near record highs. (Gallup website above)

The other interesting aspect emerging from the polls is the role of religions, and how closely opposition to same-sex marriage and accepting gay relations track with religious practice. For example, for those who said that religion is very important in their lives, 27% accepted same-sex marriage. For those who said it is not important, 71% say that such marriage should be legal. I note this because about 83% of Bulgarians identify themselves as Orthodox Christians according to the 2001 Bulgarian census, but in a 2005 report by the Bulgarian Academy of Sciences (Wikipedia: http://en.wikipedia.org/wiki/Freedom_of_religion_in_Bulgaria),
only 50% of them identified themselves as practicing. Anecdotally, I have heard that this means only rare or occasional attendance at church, usually for Christmas or Easter. In the U.S., by contrast, 39% of Americans in 2009 said that they attend worship services at least weekly (Pew Forum on Religion and Public Life, at

http://pewforum.org/Religious-Attendance/Is-a-Bad-Economy-Good-for-Church-Attendance.aspx, accessed 1 July 2012).

The Pew Forum writes in broad terms:

> Pew Forum surveys over several years show that Americans are generally more comfortable with religion playing a major role in public life. In contrast, Europeans generally place much less importance on religion in their lives, and general indicators show that major churches in Europe are declining in terms of membership, recruitment of clergy, financial contributions and overall public influence. (http://pewforum.org/Politics-and-Elections/Secular-Europe-and-Religious-America-Implications-for-Transatlantic-Relations.aspx, accessed 1 July 2012)

I should add that the Pew Forum study did note that the decline in religious practice is more common in Western and Central Europe than in Orthodox Europe. This will be of interest when we look at the influence of the Orthodox Church in Bulgaria, below.

There have also been shifting attitudes in America on whether one is born with a gay orientation or one chooses such a lifestyle:

> There is one surprising area where young people differ from their elders about homosexuality. Since the pollsters started asking about it in the late 1977, the number saying homosexuality is something one is born with has been growing. But today, more young people than older ones believe it is a lifestyle choice. In May 50% of 18-29 year olds told CBS News pollsters that being homosexual is something people choose to be; 47% said it was something a person couldn't change. Among those 65 and over, however, 25% said it was a choice, 55% said it was something

that couldn't be changed. (Karlyn Bowman for American Enterprise Institute, at http://www.aei.org/article/102442, 20 August 2010)

Though there may be no clear trend in whether young Americans believe that homosexuality is either inborn or a lifestyle choice, what is evident is that they increasingly see it as something that cannot be changed, and therefore not a sin in religious terms, but something that should be accepted.

The chief vehicle to promote gay rights in both the U.S. and Europe in recent years has been the annual gay "pride" parades, a demonstration that LGBT people are here to stay, proud of who they are, and won't go back in the closet. The Gay Pride march, as it was originally known, has its roots in the gay community of New York. In a public climate in which educators and political leaders warned children about the danger of molestation and abduction by homosexual predators, and gay acts illegal nationwide, the New York police raided a popular, demimonde gay bar, the Stonewall Inn, on 28 June 1969. In the wake of decades of protest under the banners of black, women's and other liberations, the gay community felt the sting of victimization, and took to the street to demand their rights. Hence was born the first Pride Parade.

Having expanded across the U.S. and into Europe, the Parades are sometimes accused by detractors as a tool steered or manipulated by outsiders, and they have been met with various degrees of violence and hostility, especially in the more socially conservative cities of Eastern Europe. Such parades have been held in Sofia each year from 2008 to 2012. The first, with about 150 participants, provoked attacks by far-right nationalist and football hooligans, who threw gasoline bombs and bottles of urine. No one was hurt, but of course many were unnerved and intimidated. In the demonstration of 2010, which I observed, there were more participants, and still apparently hostile elements lining the route—and many uniformed police—but no violence. The mainstream Orthodox Church rasied its voice against the gay parades and the openly gay lifestyle, saying that it undermines Christianity, the offical religion of Bulgaria (Novinite, 18.4.2011:online). American gays face the same oppposition from domestic conservative, often southern U.S. churches and others, which opposed the opening of *Angels in America* in the 1990s, such as in east Texas (discussed in chapter five, below).

What all this data tells us is something evident to those who have lived in the U.S. or Great Britain and see the shifts in attitudes toward LGBT there, but not yet in Bulgaria. As British Ambassador Steve Williams said at his farewell in Sofia on 14 March 2011 about sexual orientation:

> In the UK, there has been a huge change in the last 20 years. With the exception of a few "macho" professions – most especially, regrettably, professional sport – it is simply no longer a big deal whether someone is straight or gay, any more than whether they are black or white, or left or right handed.

> Here in Bulgaria the subject is still sensitive, but much less so than in the 1980s when it was taboo. I was heartened by the fact that last year for the first time some of the mainstream media and some of the mainstream political parties publicly came out in support of Lesbian, Gay Bisexual and Transgender (LGBT) rights. That puts Bulgaria ahead of many countries in the region and you should be proud of that. Amusingly, an extremist in Bulgaria criticized me for supporting LGBT rights, and emphasized the fact that I was married with 3 children, as if it was therefore somehow impossible for a heterosexual to support the rights of homosexuals.

The Pride parade rolled out in June, 2011, but again by hundreds of police that kept hostile forces at bay. According to the police, there was only one NGO protesting, called "Forum for Defending Children and Family," whose protest consisted of handing out brochures entitled, "The Myths about Homosexuality." After the parade, however, according to news reports, five activists from LGBT Action, a supportive NGO, were attacked as they were walking away, by about six hooligans. Though their injuries were light, the police made no immediate arrests.

As noted above, the Orthodox Church in Bulgaria is leading the conservative forces against the parades. Prior to the 30 June 2012, the Orthodox Holy Synod declared that it is "categorically against" the Pride parade, which it called "immoral" (*24 Chasa*, 2012:4). *24 Chasa* also quotes the president of Alexander Nevski Cathedral in Sofia in a Darik Radio interview saying that

> it is unacceptable for an American president to try to convince us that we should tolerate homosexuals at

> all costs. I would not be surprised if they impose gay marriages on us. No one stones and beats homosexuals with sticks; they can do whatever they want in their private space, but should stop overexposing themselves. (ibid.)

Things in Bulgaria took a darker turn just on the eve of the parade, when Priest Evgeni Yanakiev from the Bulgarian Orthodox Church in Sliven stated that citizens should throw stones at the participants in the Pride Parade. This generated a letter from a Human Rights Watch official to Minister of Justice Diana Kovacheva, which expressed concern about the priest's calls for violence. Kovacheva then issued a statement saying, "Bulgaria is a tolerant country which abides by the European principles of non-discrimination on the basis of sexual orientation" (*Trud*, 28.6.2012:7). There were no incidents at the actual parade, in which about 2000 people took part, but one participant was attacked on his way home and about 200 people organized by far-right parties participated in a counter-demonstration (Novinite, 1.7.2012:online).

The climate surrounding the gay Pride parades perhaps suggests best of all the continued gap in public attitudes toward LGBT between American and Bulgarian social leaders. But the gap in attitudes toward LGBT can also be seen in the theatre worlds. The American story might start with Mart Crowley's *The Boys in the Band* (1968), an off-Broadway hit about gay men at a birthday party, which is often cited as the first homosexual play (Kaufman, 1994:774) and later a successful movie by William Friedkin (1970). Openly gay-themed plays began to appear on the New York stage in the 1970s and 1980s, including Terence McNally's *The Ritz* (1975); Martin Sherman's *Bent* (1980), about the persecution of gays in Nazi Germany; and *Torch Song Trilogy* (1981), about a Jewish drag queen's longing for love, by the actor and writer Harvey Fierstein.

The biggest play on a gay theme was also penned by Fierstein, *La Cage aux Folles*, in 1983, a musical with lyrics and music by Jerry Herman, it won the Tony Award for Best Musical. The story of a gay nightclub owner and his straight son, it was based on a 1973 French play by Jean Poiret. A hit movie followed, and the play has become a standard, both in revival on Broadway (2011), and on national tour.

Many gay-themed plays followed, but among them one should note *The Normal Heart* (1985), by Larry Kramer, about an anti-AIDS crusader. Thus it is clear that Kushner had many successful predecessors in the gay theatre: Contemporary hits include the musical *Kiss of the Spider Woman (1993)*, and the comedy, *The Sisters Rosensweig* (1992), so he knew that there would be a receptive audience in San Francisco and New York for a play about gays and AIDS. As for the political climate, as *Time* magazine noted, Kushner "and the delighted spectators reflect an evolution in attitude akin to what happened among blacks and women: one generation sought empathy; the next demanded justice; the generation equivalent to Kushner's just flat-out asserted equality and spurned any more debate" (quoted in *Commentary*, 2011:82). In fact, several social and arts commentators have noted that with *Angels in America*, despite what some called the persistence of self-loathing in the play, a new movement was afoot:

> in the theater, long a haven for gay artists provided they addressed straight topics, gay characters and stories have abruptly taken center stage. After decades on the fringe, gay-themed works are increasingly enjoying lavish Broadway productions and being embraced by mainstream heterosexuals. "The trend really peaked this year," says John Harris, editor of TheaterWeek. "All the hot properties seem to be gay." (Henry, 1993:online)

Albee has also addressed similar themes, but despite his gay identity, they have not been the centerpiece of his work. I will return to the gay theatre-gay audience issue in the discussion of *Angels in America*, below.

CHAPTER FOUR: *One Flew Over the Cuckoo's Nest:* A Free Adaptation

History of the Play's Productions

One Flew Over the Cuckoo's Nest opened at the Cort Theatre in New York City on 13 November 1963. Written by Dale Wasserman, produced by the solid team of David Merrick and Edward Lewis, and directed by Alex Segel, it starred Kirk Douglas as Randall McMurphy, Ed Ames as the Indian Chief Bromden, Gene Wilder as Billy Bibbit, and Joan Tetzel as the formidable Nurse Ratched. Those who know something of the storied later success of this play will be surprised to know that despite this stellar cast, the original production flopped on Broadway. In fact, this production was savaged by the critics and closed after 82 performances, in just ten weeks of performances (DeDanan, 1995:12). What this indicates, I believe, is that even outstanding performances by the best actors – *New York* magazine's erudite theatre critic John Simon attested to the outstanding performances by Douglas and Wilder (2001:online) – may not rescue a play that is poorly conceived or staged, in the view of most of the reviewers. Part of this problematic concept may be the crucial role of McMurphy, as we shall see in later productions. Already here, some reviewers dismissed the play as a comic melodrama, and Wasserman himself disowned the production on the grounds that "Douglas demanded a lovable McMurphy" (Campbell, 2001:7), while he wanted a more textured personality.

Sterling Lord, Kesey's and Jack Kerouac's literary agent, and therefore not really an objective observer, nevertheless had a positive, first-person reaction to the play's premier:

> Opening night for *Cuckoo's Nest,* at the Cort Theatre...was memorable. The house was packed, and Dale Wasserman's dramatization was superb. But the subject of a mental institution was not yet acceptable to all the theatergoers. Although it was a riveting performance, by the end of Act I about 15 to 20 percent of the audience had walked out. Those of us who remained were spellbound. (2011:online)

In other words, the play's downer subject matter was not in tune with, or rather perhaps ahead of, its time. It's curious in any case why the later blockbuster play failed to ignite. Let's look at the bestselling and countercultural classic Kesey novel it was based on, which was published the year before the opening. Kesey wrote a freewheeling novel influenced in style by the 1950s Beat poets, such as Lawrence Ferlinghetti and Allen Ginsberg. Kesey became a heavy drug user and drew from his experience working as an orderly in a Menlo Park, California mental health facility, where he was introduced to psychedelic drugs. His novel has been credited with sparking the Psychedelic Generation associated with the drug-popping advocate, Timothy Leary.

Unlike the play and later movie, the novel's central voice and narrator is Chief Bromden, the delusional psychiatric-ward patient who sees the civilized world as a "Combine," or huge manmade apparatus, with robotic people, and nefarious machinery hidden away in the walls of buildings. The story is necessarily simpler in the Wasserman play than in the novel or movie. The free-spirited McMurphy, posing as mentally ill in order to escape a work farm, undertakes to cure the patients with laughter—which "rings big and free, and its vibrations jolt the Patients open-mouthed" (Wasserman, 1970:12)—spontaneity, rule-breaking, and lusty sex. After asserting his authority among the patients, McMurphy learns the rigid policies hammered in by Nurse Ratched at both the group therapy sessions and in everyday rules of behavior. McMurphy regularly engages the patients in gambling and even bets them that he can dethrone the tyrannical head nurse without losing his temper or "cussin' her out." He also soon cannily discovers that Chief Bromden is neither deaf nor incapable of speaking, and with his help, pushes through a vote on watching baseball on the ward's TV. But because of his rebelliousness and defense of Bromden, Ratched sends him to electric shock therapy. Later, McMurphy arranges a ward party with two prostitutes so that Billy, a virgin terrorized by his mother, can experience sex with one of them. But this backfires when Ratched catches the couple after the act, and Billy commits suicide when the nurse threatens to report his moral lapse to his mother. This provokes McMurphy's attack on Ratched, and results in the institution's administering a lobotomy on him. This punishment fully removes him as a threat to her authority. Ratched later returns as supervisor of the ward, but unable to speak, and greatly diminished in stature. McMurphy, now a mere vegetable, is smothered to death with a pillow by Bromden. The Chief then chooses a water console that McMurphy had earlier tried and failed to lift, and rips it from the floor, proving, as he says, "I am full size again." He then escapes the hospital for good through an open window.

In the course of McMurphy's battle with Nurse Ratched, a symbol of manipulative and cruel Establishment authority, he liberates the spirit of the other patients, especially Bromden, who is not only encouraged to break free of the hospital but, symbolically, to break out of his psychological prison.

The story was a natural for Wasserman, who was orphaned at the age of nine and described himself as "a self-educated hobo" (McLellan, 2008:online), or someone in synch with the freewheeling McMurphy. Wasserman had only one year of high school in Los Angeles before starting theatre work for the illustrious producer and impresario Sol Hurok, and was 50 years old when he wrote the play *One Flew Over the Cuckoo's Nest*. Despite the flop of the first Broadway run, its later success around the world, as we shall see, rivals Wasserman's huge success three years later with his book for the Broadway musical classic, *Man of La Mancha* (1966). Unsurprisingly, this is another story about a crazy outsider who marches to a different drummer.

Apart from the formal differences noted above between the novel and the original play, there is another significant element in the Merrick-Lewis production that differs from the novel and many later performances, including both stage and movie versions. This is the conclusion of the story. In the original 1970 and 1974 Wasserman texts, some time after the night of sex and boozing, the lobotomized ringleader McMurphy is wheeled out on the floor and all the patients gather round to debate whether the abject figure is really McMurphy. Later that night, Bromden smothers McMurphy and pulls out the water console, as in the other versions. But only in Wasserman's texts does Bromden also cry and say, "I'm afraid." With some encouragement from a fellow patient (Scanlon in the novel, Harding in the play), Bromden escapes from the hospital, but has to be practically pushed out the window by Harding.

The dramatic weakness of Wasserman's ending seems clear now: McMurphy is sacrificed, but only after transferring his strength and confidence to Chief Bromden, as well as to the other "acutes," most of whom, Kesey writes, are discharged from the hospital or get internal transfers off Ratched's ward. Yet at the end of the original Wasserman play, Bromden is still wimpy and whining, which halts the emotional locomotive. Even worse, Wasserman removed Kesey's outstanding symbolic device: the very console that earlier proved too heavy for McMurphy is not only ripped out by Bromden, but hurled through the grated window, bursting it open and clearing the path to freedom. This clear symbolism is in the novel, and retained in later, highly successful versions of the play, as well as in the Milos Forman movie. So it seems that Morfov made the right decision in ignoring Wasserman's script and keeping to the Kesey story (page 42, above).

Despite the troubled first production on Broadway, a 27-year-old unheralded local San Francisco director, Lee Sankowich, undertook the play seven years later in this countercultural capital, toward the end of the rebellious sixties. Opened at the Little Fox Theater in 1970, it did not do well with the critics either. According to Mary DeDanan (1995:12), "With Wasserman's blessing, Sankowich had rewritten parts of the script himself, using the novel for inspiration. 'I went much further than I had a right to go,' he says now. It worked, though."

The most fundamental rewrite was the suicide of Billy Bibbit. Sankowich wrote (in an email to me, January, 2012), that Wasserman, "said it didn't work when the Kirk Douglas production was trying it out in Boston so he scrapped it. He was very upset when he read I put it into my production in SF. However, upon seeing it he loved it and put it into his republished script [1974]." It is hard to imagine how the drama could be effective without the suicide, and I have to wonder if this is one key reason the original Broadway production failed to thrive. Most later revival reviews or critiques cite the pivotal importance of Billy and his suicide, and certainly Brad Dourif, who was nominated for a Best Supporting Actor Academy Award, contributed to the movie's success, and defined the role for many later interpreters.

Sankowich said, in a phone interview for me on 18 January 2012 (all of his subsequent remarks are from this personal interview), that he also added Chief Bromden's voiceover, or "head trips," which several reviewers particularly liked. His San Francisco production ran for five and half years, till 1975, and revealed the dramatic and commercial potential in the story.

Sankowich also said that Bromden did not hurl the water console through the hospital window to escape in all the early productions he knew of, since that was difficult to stage in some of the theatres. This has become standard, however, since then.

Sankowich recalled the critical reaction to the play. The premier was panned by San Francisco's two major newspaper reviewers (*San Francisco Chronicle* and *San Francisco Examiner*), but a highly influential non-critic, the *Chronicle* columnist Herb Caen, championed the play, and played a key rule in building the audience. It was particularly popular with young people and students, who idolized the anti-hero McMurphy as well as his rebellious creator, Ken Kesey. According to Sankowich, Kesey was in fact the real hero, and the reason that students who had read the novel formed lines around the block every play night for rush tickets.

Sankowich says he abridged the long play from the original, which was over three hours, to one with the curtain down after two hours and forty minutes. He also restructured the play from three acts to two, with the only intermission just after the patients pretend to watch the exciting World Series baseball championship on television. This seems to be an excellent moment in the story to pause, because it is a high point of McMurphy's power and influence. Sankowich did not take credit for introducing the final scene revision, in which Bromden tosses the water console through the window grille to break it open, but when we spoke he was aware of it from the 1975 Forman movie.

Sankowich told me that Kesey and Wasserman both saw his first production and highly approved of it. (As noted above, Wasserman was at first jealous of his playwright rights, though he told Sankowich that he did not at all like the Kirk Douglas version on Broadway.) Shortly before show time, Kesey arrived with his large family and the notorious Merry Pranksters, for a party of thirty-five in all, and filled the theatre aisles. This of course added to the show's celebrity buzz. Kesey told Sankowich that all the characters were indeed from the veterans hospital where he had worked—except significantly, McMurphy, a product of his imagination.

While *Cuckoo's Nest* continued to fill the house at the Little Fox until 1975, Sankowich also had great success with it on the road. He was responsible for the first successful New York production, an off-Broadway revival in 1971 at the Mercer-Hansberry Theatre, which ran for two and half years, good by any measure. McMurphy was portrayed by William Devane, who later went on to a successful film career. Christopher Lehmann-Haupt, The New York Times critic, wrote (2001:47) that this production was done "in a slightly different form" from the original Broadway production, but I am skeptical if he was aware of the actual scale of the changes, and Sankowich did tell me that he changed a lot of the original Wasserman text.

In all, Sankowich says he was responsible for eleven productions of *Cuckoo's Nest*, including those in Boston, Los Angeles, Baltimore and Israel, and two record-breaking tours at colleges. I saw his successful production of it at Philadelphia's Walnut Street Theater in the early 1970s, and remember the excitement the sold-out show generated, especially among young people. (I was a college student at the time.) The multiple Oscar-winning movie, directed by Milos Forman, starring Jack Nicholson, appeared in 1975. Notably, the screenplay, which also won an Academy Award for best adaptation from other material, was written by Lawrence Hauben and Bo Goldman, and was said to be based on the novel, not Wasserman's play, confirming that the trend was moving away from Wasserman's version (Horwitz, 2001:21). But Kesey was not at all happy with how the movie was being developed, and never saw it (Lord, 2011:online). When once asked why he hadn't seen the movie, Kesey was reported to have said, "It would be like watching your under-aged daughter raped in a parking lot to a standing ovation" (Sankowich interview, 2012). More prosaically, it was reported that he quarreled with the movie's producers about their creative choices, later sued them, and accepted a settlement (Lehmann-Haupt, 2001:47).

Sankowich's major New York production was enough to capture the attention of the largest commercial and foreign English-language theatres. The first London production was staged at the Playhouse Theatre in April, 1988. The play's production history seems to have been well-timed, capturing the counter-cultural zeitgeist of the sixties, and then riding the wave of anti-establishment, antiwar sentiment – since the Establishment that brought the Vietnam War is fit for an insane asylum – into the early seventies. The flavor of the movement is captured in both the film depiction of a nuclear Armageddon set off by a deranged Pentagon general, Stanley

Kubrick's *Dr. Strangelove* (1964), and in an activist NGO of that era, the Committee for a Sane Nuclear Policy (SANE). Even the acronym for U.S. nuclear defense policy, MAD ("mutually assured destruction"), reflected Kesey's apparent theme that it was the American political leaders who were crazy, not the protestors or rebels. And one must also mention Joseph Heller's antiwar bestseller, *Catch-22*, which appeared the same year as Kesey's novel (1961). Its famous "catch-22" paradox refers to a putative U.S. Air Force regulation, which says that willingness to fly dangerous combat missions must be considered insane, but if pilots protest it on mental grounds, their request proves their sanity.

The most recent major American production of *Cuckoo's Nest* was created by the highly-regarded Steppenwolf Theater in Chicago, with Gary Sinise (a Steppenwolf Theater co-founder) starring as McMurphy. The production premiered in April, 2000, and was directed by Terry Kinney, with major roles by Amy Morton, Tim Sampson, Eric Johner, and Ross Lehman, several of whom went on to lucrative Hollywood film careers. The ensemble production sold out immediately and had a similarly successful commercial run starting on July 27 at London's Barbicon Centre.

This production reached Broadway in another successful run at the Royale Theatre in April, 2001, which was later extended for three months. It won the Tony Award that year for Best Play Revival, and Gary Sinise was nominated for another Tony for Best Performance by a Leading Actor. Overall, however, critical reviews were decidedly mixed: according to Robert Hofler in a *Variety* magazine survey (22.6.2001:2), the Broadway production received six favorable, six unfavorable, and six mixed reviews.

Given the relative availability of literature on Kinney's version, and its status as the latest Broadway version, with its ending consistent with both the novel and the National Theatre version, I will focus later on reviews and critiques of this production to make comparisons regarding the critical and audience receptions.

I should note, in any case, that revivals of this popular show have never really stopped. Apart from the string of productions by Lee Sankowich through 1975, *Cuckoo's Nest* was staged in Paris, Mexico, Sweden, Argentina, Belgium, Japan, and most likely in many other cities, both commercially and by non-profit theatres. Wasserman claimed in 2006 that the play had been produced 140 times in the last 40 years (Cox, 2006:41). Another source says that "more than 150 productions are staged each year around the world" (Kirkpatrick, 2001:1).

Among the more recent productions was a British production in 2004 with Christian Slater, at both the Fringe in Edinburgh and later at the West End Gielgud Theatre in London. Then in 2007, Linda Hamilton took on the role of Nurse Ratched at the Berkshire Theater Festival in Stockbridge, Massachusetts. As late as July, 2011, Nicholas Cage was rumored to be considering the McMurphy role in a new production to premier in 2012. The persistent interest of A-list Hollywood stars in this play testifies to its durable public appeal.

The Forman movie quickly struck a chord in Bulgaria, which generated interest in mounting Wasserman's play. The first production was in Burgas in the 1978-79 season, shortly after Mariana Nedelcheva's Bulgarian translation of Kesey's novel appeared. The production was directed by Simeon Dimitrov, who won the best young director award from the Union of Bulgarian Artists. Dimitar Elenov played McMurphy and Elefteri Elefterov was Billy in his debut performance. This was quickly followed by a production in Varna directed by Stancho Stanchev in the 1979-80 season. The Salza i Smyah Theatre mounted it in 1980. The huge hit was directed by Krasimir Spasov, with Marin Yanev as McMurphy and Ani Bakalova as Nurse Ratched. There was another production by Simeon Dimitrov, this time in Pazardzhik in 1994-95, with Emil Emilov as McMurphy. This string of successful stage productions most likely created a favorable public climate for the next production, at the National Theatre. The America for Bulgaria Foundation directors may have selected this sure thing to balance the difficult works by Albee and Kushner when they made up their slate for the American season.

The Ivan Vazov National Theatre Production

One Flew Over the Cuckoo's Nest opened on 1 December 2010 with a creative team that was a close as one comes in Bulgaria to a sure thing. Two guarantees were the enormously popular director, Alexander Morfov, and the pop-star lead actor, Deyan Donkov, in the role of Randall McMurphy. Morfov is perhaps best known for his long-running National Theatre play, *Outcasts (Хъшове,* 2004), but he also caused a stir with what Albee would call a "free adaptation" of *One Flew Over the Cuckoo's Nest*, re-titled *Eclipse*, at the Lenkom Theatre in Moscow, in 2006. The Bulgarian adaptation had a title closer to the original of Kesey: *Polet nad kykyviche gnezdo*, or, *Flight Over Cuckoo's Nest*, but one would err to infer that this meant a faithful adaptation. The huge Russian-language hit taught Morfov to cast a dynamic pop icon as McMurphy, which he did with Donkov. Each of the three evenings that I've seen the play, the National Theatre was filled or was close to filling the 780 seats in its Grand Hall, confirmed also by newspaper observers (*Trud*, 21.1.2011:20).

In looking at this production, one must start by citing what is written publicly on the National Theatre website: "Alexander Morfov is not afraid of comparisons and makes an absolutely distinct work that cannot be compared to previous works with this title." In other words, the director Morfov alone is the "auteur." In fact, I suspect he may even dispute the term "co-author," since the phrase "absolutely distinct work" suggests that he is the sole author. The Theatre's website says that the Morfov production is based on the novel by Kesey, with no reference to the Wasserman play. National Theatre sources have told me that Morfov worked on the Bulgarian translation of the novel by Mariana Nedelcheva, but that his production is only vaguely based on it, and that it includes more of his own dramatization. This includes added scenes, such as the dance with brooms that opens scene two, and an extended party scene. Total additions pushed the premier to over four hours, whereas Sankowich's version was just two hours and forty minutes. But Morfov's version was is in the spirit of Elia Kazan, who needed to express his own artistic vision (see p. 14, above).

If we look back at the critical appraisal of the Kinney production, we can understand some of the challenges that the National Theatre faced in mounting it in 2009. To start with the most obvious hurdle, though the characters and themes undeniably struck a chord in the 1970s, especially for left-leaning young people, more recent critics have persistently called it out-of-date. For example, *Daily Variety* reviewer Frank Rizzo cited the "script's dated indulgences, especially the Chief's rambling flights of woeful poetry" (2007:2). Julia Keller, the *Chicago Tribune* theatre critic, asks a fundamental question about it:

> Since the play reflects attitudes toward mental illness that are out of sync with current science, should it continue to be staged? Can works of art embody metaphorical truth even if they are factually unsound?...We no longer believe that mental illness is a device strategically employed by creative geniuses or a political gesture designed to subvert the dominant paradigm. We know that psychiatric problems are caused by brain chemistry. We know that certain drugs can alter that chemistry and thus change behavior (2000:online).

Keller cites a mental health expert, who says, "Not only does it perpetuate stereotypes about the mentally ill, but also might dissuade people in need of psychiatric treatment from seeking it" (ibid.).

The play carries additional elements that are hardly politically correct today. The roles of Nurse Ratched as a manipulative dictator, and the bimbo prostitutes (one is named "Candy Starr"), not to mention the offstage castrating mothers and wives who caused the patients' mental disturbances, are counterbalanced only by a marginal, sympathetic Japanese nurse, Nakamura. Wasserman admitted in a 2001 interview that misogynistic stereotypes flourish in the play: "The book and the play are fearfully misogynist, and the women are treated terribly," but explained that he felt an obligation to be faithful to the novel (Kirkpatrick, 2001:E1). He also said, "It puts me in a peculiar position because I don't have those views; they make me uncomfortable and always have, even back in 1962 when I read the novel" (Horwitz, 2001:21).

So too Gary Sinise has been discomfited. He admitted that he doesn't talk about the "show's legendary sexist subtext." Terry Kinney, however, has said, "If the play seems mildly sexist, the novel is overtly sexist...I put 'Cuckoo's Nest' in the world of myth, and these symbols are mythological" (Hofler, 2001:9). He also apparently strove already in the original Chicago production to keep "both McMurphy and Ratched from ever going over the top – as they have in many productions – Kinney keeps this *Cuckoo's Nest* from fully whipping up and manipulating audience emotions" (Abarbanel, 2000:15).

Another element that dates the play is its casual racism. There are no African-Americans patients or nurses, and the only black characters are the irresponsible night aide Turkle and two dim black orderlies, all of whom are written largely as foils to amplify McMurphy's energy and cleverness. Completely unsympathetic, the orderlies are scornful toward the patients, yet servile toward Ratched, who calls them "boys," in outdated, condescending language.

In Wasserman's play, the black aides are introduced talking African-American vernacular while making fun of Chief Bromden:

Williams: What you want, baby? Yo' broom? (Going to fetch it.) Thassit. He want his broom.

Warren: Ol' Chief Broom. Thassit, baby, thassa good loony. (1970:7)

After this puerile exchange, Wasserman's stage notes say that, "They bray with laughter." One might interpret these characters as fellow victims of the oppressive system, and not as flunky cogs in the power structure, were they not so two-faced, malicious, and contemptible.

But the orderlies' roles are actually more balanced in Kesey's novel, where they are ugly and hate-filled, but also clearly victims of Ratched's manipulation. As Bromden says: "When she finally gets the three [two in the Wasserman play] she wants—gets them one at a time and over a number of years, weaving them into her plan and her network—she's damn positive they hate enough to be capable" (1962:31).

At the National Theatre, Alexander Morfov was responsible for solutions to these inherent problems. One of these is the datedness, which includes the patient Harding, someone we would now call a closeted homosexual, taking offense at being called a "fairy"

(Wasserman, 1974:24). Morfov and his creative team at the National Theatre addressed this issue head-on. As he said, during the process of adaptation, geographical and political issues were taken into consideration to form a play that would be understandable for the viewers with certain characteristics, that is, for modern Bulgarians living in 2010, in a different political system. (All remarks by Alexander Morfov, and later by the actor Rusi Chanev, are taken from a personal interview with them on 16 January, 2012. I have used only paraphrases drawn from my notes, not tape-recorded remarks.)

To start, little could be done, I think, to change the story's essential mechanism of society's brutal treatment via lobotomy of the rebel McMurphy without eviscerating the narrative and theme. If lobotomy is no longer employed in psychiatric practice to treat putative aggressive or anti-social behavior, knowing viewers of the play must then accept that this is a historical drama, not a contemporary one, either in the United States or Bulgaria. In my view, this shouldn't detract from the effectiveness of the play any more than does the datedness of Shakespeare or Molière. We simply accept the history, and don't demand anachronisms or changes on stage. I agree with Morfov when he says that the datedness is, relatively speaking, not as serious as it would have been if, for example, it had concerned use of a guillotine instead of lobotomy, since the latter has the echo of modern medicine.

Morfov is correct when he said that electric shocks are still employed to treat mental illness. According to Dr. Herb Campbell, a psychiatrist based in Athens, Greece, it is currently called ECT (electric convulsive therapy), and is occasionally used to help patients locked in a cycle of depression, since it works like turning off and on a circuit breaker. Incidentally, Dr. Campbell says that "Nurse Ratched" is an epithet known today among psychiatrists for a type of rigid, harsh, and controlling mental health practitioner.

Morfov had insightful observations on this matter. He showed that he clearly respects the National Theatre's audience, and its ability to accept the contemporary issues in the play. The veteran National Theatre actor Rusi Chanev, who plays Scanlon, a patient in the play, added that the Bulgarian public has seen or knows the novel, play, and movie. They are open-minded, he said, and see the better parts of the play, disregarding what is out of date. Morfov said that he felt he could mount *Cuckoo's Nest* while avoiding the issues that are typically American and not understandable for Bulgarian audiences. True to his word, he also avoided some of the medical issues: he says he could have focused on the medical "experimentation," but downplayed this element of the play. Chanev added that the challenge in using older stories, as Shakespeare did, is to transform or interpret them, and make them interesting to one's contemporaries. You need to recreate a true and authentic picture of those distant times or foreign places for those who have never lived in them, he said.

Regarding the play's sexism, in Sofia Nurse Ratched is still the antagonist, the other nurses are still female and subservient, and McMurphy's girlfriends are still floozies. American producers and directors have for some time made creative adjustments to address such issues, and Morfov seems to have done the same. According to Vyara Tabakova (personal interview, 16 March 2012), he made her character, Nurse Flinn, a kindly person, as she says, "I am good, the opposite of Ratched. Not as 'sweet' as her on the outside, but I like everyone, I laugh all the time."

As for the prostitutes, one of them could have a witty or intelligent line or two, rather than just be introduced as American-style sex symbols: In Morfov's version, one of them even wears a red, white, and blue vest and hotpants. This may add to the humor and fun of the production, if not to the political correctness.

The final controversial issue is the handling of the racial issues, which Morfov and company do with one decision: All the black characters are eliminated. To be sure, Bulgarian characters portraying Africans using makeup is commonplace, but Morfov chose not to address or interpret the racial elements in Kesey's story.

This is a valid and responsible approach, I believe, to an unfortunate component of the novel and play. It should be said, however, that American theatre producers and directors often go further in addressing this situation. As I wrote above, Morfov could have made one or more of the female characters more positive. It would have been even easier to make a statement about racial attitudes in a choice of characters. As far back as the 1970's in America, Joseph Papp, the enormously influential director of New York's Public Theater and the New York Shakespeare Festival, broke new ground by casting African-American actors in lead

Shakespearean roles—and not only as Othello (Turan and Papp, 2009:86)—to the consternation of much of the city's critical establishment. Sankowich also told me that he considered making one of the black orderlies a white, but that his audiences had no trouble with this aspect of the play.

Similarly, rather than sidestep the issue, Morfov could have made at least one of the patients black, or, to address the sexism, introduce a male nurse. This is what a contemporary American director would do, since it is fairly routine. For example, for the 2011 staging of the classic 1943 musical *Oklahoma!* at Washington's Arena Stage, the theatre's program notes explained that, though the show traditionally contained no black characters, in fact, non-native setters in the Oklahoma territory in the nineteenth century, the venue for the story, included a large number of African-American families. So in its production, the innovative Arena team turned farm girl Laurey Williams and her Aunt Eller into a black family. The audience had no trouble buying into the spark that arises between the attractive young woman and the handsome white suitor, Curley.

Morfov's decision to drop the racial subplot is consistent with his reaction to Desi Shpatova's *Angels in America*: see page 165 below.

Another significant change was Morfov's decision to drop all of Bromden's delusional voiceover in the Wasserman text, based on his interior monologues in the Kesey novel. These might have been understood, he said, but would have had no emotional impact. This is a notable example, since Sankowich said these "headtrips" were among the most effective devices in his 1970 San Francisco production. Surely the drug culture of that audience determined their welcome reception of the device. They were also retained in the Kinney production and praised by some of the critics.

Brecht had another view of this psychological spotlight: He wrote that in his theatre he is less interested in personal psychology than in the social man, that he disdained psychological realism because it diverted attention from the social and political structure of the characters' world ("issues of individual morality rather than with larger social structures"), and wished to avoid looking at the world "through a keyhole" (Bennett, 1990:23).

Based on Morfov's many public comments, he seems to share this view. In his *Dnevnik* (29.11.2010:7) and *Trud* interviews (26.11.2010:22), for example, he talks at length about the character and struggles of the Bulgarian male as a social animal, but never employs the language of pop psychology. I find it somewhat strange and ironical that, in a play about mental ward patients, Morfov is not particularly interested in their inner lives or personal psychology.

Of all the latent themes in Kesey's work, I believe that Morfov's focus on the outward or social animal determined his interpretation. Here is what he told the newspaper *Duma*:

> The play is about the whole world, which is going mad. All actors have been given suitable roles. Some roles are stronger and consume the weaker ones in order to gain even more strength, and unfortunately, in reality we are the weak ones and most of the time we are the ones who are eaten (4.12.2010:26).

In this same interview, Morfov does mention his usual tropes that we are all living in a worldwide madhouse, and that man must rebel against rigid principles and rules. But it is interesting how he picked up so accurately one of the play's themes, articulated by the intellectual patient, Harding: "the world belongs to the strong, my friend. The rabbit recognizes the strength of the wolf, so he digs holes and hides when the wolf is about...All of us here are rabbits" (Wasserman, 1970:27). This is also laid out on the National Theatre's website background information on the play (30 November 2011), which tells us that the theme is freedom, and that today's "freedom by schedule" has a basic law: the law of the strong.

True to his claim, however, Morfov probably derived his theme directly from Kesey's more explicit novel, in which Harding tells McMurphy:

> This world . . . belongs to the strong, my friend! The ritual of our existence is based on the strong getting stronger by devouring the weak. ... The rabbits accept their role in the ritual and recognize the wolf as the strong. In defense ... he digs holes and hides when the wolf is about...All of us here are rabbits of varying ages and degrees. (Kesey, 1962:60-1)

Among Morfov's most interesting interview comments was his description of the play's history in the Soviet bloc. Although it was popular throughout the Western world up through the fall of the Berlin Wall, it was forbidden in the Soviet Union prior to perestroika. This may seem counter-intuitive, since *One Flew Over the Cuckoo's Nest* is *prima facie* an attack on American medical practice and power structures, and the Soviets preferred to publish and celebrate critical or left-wing American writers, such as John Steinbeck and Kurt Vonnegut. But for the 1960s Kremlin, the Kesey story was seen as equally an attack on the Soviet government, and attacked too clearly Soviet illusions, according to Morfov. The Soviets seem to have been right: Nedyalko Delchev, a theatre professor at the American University in Bulgaria, told me (personal interview, 11 March 2012), that when he first saw *Cuckoo's Nest* at the Salza i Smyah Theatre when he was 12 years of age, he realized afterward that, "I lived in a prison camp and can't leave." That is why for him, as for others of his generation, the play is about freedom. This is how Daniel Nenchev (2010:11) and other critics interpret it.

What's more, the play recalled too sharply the Soviet practice of consigning dissidents to mental hospitals. According to a *Variety* review of the Steppenwolf production, Kesey makes the case that, "folks judged insane by a repressive society are really just victims of the government's thought police" (Jones, 2000:28).

In any case, the play gained huge popularity in the late communist era. Most East Europeans learned of the Kesey novel or play from the Forman movie (or never knew it was based on a bestselling book). It's easy to get the impression in Bulgaria that almost everyone has seen and liked it, as Chanev said, but they only first got to view it in the mid-1980s, ten years after its American premier. One not insignificant attraction, Morfov avers, is that Milos Forman is "one of us," an East European, and presumably one who shares the regional sensibility or worldview.

The question of what East Europeans, and especially Bulgarians, typically like about this play brings us to the question of the celebration of freedom, and the appeal of the antihero Randall McMurphy. This character has been depicted as part of a moral fable: "'Cuckoo's Nest" is a tale of rebellion for adolescent boys. There's no confusing the good guys (childlike men) with the bad guys (rule-enforcing women). And its rambunctious but pure-hearted hero, Randle P. McMurphy ... might as well be wearing a white hat" (Brantley, 2001:E1).

The rebel took center stage on Broadway, but already this McMurphy was not what Wasserman said he intended: "What they finally produced [in 1963] was not my play at all and the reviews were just dreadful. Kirk [Douglas] decided to make McMurphy loveable, heroic, and endearing. McMurphy should be an ambiguous character—part conman, part Christ figure" (quoted in Horwitz, 2001:21).

Sankowich told me that he agrees with Wasserman that McMurphy is part con-man, and there is textual support for that in the novel. Nurse Ratched early on tells Nurse Flinn that McMurphy is a "'manipulator,' ...a man who will use everyone and everything to his own ends" (Kesey, 29:1962). But Sankowich said he prefers the description offered by one San Francisco critic: "not a guy to invite to a family dinner, but a guy who gets the job done." *Cuckoo's Nest* has been called an adult Western, he said, meaning McMurphy is an imperfect Western hero. Clearly neither

Wasserman nor Sankowich intended the story as a one-dimensional contest of heroic rebel vs. villainous authority.

As for how to play McMurphy, it has been challenging for stage actors to ignore the Jack Nicholson portrayal since Forman's 1975 hit movie. One of them is Gary Sinise. He has said that Nicholson was one of several icons whose realistic approach to acting inspired members of his theatre company, Steppenwolf. "I was a huge fan of the film, I saw it so many times," Sinise has said, but also admitted that he was impressed by the stage versions he saw (Green, 2001:1).

Central to the character of McMurphy, is his "wall shaking" or "exploding" laugh, which he "unleashes" (Wasserman, 1974:13,16,20). Critics agree on this:

> It's part of what cinched the Oscar for Mr. Nicholson, whose visceral roar really did seem like an open invitation to anarchy…Mr. Sinise's version is lighter—more purely hedonistic and friendly, without the unsettling wildness with which Mr. Nicholson blurred conventional notions of sanity…This McMurphy has the adrenaline to dominate the stage, all right. Mr. Sinise, whose satyr's smile is truly infectious, can't seem to take a step without stomping (Brantley, 2001:E1).

The frequent, loud laughs of Deyan Donkov hardly struck me as "infectious." To the contrary, my American sensibility found them aggressive, almost hostile, just as I found his McMurphy swagger a little over-the-top, at least early in the National Theatre run. Donkov seemed to tone it down later on. Nevertheless, it was hard to see Donkov exhibiting the "happy chortling" and companiable laugh of

Wasserman's McMurphy (1974:36,37). Morfov said his creative team discussed the laugh, and agreed that it was very important, but not the most important element in the play. In the end, they decided that it held two aspects: it served to defuse moments of intense drama, and to add "paradoxical emotions." Thus it is not an element of McMurphy's charm, but of his ambiguous nature.

At least one Bulgarian critic agreed that the McMurphy laugh was crucial to his character, and to the viewers' reception of the play. He wrote that "the deep philosophical subtext and impact" of the play owes extraordinarily much to the work of Deyan Donkov. "In his rough way he returns the patients to their lost reality and dignity" with "his deep laughter [that] will echo in the consciousness of the viewers not only after his lobotomy, but also long after the end of the production" (*Novinar*, 7.12.2010:21). It seems very subjective when some viewers perceive the McMurphy laugh as rude and aggressive, while it penetrates into the deep consciousness of this critic and others as a sort of poignant symbol of heroic rebellion.

So in addition to the Nicholson-like appeal, Morfov wished to add some balance, clearly to emphasize the uncivil side of McMurphy's character. As he told the nespaperer *Dnevnik*, "independent of whether he enters like an elephant [in a china shop], as a bandit or as a locomotive, or with muddy shoes in a fallen world—he really had the unrealized dignity of the male, of a real man" (29.11.2010:7).

I have heard Bulgarians elaborate on this myth of the traditional strong, "real" Bulgarian male. He is literally an earthly character, one who, since the 1930s, has lost his strength since he was uprooted from the farm, stopped working in the field, and took to the city. This myth is consistent with Kesey's tale. McMurphy and his Indian soulmate Bromden (in American myth, often a noble savage) come in from the country, and society tries to "civilize" them (Huckleberry Finn's term). Perceptively, Forman frames his movie with an opening scene of McMurphy entering the hospital ward from the bucolic countryside, and ends it with Bromden escaping back into it.

During his two productions of *Cuckoo's Nest,* in Moscow and in Sofia, Morfov gave a lot of thought to this key personality. He used a bundle of adjectives to describe McMurphy to me: brutal, manipulative, mercantile, gambling, aggressive—hardly attractive attributes. More importantly perhaps, though, Morfov linked McMurphy to the image of the rebel in the popular imagination. Bulgarians, he said, always like the "not so positive heroes," such as bandits, gangsters, and brigands. A lawbreaker—but with a pure soul, he said. Arguably, the most popular Bulgarian literary figure, Bai Ganyo, has a host of unsavory personal traits, and Bulgarians do not necessarily emulate him or his character, it seems to me, but they identify with his powerful motivations to survive in a corrupt and difficult world.

Vyara Tabakova suggested another reason why Bulgarians like McMurphy (personal interview, 16 March 2012). No Bulgarian would admit that he or she needs to see a psychiatrist, and shame attaches to mental illness. Such patients have even been isolated from others, and it has been unusual to enter a mental ward voluntarily, as in the play. Consequently, part of the appeal of McMurphy is that he makes fun of the psychiatric hospital, confirming the national prejudice that it is not really necessary. In a less attractive way, he also makes fun of the patients.

Morfov strove for a balanced McMurphy, as did Kinney, but also for a more human Nurse Ratched. Morfov told me that one possible interpretation of the story is that McMurphy enters a perfect (or perhaps stable) society and destroys it from the inside. By this reading, Ratched is a positive character: she has organized the society well, and protects her patients in her way. The problem arises because she doesn't notice when her professional attitude changes from concerned and loving to dictatorial. (Some critics would argue that this staging tones down the melodramatic villainy in the novel.)

In any case, Morfov's reading confirms that he has ignored the earlier melodramatic stage productions and gone back to the richer characters of Kesey's novel. (See my discussion below on the accuracy of Morfov's characterization of Nurse Ratched.)

Morfov may have toned down the villainy, but he amplified the music and the directness of the original Wasserman play. Wasserman calls for music that is "miserable stuff, lawrence-welky in mode" (1974:17) because, as Ratched says, Lawrence Welk music is therapeutic (Wasserman, 1974:18). Morfov, with an ear for the entertainment value, played the Beatles' "All You Need is Love," "Don't Worry Be Happy," and the anthem-like "YMCA." He also revs up his climactic drinking party with Metallica's "Die Die My

Darling." (Morfov told me that he tries to play his personal musical favorites in his plays.) In this case, Morfov is more in sync with Kesey than Wasserman, since Kesey saw the Kinney production on Broadway, and told Gary Sinise that he admired the production's spirit, especially the music: "'Adding Jimi Hendrix and the other stuff really helped bring it up to date,' he said" (Kirkpatrick, 2001:E1).

For the language too, Morfov says he disregarded Wasserman and turned to Kesey's novel as his source, but both the novel and the 1974 rewrite of the play are in line with the frank contemporary use of vulgarities, as in both *Angels in America* and *The Goat*. For example, in Kesey's novel, Harding asks McMurphy if he believes Nurse Ratched is a

> "giant monster of the poultry clan, bent on sadistically pecking out our eyes. You can't believe that of her, can you?"
> "No, buddy, not that. She ain't peckin' at your *eyes*. That's not what she's peckin' at."
> ...
> "Not our eyes?" he says. "Pray then, where *is* Miss Ratched pecking, my friend?"
> "McMurphy grinned. "Why, don't you *know*, buddy?"
> "No, of course I don't know! I mean, if you insi--"
> "At your balls, buddy, at your everlovin' *balls*."
> (Kesey, 1962:56-7)

Morfov hews pretty close to Kesey's graphic text:

ХАРДИНГ. Да, сестра Речид може да е

строга дама, но не е някакво кокоше чудовище, копнееща да ни изкълве очите.
МАКМЪРФИ. Не оченцата, пич! Кълве те право в топките, в ташаците!
ХАРДИНГ. Нашата мила мис Рачид? Нашият усмихнат, нежен ангел на милосърдието, ни кълвяла...? О, приятелю, твоята диагноза е сериозна... (Morfov, 2010:13)

Or in English:

HARDING. Yes, Nurse Ratched may be a strict lady, but she is not some sort of poultry monster panting to peck at our eyes.
McMURPHY. Not at your eyes, buddy! She's pecking you right in the balls!
HARDING. Our dear Miss Ratched? Our smiling, sweet angel of mercy, pecking at our ...? Oh, my friend, your diagnosis is serious ...

This is actually not too distant from Wasserman's revised text:

McMURPHY: She ain't peckin' at your eyes. She is aimin' at a spot about three feet south—right square at the family jewels! (Wasserman, 1974:26)

So Morfov, in 2009 Sofia, could be more direct and graphic on the stage than Wasserman could be even in 1974, and actually put more of Kesey's language on his stage.

According to Sankowich (18 March 2012 email to me), however, he put the first swears into the text in his 1970 production. "At the time swear words were not in the text and after my using them Wasserman included them when he republished the script in 1974." The original, rather prudish Wasserman text (1970) had euphemistic expressions like "frig them all" and "put a burr up her bloomers,"

Sankowich said. So the 1974 text, with vulgarities like "shit" and "fuck" (pp. 32 and 61, respectively), match the ribald coarseness of Morfov's text. The singular oddity of Kesey's text, which is outdated in its peculiar way, is the use of racist slurs, which are much more inflammatory in contemporary American public life than mere profanity. McMurphy cries, "Goddamned motherfucking nigger!" (Kesey, 1962:229). If today's young admirers of the McMurphy of Wasserman's play or Forman's film heard this racist rant, they would surely temper their enthusiasm for him.

In the end, there are some scenes from the novel that are missing in Morfov's play, and Morfov apparently added new scenes which he thought would resonate for Bulgarians. But this change was only in the story, not in the feeling or the ideas of Kesey, he told me. His goal was to retain the "poetic atmosphere" of the novel, even if the scene or event is different. For example, Morfov added the dance with brooms that opens the second act, freely used his favorite music, such as that of the Beatles and Metallica. He also added slapstick for big laughs, as when the patients drop the big birthday cake for Ruckly (the habitually "tired" patient, called Pete Bancini in the novel). He drops the Chief Bromden voiceover since he's not interested in the characters' obsessive inner lives. I would argue that Morfov wanted to add striking visual elements, for theatrical or entertainment value, but also consistent with the storyline that McMurphy brought fun to the ward. Morfov also dispenses with McMurphy's and Bromden's conversation about the play title's eponymous children's rhyme, since it would have no emotional impact for his Bulgarian audience.

The Critical Reactions

A look at the table of American reviews in appendix A.1 will show that the critical reaction to the Steppenwolf production, in both Chicago and New York, was only slightly on the positive side. Of the reviews of this production from 2000 and 2001 that I have read, six were favorable, one was mixed, and four were negative, similar to the tally reached by Hofler in *Variety* (p. 60, above). Of the reviews I read, it's curious that of the four publications that panned this anti-Establishment play in 2000-01, one was a conservative newspaper, one was generally conservative, and one was written by a usually conservative arts critic for a liberal magazine. Only the pre-eminent American reviewer, Ben Brantley, chief theatre critic of the liberal *New York Times,* expressed mostly negative views. Curiously, the arch-conservative *Wall Street Journal* was mostly down on the original Chicago production, but turned around and issued a mostly positive notice on the New York play. We will see a similar correlation of reviewers' political ideology and artistic judgment in regard to *Angels in America* too.

Brantley's criticisms partly cited the Kesey-Wasserman story, and partly the production itself (9.4.2001:E1). For him, the story is too simplistic a fable of a battle between good guys and bad guys, and though the staging had "top of the line" production values, it was "cute instead of confrontational." Like the critics cited earlier, he wrote that McMurphy's laugh is crucial, but that the play in the end is "disappointingly sane."

The Wall Street Journal's Joel Henning, took aim at the datedness cited above, by calling the original Chicago production a "superficial period piece," like the Kesey novel (2000:A46). His complaint about the production was odd and unique among critics in calling Sinise's performance weak, and said the same about the other actors. He otherwise appreciated the play's mockery of 1960's sacred cows like women's lib and civil rights.

The Wall Street Journal's Amy Gamerman, reviewing the later New York production, also cited the misogyny – Nurse Ratched is a "castrating witch"—and how the audience laughs, but in a cheap way, at her coldness (2001:A16). She attacked the script as trite and sentimental, but highly appreciated the ensemble performance and "full-bodied" production.

The other reviewers formed a broad consensus about the Steppenwolf production's strengths, both those cited already, and others. One called it a "lurid melodrama"—and one can understand that aspect of the play—with moments of greatness in the acting and faultless direction (Burke, 2001:online). These reviewers were more forgiving of the datedness ("somewhat updated adaptation…fresh and vigorous," Sommer, 2001:online). The reviewers found it powerful, with excellent performers, and though they knew that it was melodrama, if they liked it, they did so because they did not think it went overboard into sentimentality or manipulation. A forgiving example of this latter reaction is Michael Sommers, who wrote, "Manipulative as it may be, 'One Flew Over the Cuckoo's Nest' still brings you to the edge of your seat until you jump with applause at the final curtain" (2001:27). Very similar language is used by Jonathan Abarbanal: "Kinney keeps this Cuckoo's Nest from fully whipping up and manipulating audience emotions" (2000:15). Finally, Charles Isherwood, in the influential entertainment daily, *Variety*, wrote that the play is an "emotional buttonpusher, wringing tears and cheers with mechanical precision" and with "calibrated doses of laughter and tears." Despite this somewhat patronizing tone, he also wrote that this is an "expert ensemble" and that the show is "irresistible" with "heart-tugging pathos," and "a natural response to American culture's warped values" (2001:37). I note how the leftist ideology drives this reviewer's positive review.

In all, it appears that the reviewers who panned Kinney's *Cuckoo's Nest* thought that its melodrama and manipulation destroyed the play's value, while the positive reviewers accepted the play for what it is and recognized its humor, entertainment value, or emotional impact. In fact, the 1963 Broadway premier was panned by critics who dismissed it as a "comic melodrama" (Campbell, 2001:7) without giving it further credit. Indeed, even in a poor production, the Wasserman script had choice language with undeniable humor:

HARDING: [You] have already simplified the work of Freud, Jung, and Maxwell Jones…

McMURPHY: I'm not talkin' 'bout Fred Young and whosis Jones, buddy… (Wasserman, 1974:25)

In Sofia, in contrast to this diversity of positive and negative reviews, Alexander Morfov's *auteur* production met with a massive and almost complete critical love embrace, with just two dissents. This was odd for an American used to a critical environment in which even the most ballyhooed and celebrated plays, including Pulitzer Prize winners, always provoke a few contrarian voices. Not so in Bulgaria. From the many tabloids and mainstream daily newspapers to website reviews, there was a strange and even suspicious near unanimity about this play. The daily tabloid *Telegraf*, in a short summary by Georgi P. Dimitrov (3.12.2010:23), reports that "hysteria is total" for a play with a "perfect" director, who has achieved, critics say, "total balance with no wavering into extravagance." *Trud*'s Patritsia Nikolova tells us that Morfov has achieved a masterful adaptation, and one still timely 20 years after the transition from totalitarianism, with a "virtuoso ensemble cast" that has "a perfect grip" on the material (2010: online). The eva.bg writer gushed that she loved the acting, that the production is the "absolute hit of the season," and that she gave the play a standing ovation (undated on website).

This sort of exuberance reflects not only Alexander Morfov's reputation as one of the great creative talents in contemporary Bulgaria, but what several Bulgarian theatre experts have described as the reluctance of the critical establishment to make genuine critical comments or reviews. Peter Kaukov, a director at the Nikolay Binev Youth Theatre in Sofia, ascribes this to a cozy club in the national theatre society of people who know each other personally and are either friends or are afraid that a severe review will cause retaliation from a theatre's administrative or creative team, and that future favors or invitations might be curtailed as a result (personal interview, 4 December 2011). An American theatre director and student of the Bulgarian theatre concurred, saying that Bulgarian critics won't insult people like Morfov, and that "everyone is covering his back." We should bear this in mind when we read the overwhelmingly – but not entirely – positive reviews of the play (summarized in appendix A.2).

It should be noted that though American reviewers tend to be more critical, they are not above a different sort of criticism themselves. "Theatrical coverage in *Time*, *Newsweek*, and *USA Today* is brief, random, and often vapid," according to a survey in *American Theatre* (Cote, 2011:30). So critiques of the putative shallowness of critical commentary can be found in both the U.S. and Bulgaria.

The most notable exception to the chorus of kudos for Morfov was a densely written evaluation in *Kultura* by Stefan Popov (2010:8). Although this critic calls the production a "milestone" for the Bulgarian theatre, his mixed review faults Morfov for the timidity of his adaptation. He charges that the outdated story of a social power structure without human feeling, among many other possible themes, is well explored in both Kesey's novel and Forman's movie, but that Morfov neither gives shape or focus to the themes nor updates them in any meaningful way. Instead, he sticks too close to the novel and renders a literal adaptation. Furthermore,

Popov criticizes Donkov's overly physical portrayal of McMurphy (here he is in agreement with the Americans who saw the Morfov version, below), and says both his overacting and the party orgy scene seem more geared to Bulgarian TV audiences than to those in the National Theatre.

Popov was not the only critic, however, who found the orgy scene either too long or inappropriate to the drama. A young poet and television script writer, Ivan Landzhev, told me (personal interview, 5 April 2012) that he thought the party scene is much too long and not justified by even Morfov's Bulgarian text. Interestingly, he also said that though the play is genuinely funny, the viewers seem to "laugh for the wrong reasons." That is, they like the old jokes, the cruel teasing of the patients by McMurphy, who calls them retards or worse ("we have gathered a nice company of idiots, cretins and retards"/"много готина компания сме се събрали, идиоти, кретени, дебил до дебила," p. 40 of the National Theatre script), the slapstick, and the overacting in scenes like the party one. These, he says, neither advance the story, nor, I would add, develop the characters, hence are arguably not dramatic, but extraneous. The cruel jokes do however add unsavory elements to McMurphy's character, who is arguably both a racist and sexist in the Kesey novel.

For the record, despite the American critics' frequent charges of manipulative melodrama about the Kinney production, I found no Bulgarian critic who used such vocabulary about Morfov's production. Several did, however, find a different sort of manipulation, and described both McMurphy and Nurse Ratched as manipulative characters (e.g., in *Novinar*, 7.12.2010:21).

I believe that most of the Bulgarian critics were right to avoid the language of manipulative melodrama because Morfov indeed provided a richer character drama than that. Morfov found the language he wanted in the Kesey novel to source his strict but not monstrous Ratched and his charming and rebellious but manipulative McMurphy. The character of Ratched is described by the patient Harding (the fuller text of the quote on page 74, above): "The staff desires our cure as much as we do. They aren't monsters. Miss Ratched may be a strict middle-aged lady, but she's not some kind of giant monster of the poultry clan, bent on sadistically pecking out our eyes" (Kesey, 1963:56-7). That is, in the eyes of her manipulated patients, there is no knife visible in Ratched's sheath.

Despite Morfov's authentic source material, and deeper and more textured characterization, several of the Bulgarian reviewers missed the point entirely. "If in the Kesey novel and in the movie with Jack Nicholson, she [Ratched] is a monster, now she is good and she believes she is right and she is merely unable to grasp what people really need" (Baichev, 2010:23). Kaukov had a similar problem, when he told me that the battle between McMurphy and Ratched was diminished when Morfov displays a hospital that is not dreary and depicts Ratched as "caring," but this surface concern is clearly justified by the novel.

Closer to understanding Morfov's adaptation, is the uncredited reviewer who says that McMurphy and Ratched "are absolute opposites only at first glance. She embodies the stability of the system and its strict rules, and he works for full destruction and meaningless," but, "they are both virtuoso manipulators." The insightful anonymous reviewer has an eye on the larger elements that these two characters represent when he or she writes of the play's eternal conflict between order and chaos, or between freedom and dogma, which "acquires the scale of struggle between giants who bow before different gods. They will both be destroyed in the storms they create" (*Novinar*, 2010:21). The depth of Reni Vrangova's achievement as Ratched was also picked up by Mariana Parvanova in her review, in which she writes that Vrangova has managed to create "a complex image that both repels and builds empathy" (4.12.2010:37).

In conclusion, though too many of the Bulgarian reviewers were fawning in their praise of the Morfov adaptation, several captured the particular tilt he gave the story in two senses: giving shades of gray to the characters of both McMurphy and Ratched, and yet retaining their symbolic stature in representing the clash of values: freedom/chaos vs. order/oppression.

The Public Reception: Results of the Audience Questionnaires

The questionnaires for *One Flew Over the Cuckoo's Nest* were distributed manually courtesy of the National Theatre's marketing and sales office, and by me to acquaintances, in both Bulgarian and English. The questionnaire was also posted on the Theatre's website, with readers directed to send their responses to the Theatre or directly to me. Questionnaires were not distributed in the Theatre during performances due to the objection of one of the actors, who worried that the play was already lengthy, and did not wish to ask the playgoers to stay any longer to fill in a questionnaire. The survey started in June, 2011 and the last questionnaires were collected in June, 2012. Forty-four playgoers responded.

The Bulgarian public reaction to Alexander Morfov's production was overwhelmingly positive, and to a degree that would be exceptional on Broadway, even with the theatres' typical, pricey promotional campaigns. The questionnaire is in appendix A.7; appendix A.9 has the results and respondent comments.

Asked simply if they enjoyed the play (question 1), 32 of 44 spectators answered that they liked it *"very much,"* which is a very impressive 73 percent. (All fractions are rounded off.) Another 4 spectators (9 percent) enjoyed it, 7 liked it "somewhat" and *only one single person* said he did not: 2 percent. Total positive audience reaction: 82 percent.

Other audience survey results are (numbers below keyed to questionnaires):

2. Almost all respondents said that they think they understood the play: 40 said they understood or understood very much (93 percent), and only 3 replied that they understood it "somewhat." So in the broadest measure, that of liking and understanding, Morfov and his team matched the critical approval with comparable audience bravos.

3. Though fewer respondents answered the question about the play's theme, almost all of them chose the most reasonable of themes that I proposed, showing that they did understand the production. Thirty-one choose the theme, "Society demands conformity and represses creative and energetic individuals," and only one chose the teaser, imperfect answer, "Nurse Ratched is a controlling monster, but Dr. Spivey represents a more humanitarian social elite." Clearly many elsewhere do indeed read Ratched as a monster, especially if they've seen Louise Fletcher's interpretation in the Forman movie or other productions of the show (see Abarbanal citation, page 77). But Morfov said he strove for a more balanced portrayal (page 73). So this theme is not right in this case, and his audience got it, while many of the play's directors and erudite critics have agreed on theme "A" regarding society's repression of creative or non-conformist individuals. Only three respondents chose themes clearly at variance with those of both Kesey and Morfov.

4. Many audience members, 17, tended to see the hospital characters as more American than Bulgarian, despite Morfov's liberal adaptation (which would allow more Bulgaria-specific content), but slightly more (19) said they were just as much Bulgarian as American. Only four found them more Bulgarian. This is perhaps unavoidable given an Indian "Chief" Bromden. Morfov also provides girls dancing in hotpants made from an American flag, and a disabled war

veteran warbling the American national anthem and practically waving that flag. There is also basketball played and watched on TV (in lieu of the World Series in the novel and the Wasserman play) and some talk about democracy. Basketball and democracy can be found worldwide, of course, but are still generally identified with America. My own interpretation is that there are not more respondents calling the characters American because of the strong "Bulgarian" personality of Donkov (see next question). Interestingly, Vyara Tabakova (the nurse Miss Flinn), told me (personal interview) that she is "an international nurse," neither American nor Bulgarian.

5. When asked if McMurphy is a "recognizable Bulgarian personality," most, 20, said yes, and only 5 said no. Eighteen could not decide. One of these wrote in that he is, "just human." I can't help but interpret this as Bulgarians having a hard time identifying the well-known icon, Donkov, as something other than Bulgarian. And this is even though the same audience respondents saw the play's characters *in general* as more American than Bulgarian (question 4).

6. Respondents clarified their feelings about McMurphy when asked to choose his personality. Twenty-four said that he has, "good and bad points (e.g., energetic, but a little manipulative and calculating)." Nine spectators went for "Generally winning, attractive, natural," overlooking his boorishness, and 7 wrote in their own appraisals. Per my

comment on question 3 above, most respondents correctly read Morfov's intention, that is, to present a broadly human, controversial or balanced McMurphy, and not a cartoonish hero. Even the 9 who found him generally winning can be excused for being carried away by Donkov's charm. (See below, where American playgoers at the National Theatre disagreed most strongly.)

7. Surprisingly, given the robust laughter in the theatre, that a plurality of respondents, 20, said that the show is only "somewhat funny," and perhaps, not primarily a comedy. Thirteen respondents said it was "very funny" (6) or "funny" (7), while ten did not see the humor in the production. I wonder if the mere 14 percent (6 of 43) who said the show was "very funny" were modeling themselves on McMurphy's aggressive laugh, and caused louder or longer laughter from other spectators.

8. Almost all respondents had a sense of the meaning of the title of the play, identifying it as an American children's verse that suggests that McMurphy wants to visit the hospital but not stay long, or that it simply refers to a hospital for the insane. (Wasserman's script includes children singing the verse on tape; Morfov did not include it.) Only 6 admitted that they don't know what it means, and 9 had plausible or even clever interpretations of their own. For the relatively few spectators who bought programs at the National Theatre, the notes identify the title as an American children's verse.

And they could select the interpretations of the title I suggested, even if they really don't know that Kesey took his title from such a verse, because any perceptive viewer could see the aptness of the verse. Selecting either of the verse interpretations underscores the respondents' understanding of the play.

9. Most respondents, 22, chose the best answer to the question why Chief Bromden chose to break out of the hospital, that is, that McMurphy has given him the confidence to live independently. The other two replies—either to fight "the combine," 9, or because Bromden has returned to "full size," 7—are actually plausible only if one buys into Bromden's imagination, but they are fictions of his mental illness.

10. A plurality of respondents, 20, chose the most suitable answer to the question of what should be done with the "acute" patients in the play, that is, that some of them could probably do better without treatment. Eleven took a more radical (socially critical) line and replied that hospitals generally do a disservice to the mental patients. Nine others offered answers of their own. They were all generally critical of contemporary treatment of mental illness, and would reject the notion (chosen by only two respondents) that the acutes need to be kept in hospitals. This question probes the audience's acceptance of Kesey's and his adapters' social criticism. Kesey himself has written that the story is, "an attack on tyranny of the sort that is perhaps more

predominant in mental hospitals then [sic] any place else in our land" (Kesey, 2011:online).

11. About half, 18, said this play changed their view about society's treatment of acute mental patients, and about half, 21, said it did not. This question is driven by Wasserman's goal, cited above, page 43, that theatre is a form of propaganda, implying that this is a "problem play." This is seconded by Morfov, who has openly criticized Western and Bulgarian society, and has said repeatedly in interviews that we all live in a madhouse, implying that certain individuals should not be singled out for confinement (e.g., Dimitrova, 2010:online), and, "We have become crazies. Fifty percent of people on the streets are crazy. They have deep complexes and are maniacally depressed" (*24 Chasa*, 30.11.2010:11). In the end, the tricky part of interpreting these responses is whether, when a spectator responds that his or her mind *wasn't* changed, this means that he or she was not persuaded by the play's propaganda, or rather that he or she already accepted the play's polemic. I would conclude that given this unresolved question, Morfov could take satisfaction is registering the changed minds of about half of his audience.

12. *One Flew Over the Cuckoo's Nest* attracted a very young audience: Two-thirds were under 35 years of age (30 of the total 44 respondents). This duplicates what Sankowich said about the audience for the play in San Francisco, where its

counter-cultural message, as well as the personal renown of Kesey, drew queues of college students outside the theatre.

13. and 14. The play also drew mostly well-educated, regular theatre-goers. Only 8 of the 42 respondents, 19%, said that they attend the theatre less than once every six weeks, with about 32 percent saying they also enjoy *avant garde* or challenging theatrical work. All but 5 of the respondents have a bachelor's degree or higher. This may indicate to some degree that such educated and inveterate theatre-goers are the ones more likely to take the time to fill out questionnaires.

Many of the respondents provided subjective insights on the play in their additional comments in the questionnaires. Many of them are close to what Morfov has said in interviews about who is really sane, e.g., the comment, "If you are different, you're labeled 'insane'." Others picked up on his depiction of McMurphy as a sort of spiritual liberator, or representing human freedom. Given Morfov's free adaptation, these write-in replies are actually very accurate, since they tally with what Morfov wished to emphasize in the Kesey story.

Several respondents who agreed that McMurphy has positive and negative traits (in question 6, answer C) also said that the positive qualities outweigh the negative, in that he has "a free loving spirit, loyalty, and honesty." Others appreciated his energy and "unwillingness to conform to the limits invented by society," which surely Kesey and Morfov would accept. No one mentioned tragic flaws, but one spoke for the many who were moved when he or she wrote that McMurphy is a "wonderful and inspiring person with tragic destiny."

As I have written above, I tried to get at the issue of whether an adaptation should try to represent the source or target culture, so I asked the playgoers whether they thought the play depicted Bulgarians or Americans (questions 4 and 5). For reasons stated above, most believed the characters seemed to be Americans, but the only comment on this question was, tellingly perhaps, "Can we seek the nationality of people in the 21st century?" (I.e., we're all the same by now.) Commenting on the themes and the character of McMurphy, though, respondents strongly underlined both American and Bulgarian characteristics. For one, the play was about, "Everyday problems of the U.S. in the 1960s-70s." Though most described McMurphy in universal terms, as an inspiring rule-breaker, when more specific, they clarified why he seemed Bulgarian. A "Bai Ganyo and the city 'wise guy' [тарикат]," wrote one respondent, while others cited his "undisciplined behavior" and nonchalance. Clearly, several conveyed their own view of the Bulgarian national character, as in this comment why McMurphy is not a Bulgarian type: "In the past 60 years Bulgarians consistently lack energy, determination and passion and are forced, trained and 'educated' to avoid them in life."

The thoughtful written interpretations of the play's title indicated the audience's higher education, or at least its attentive reception. (One also discussed the play's themes in terms of the theories of

French philosophers Michel Foucault and Jacques Derrida!) Though several stated the obvious, that the "cuckoo's nest" is the insane asylum, others were more creative: Two respondents said in effect that the "flight" (полет) of the Bulgarian title was an opportunity to peek in, over the wall as it were, on an unseen world. Another wrote that the "cuckoo" is not just a crazy person, but that the cuckoo bird leaves its eggs in the nests of other birds, so that the chicks have to "eliminate all competition" after they hatch, which would explain McMurphy's aggressiveness. *Pace* Sontag, this is a clever and apt interpretation.

Several written responses seemed to indicate some knowledge of psychology or experience with mental patients, especially regarding how society should handle the play's "acutes." They struggled with the patients' need for help, but questioned the care they are provided in the play. E.g., "Isn't it true that there are acutes who are not appropriate in society?" and, "They need to regain their sanity." I heard the apparent voice of a professional care-giver whose advice about how to handle such cases was simply, "Listen."

Apart from the numerical evidence provided by the questionnaires about how much the audience liked the play, the depth of their appreciation could perhaps only be sensed in their written comments, particularly in the obvious inspiration they drew from it. One wrote, for example, that the theme is, "that man should never forget who he is and what he wants to be, regardless of the situation in which he finds himself. The strength of spirit can topple mountains."

I should also cite this additional testimony to Morfov's achievement: "I have seen almost all of the Bulgarian stage, but for the first time I have a total favorite, I saw this production of 4 full hours, completely already 3 times! Wonderful acting, unbelievably touching and at the same time full of small things from life!" (The play's duration was actually cut during the first season from 4 hours and 10 minutes to 3 hours and 40 minutes. The cut seems to have been done so skillfully that I could not identify what was missing. The intermission might have been shorter too.)

Many of the National Theatre website's comments have also been very enthusiastic. For example, one questionnaire came to me via the website with this email language: "Unique production, masterful acting! There is a lot to think about, and after you see it, it carries messages! I will have to recommend it to my friends. Regards to the entire team!!!" (24.2.2012). (Уникална постановка, майсторска игра! Има върху какво да се замисли човек след като я гледа, носи и послания! Ще я препоръчам на приятелите си задължително. Поздрави на целия екип!!!!) Of course I had no way of determining gender for the unsigned questionnaires received, but the preponderance of exuberant signed responses from women suggested Donkov's appeal to them. Of course the subject matter also appealed to youth.

Additionally, all of the ten or so comments about the play on the NationalTheatre website, as well as the four questionnaires sent directly to me via the website, were from women (i.e., had apparent women's names, through 25 September 2011). All of them were positive. Most celebrated the terrific acting, including that of Donkov. One woman wrote that she was inclined to like him because he acts macho but probably is not ("Бях предубедена малко към Деян Донков , мислех ,че го раздава малко "мачо" , но игра невероятно.")

A control group of 8 American viewers, on the other hand, did not at all share the enthusiasm for Morfov's *Cuckoo's Nest* that his Bulgarian audience displayed. Asked if they enjoyed the play, 6 of them said, "somewhat." Only 2 said, "yes" or "yes, very much." Despite having college degrees in excess of the average Bulgarian spectator at the play, a lower percentage said they thought they understood the play (question 2): 3 of the 8 had doubts about that. This could reflect modesty about overcoming the language or cultural barrier. Nevertheless, the Americans understood the main theme of rebellion and conformity (question 3).

The American playgoers had a sharp split about whether Morfov's interpretation of the characters rendered them more like Americans or Bulgarians. Half of them said they are in general more like Bulgarians (question 4), while 5 felt that Donkov portrayed a Bulgarian McMurphy (question 5), with some reflecting their strong views of Bulgarians. For example, for those viewing him as Bulgarian, one commented that Donkov, "seems to exaggerate some qualities that are stereotypically 'Bulgarian male'—smoking, brash, macho, anti-authority, work-adverse." Another agreed, writing that he "played into the idea that Bulgarians have about male gender roles in the worst way." Another American commented that

Donkov's McMurphy was Bulgarian in his rebelliousness, and one compared him to Bai Ganyo (as did a Bulgarian respondent above). Despite my hesitation to define Bai Ganyo's character, I would venture to say that he bears resemblance to Kesey's McMurphy in being both raffishly attractive and repellent at the same time, and that Donkov may have captured this McMurphy. (See pages 107-08.)

Interestingly, Americans who did not agree that Donkov's portrayal seemed like that of a Bulgarian personality had these two contrasting comments: "Have not seen the same level of confidence in a Bulgarian," and, "Bulgarians, especially with mental problems, are not the 'can do' sort of people." This respondent's comment actually echoes something Kesey said when he admitted that, even in the United States, McMurphy is not really the personality type one would find in a mental hospital, but, "of course, fictional—a dream, a wild hope," a character fabricated to rescue the "broken and defeated men of our society" (Kesey, 2011:online). The most unexpected comment pegged him as Bulgarian because his mannerisms were such—though he could have been American because he handled the basketball so well. Very few respondents noticed body language in this way in deciding the nationality of the characters.

The most complete divergence between American and Bulgarian audience reactions was just on this topic of McMurphy's personality as portrayed by Donkov. While almost a third of Bulgarians found him generally winning, attractive, or natural, none of the American respondents agreed. Three said he was "mostly overbearing and obnoxious" (only 4 of 44 Bulgarians checked this answer), but half said he had good and bad points, about the same percentage of the Bulgarians. So the only difference between the Americans and Bulgarians was that the Americans were more critical of this personality type, with one going so far as to criticize the actor Donkov as looking "fake" and "motivated by ego, stardom." This response, from an American male theatre director, is opposite to the largely young and female Bulgarians who were captivated by the performance.

On the question of whether the play was funny, how to interpret the title, and why Chief Bromden decides to break out of the hospital, the Americans generally tracked the Bulgarians' responses. There was a diversity of views, including individual opinions, about what to do with the acute mental patients, and whether the play changed their minds about treatment of mental disease. In general, the Americans were older than the average Bulgarian playgoer, but attended the theatre less frequently. All but one of them had advanced degrees.

Although one might question the value of Americans' reactions to a play expressly adapted for a Bulgarian audience and sensibility, still I find some of the reactions telling by the American theatre professionals who saw it. One director wrote bluntly that, "they missed the boat on this one!" (The full comment is in Appendix A.10.) His criticisms, in brief, were clearly based on his belief in the "faithful" adaptation, and he stated that, "the director has a responsibility to tell the story first and add his 'vision' second." He faulted the excessive length of the production, and implied that this is due to a lack of discipline and the unjustified additions, such as the "broom dream ballet." He acknowledged the humor, but wrote that it was not supported by the text. (Tabakova told me that Morfov added jokes that Bulgarians would like.) Finally, he said (agreeing with a Bulgarian theatre director he has worked with) that Morfov did not stage the play well. Their view is that the huge National Theatre stage space was "completely antithetical to the intention of the script," or to the "suffocating world" of *Cuckoo's Nest*.

Since other Americans were similarly caustic in their response to the National Theatre production, I have to ask whether Morfov, in adapting *Cuckoo's Nest* to his Bulgarian audience or to his personal vision, made it necessarily less appealing to Americans or other foreign audiences. Another American director said that he observed rehearsals and that Morfov had no interest in the choreography of the broom dance. Yet it clicked for Bulgarian audiences. Morfov's history of directing smash hits is clear; he knows his audience, so perhaps a perfunctory look at his choreographer's final work is enough for him to sense that it carries the right emotions and tone. In the final analysis, the objections of foreign viewers do not detract from his intended goal and success.

In conclusion, it is fair to say that Morfov's *Cuckoo's Nest* was a critical and commercial success. It has been especially popular with women. A number of theatre professionals have criticized it as thematically closer to Morfov's vision than to Kesey's, and several of them have also said the production is so big that the emotional impact is lost. What many enjoy as Morfov's added entertaining elements, such as the broom dance and the party scene, others have criticized as indulgence and distractions. I will return to a fuller discussion of the lessons from this play in the conclusion.

CHAPTER FIVE: *Angels in America*: A Faithful Adaptation of Political Message

History of the Play's Productions

Though Broadway shows, especially the musical comedy, typically opened first as previews in cities such as Philadelphia and Baltimore, few Broadway hits had as long a gestation period as *Angels in America: A Gay Fantasia on National Themes*, which premiered in New York City in 1993. Robert Brustein wrote in *The New Republic* (1993), that "Tony Kushner's *Angels in America* – or rather the first of its two parts, *Millennium Approaches* – may very well be the most highly publicized play in American theater history. It is certainly one of the most peripatetic."

Millennium Approaches had its debut planned in a friendly theatre in 1989, the Eureka Theatre Company, "part of an epic theater in San Francisco that held the promise of a genuinely American appropriation and transformation of Brechtian dramaturgy" (p. 234 Janelle Reinelt, "Notes on *Angels in America* as American Epic Theater," in Geis, 1997). This "politically engaged, left-wing theater on epic principles" (Reinelt, p. 235) allowed Kushner to develop his theatrical ideas in both thematic and stylistic areas, and reflected his debt to Brecht, as well as to the playwrights John Osborne, Edward Bond, David Edgar, and Caryl Churchill (Hitchens, 1993:72).

The play was first staged in a workshop at the more up-market Mark Taper Forum in Los Angeles, and later produced by the Eureka Theater in 1990. From there, it headed to the Cottesloe Theatre in

London, in a production by the Royal National Theatre in early 1992, where *New York Times* veteran critic Vincent Canby said the reviews were "ecstatic" (1994:A4), and was then staged along with *Perestroika*, its second part, at the Mark Taper Forum in November, 1992, as well as at the New York Theatre Workshop the same year.

Millennium Approaches arrived on Broadway in 1993 at the Walter Kerr Theatre after also playing briefly at the New York Public Theater, one of its sponsors. Having "received unanimous praise at every step in its journey," (Brustein, 24.5.1993:29), it had simply outgrown the Public Theater. This approval included, notably, the Pulitzer Prize for Drama of 1993, which it won even before it opened on Broadway later that same year. It had already collected the London Drama Critics Circle Award for Best New Play in 1992, as well as the Drama Desk Award for Best Play and the New York Drama Critics' Circle Award for Best Play, both in 1993. All that was left was to scoop up the Tony Award for Best Play, which it did later in 1993.

What is the story that has generated such acclaim and fascination? *Angels in America* tells the story of two troubled young couples in New York City in 1985. The WASP Prior Walter and Jewish Louis Ironson are literate, gay New Yorkers. The marriage of the Mormons Harper and Joe Pitt, a young attorney, is strained by Joe's awakening homosexuality and Harper's addiction to Valium, partly fueled by her husband's neglect. The play opens at a Jewish wedding, where a rabbi intones in "a heavy Eastern European accent" about the noble and unique immigrant who has died. Soon after, Prior informs Louis that he has AIDS, and Louis, in a sign of moral cowardice contrasted to his ancestors, struggles with his loyalty to Prior.

Meanwhile, Joe is offered a promotion to a Washington political office by his mentor, a right-wing lawyer, Roy Cohn, who is an actual historical figure and closeted homosexual, and an ally of powerful Republican Senator Joseph McCarthy. (The actual Senator McCarthy conducted a witchhunt of suspected Communists and leftist sympathizers in the early 1950s, until he was discredited in 1954, and died in 1957. Roy Cohn died, apparently of AIDS, in 1986.) Joe tries to persuade Harper to move to Washington, but as a result of pill-popping she is soon fantasizing about trips to the Arctic and encounters with an imaginary travel agent named Mr. Lies.

Still in the first act, Louis strikes up a relationship with Joe in a courthouse men's room. Prior and Harper also meet, either in his dream or her hallucination, as the play enters the "fantasia" realm, and Prior first hears the "incredibly beautiful voice" of the Angel. The stage is split between across scenes of the couples' mounting quarrels and infidelities, while Roy tells his doctor that he doesn't really have AIDS, but liver cancer, because only homosexuals have AIDS.

In Act Two, both couples are breaking up. Prior is bleeding and in pain before going to the hospital; Harper tells Joes that she will leave him. This poses no problem from Roy's perspective, since he says he is, "the best divorce lawyer in the business," and he continues to network for Joe's promotion. Louis recoils to an anonymous sexual escapade in Central Park. A black former drag queen named Belize comforts Prior in the hospital. There are lengthy talks about Ronald Reagan-era politics by Roy, Joe, Louis, and others. Joe calls his mother in Salt Lake City to tell her that he is homosexual, but she refuses to take him seriously. The final act is suffused with fantasia. Prior meets two ancestors, a thirteenth-century squire and a seventeenth-century Londoner, and they chant that Prior is a prophet and great honor for the family. Louis and Belize debate in a coffee shop with mounting acrimony about race, religion, and injustice in America. Prior and Harper are swept up in apparent hallucinations, his of an overtly religious character, while she finds herself in Antarctica. Roy grows frustrated with both the vacillating Joe and his impending disbarment for ethical violations, and encounters a mocking Ethel Rosenberg in his own AIDS-induced illusion. (The historical Roy Cohn helped convict Ethel and Julius Rosenberg of espionage. They were executed in 1953.) The play, part one of the two-part epic, ends with Louis in bed with Joe, and Prior visited by the Angel. In part II, *Perestroika*, not mounted at the National Theatre, Prior gets access to AZT, the AIDS drug, and is living with the disease. Much of the second part is also episodic, with scenes in Salt Lake City, Antarctica and Heaven, where the Continental Principalities meet. The major characters sound hopeful as they talk about the Millennium while seated around the Bethesda Fountain in Central Park of New York City, as the curtain falls.

Despite its daunting length, and difficult and often obscene subject matter, like *One Flew Over the Cuckoo's Nest*, *Angels in America* has rarely been off the boards. Notable revivals include the first return to San Francisco in 1994, in an acclaimed production directed by Mark Wing-Davey for the American Conservatory Theater at the Marines' Memorial Theatre in San Francisco. Popular reaction to the play has not always been positive, in both the U.S. and overseas. Kushner himself notes that, in Bucharest, Romania, "an angry mob attacked the theater where *Angels in America* was being presented and tried to burn the building to the ground" (Kushner, 1999:42). This was evidently due to the controversial subject matter, and not to the dramatic quality.

The notoriety or controversy that has always surrounded this show had similar varied reactions in different cities: See my discussion of the audience reception in 5.4, below.

The play attained much wider attention when the accomplished director Mike Nichols adapted both parts for the American cable TV giant HBO in 2003, with brilliant performances by Al Pacino, Emma Thompson, Mary-Louise Parker, and Meryl Streep. The mini-series swept the Emmy Awards for television drama in 2004. This consequently became the version that people now know around the world, just as they know *One Flew Over the Cuckoo's Nest* from Forman's movie. The HBO success with *Angels in America* gave new momentum to revivals. The play was mounted in theatres in Bloomington (Indiana), Denver, Salt Lake City, and elsewhere at the same time that it returned to Broadway in another successful production at the Signature Theater, in 2010. *Millennium Approaches* is currently in a revival at Philadelphia's Wilma Theater (June, 2012).

The Ivan Vazov National Theatre Production

Angels in America premiered in the National Theatre's Grand Hall on 26 October 2010. Though one of the five plays in the Theatre's American season sponsored by the America for Bulgaria Foundation, the real driver behind the production was the director, Desislava Shpatova, who in May, 2010, approached one of the Theatre's dramaturges, Rosalia Rodichkova. She in turn brought it to Galina Tomova-Stankova, a veteran translator, and asked her to translate the play. Rodichkova became a supporter of the project and hoped it would be staged. The National Theatre's managing director and a non-English speaker, Pavel Vasev, accepted the play even before he read the Bulgarian translation. In June the show quickly went into rehearsal. According to Tomova-Stankova, Vasev had some concerns about the show after he later read the translation, but still was warm and supportive at the premier reception (personal interview, 26 November 2011).

The premier coincided with a visit to Sofia of a high-level group of American directors and theatre managers, organized by the New York City-based theatre advocacy and support group, the Drama League. They viewed the premier and blessed its production, though its artistic director, Roger T. Danforth, felt it was not as sexually charged, in its portrayal of the gay relationships, as in the Broadway production he knew. The play was mounted about twice per month, for a total of 15 shows, before the last production of the season, in June, 2011.

Desislava Shpatova, a 1995 graduate in the theatre department at New Bulgarian University, had several Bulgarian theatre award nominations when she undertook the *Angels in America* project. She was known to her colleagues as a lesbian, though this was never openly discussed. The translator Galina Tomova-Stankeva had done the works of Harold Pinter, among others. As with *One Flew Over the Cuckoo's Nest*, this became a major National Theatre production in the main hall.

In a conversation with Vasev, in June, 2011, he took pride in brushing aside my questions about the risks entailed in mounting such an edgy production, and discussed his success in mounting similarly controversial plays as a director in Russia. He said he followed the example of Vsevelod Meyerhold, who directed a highly experimental symbolist production of Chekhov in St. Petersburg (Petrograd) in the early twentieth century, despite public outcry.

Vasev has also said, in a *Teatar* magazine interview (Apostolova, 2011:17), that every detail of what happens in the National Theatre must be for the public, regardless of how it is criticized or supported. He says this in other ways about how actors must do their best and not be bothered by attacks.

Intriguingly though, in September, 2011, after the opening season, *Angels in America* did not appear in the National Theatre's program for the fall season. The National Theatre's marketing and sales manager, Milena Demireva, told me in October, 2011, that this is because audiences for the play at the end of the first season had dwindled to 20-30 people, in a hall that seats 780. At about the same time, however, Nadia Zaharieva, at the America for Bulgaria Foundation (see page 13), told me that the play's performances had just been delayed since two of the main actors in it had taken more lucrative roles in television series, but that the show would return to the theatre when they become available again.

Shpatova had one other version for the end of the run: She said that the National Theatre told her it closed for financial reasons but she did not believe it. In her view, only the second balcony was empty during performances, which is usually the case in the National Theatre. She believes that former Minister of Culture, movie matinee idol, and later Parliamentary Deputy, Stefan Danailov, ordered it to be closed. I had no way to corroborate any of these explanations, except to say that a cloud of suspicion hangs over the closure. This might be the right moment to look at the history of sex, homosexuality and other taboos in the Bulgarian theatre.

By all accounts, there was a fast loosening of censorship toward both political matters as well as sexual themes after the fall of communism in 1989. Clearly, conventional sexuality and erotic themes arrived on the scene before homosexuality, notably with the play *Casanova* (Казанова) at the Salza i Smyah Theatre in 2008, with the nakedness of the actress Borislava Kostadinova, as directors took steps away from the enforced prudery.

According to Georgi Mihalkov, who directed a play in the Renaissance (Vazrashdane/Възраждане) Theatre about a lesbian couple in San Francisco called *Taboo*, gay scenes and themes began to sell in Bulgarian theatre because people tended to find them interesting and because the themes were unknown (unsigned interview article, *168 hours*, 2010:34). Among the successful American plays on gay issues were those by Paula Vogel, whose play *How I Learned to Drive* (2003) was mounted at Theatre 199, and whose *The Long Christmas Drive Home* (1997) was featured at the Sofia Theatre. Mihalkov adds that the public was attracted by their serious themes, not by "piquant" gay sex scenes. If true, this is somewhat divergent from the emergence of homosexuality-themed plays in America, which were written and promoted by openly gay individuals like Vogel with a political agenda of liberation, who began to find a mass audience outside the predominantly gay or liberal neighborhoods of San Francisco and New York. (See my summary of the history in chapter three, above.)

Sexually frank American plays can now be found in Sofia's theatres with both the long-running (since 16 November 2000) and award-winning production of *The Vagina Monologues* (1996) of Eve Ensler at Theatre 199, and more recently in Salza i Smyah's new (September, 2012) production of Sarah Ruhl's 2009 hit, *In the Next Room (or The Vibrator Play)*. In any case, the subject of taboos and obscenity was much on the minds of the creative teams in New York and Sofia, and has also driven much of the critical and academic discussion of the play. As noted above, the Broadway version of

Angels's first long, sexually-charged gay kiss stayed long with a New York theatre professional (Roger Danforth, above), but barely registered for him in the Bulgarian version. This kiss is also deliberately extended in the Signature Theatre's New York City revival that I saw on 20 April 2011. (This could also be seen iighlighted n the Signature Theatre's YouTube promotional trailer during the play's run.)

In any discussion of taboos, it is hard to raise the topic without considering the theatre audience, since what is taboo in Peoria or small-town America is obviously not necessarily so in New York City or San Francisco. This is the essential rationale of the landmark U.S. Supreme Court decision in 1973 (Miller vs. California) that allowed local "community standards" in part to define obscenity, which could be banned in communities that could legally define it as such. In a play in which Kushner's notes say, "they begin to fuck" in the park (Kushner, 1993:57), a graphic or literal performance of this text would offend community standards in many American and European localities.

In fact, *Angels in America* ran into considerable resistance from conservatives and church officials in the United States once it departed New York. In east Texas, a Gregg County commissioner said he would withdraw a county offer of $50,000 for the Kilgore Community College's annual Shakespeare festival if the theatre department staged *Angels in America*. But the college president said that the college would go ahead despite church opposition (*Orlando Sentinel*, 1999:A16).

As it turned out, this notoriety generated not only press interest but box office buzz. "Vocal opposition from local churches and politicians to a prize-winning play about gay men has helped turn it into a box-office success." The play opened "before a sellout crowd of 264 people after weeks of angry words from local pulpits and threats from county and city officials to cut grants to the small, state-supported community college" (*Orlando Sentinel*, 1999:A20).

Given the state of gay rights in Bulgaria in 2010 (per chapter 3 above), it is not surprising that there was a forum on the play sponsored by a Bulgarian newspaper shortly following its opening, and that participants were either extremely for or against it, with verbal obscenities frequently expressed in hostility to it, according to Tomova-Stankova.

The closing of the play apparently because of weak ticket sales and not opposition from conservative church leaders, political figures, or others indicates that the National Theatre's Vasev was right in brushing aside concerns about actual protests. This may be because Shpatova's production was not as racy or explicit as in New York or San Francisco. (See discussion of the critique by Miraslava Kortenska, p. 155-157, below.)

Much of the media commentary indeed discussed the gay themes, and some of the tabloids, with unusual prurient interest, inquired which actors are gay in real life, but with no tone of opprobrium (e.g., *Telegraf*, 27.10., and *Telegraf*, 12.11.2010:34-35). On the liberal side, *168 Chasa* actually carried the position of the Bulgarian gay rights organization Gemini, which was displeased with the stereotyped portrayal of gays on the Bulgarian stage, as well as an interview with director Georgi Mihalkov, cited above, in which he notes the commercial value of exploring gay themes in the Bulgarian theatre (12-18/11.2010:34).

Tomova-Stankova disagreed with Mihalkov, and told me that gay issues are actually more difficult for Bulgarian audiences to accept than straight sex. What's more, male gays are much harder to accept, she said, than lesbianism. And though the average Bulgarian will enjoy sex in the movies or on stage, she agrees with the polls referenced in chapter three that Bulgaria is backward on the issue of gay liberation or acceptance.

The problem of depicting gays and their lifestyle on stage in cities outside the U.S. is not unique to Sofia. For example, in the London premier production in 1994, the director Declan Donnellan, "talked about the differences between the gay milieus in London and New York. 'The whole drag thing,' he said, is foreign to the English gay community. Referring to the quintessentially middle-class British department store chain, he added, 'We're very Marks & Spencer.'" Consequently some of the drag material was toned down, and the production did not include female actors playing both male roles, contrary to Kushner's instructions. Nudity, however, was not a problem, and the London version included nude love scenes that were not in the Broadway premier (Canby, 1994:A5).

As for her own translation, Tomova-Stankova says that the obscenities were not a problem, and that she avoided euphemisms and kept true to the author's text. "Audiences have heard it all before, as on *Staklen Dom* [a popular contemporary TV series]," she said, and besides, "the language gets laughs."

The particular concern in this case is that the unquestioned poetry or elevated language of the original English version – which one reviewer called "Miltonic poetry" (Brown, 2010:online) – would survive only as tiresome and obscure talk in Bulgarian. Right from the start, Tomova-Stankova told me, the team realized that the rabbi's opening monologue, about an East European Jewish woman's immigration to US, would be of no interest to Bulgarians, so it was performed quickly. It was "pointless to stress," she said.

This poetic language is perhaps, apart from the controversial subject matter, the one thing that American critics either loved or hated about the original play. Those who were moved by the story underlined its poetry; those left cold by the themes or characters scorned the play's pretentious language. *Angels in America* is a "very literate play," wrote Robert Brustein, one of the Mandarins of academic and critical opinion in the U.S. (24.5.1993:30). A popular New York critic wrote about "Kushner's approach, privileging all the characters with his mellifluous turns of speech and brightness of perception, from the Valium-dazed Mormon wife to the compulsively knowing political fixer Roy Cohn" (Feingold, 1993:218).

The translator is obviously faced with capturing the play's poetic language and metaphors. Tomova-Stankova said that she did a literal translation, with fidelity to the text, and that Shpatova was also very strict about the play and language, and opposed actors making things up or adding language. What the National Theatre saw was Tomova-Stankova's text mounted word for word.

Still, Tomova-Stankova was challenged with trying to translate Kushner's metaphors such as this line spoken by Ethel Rosenberg to Roy Cohn (Kushner, 1993:112): "History is about to crack wide open. Millennium approaches." (The phrase is derived from Walter Benjamin's essay, "Theses on the Philosophy of History," in which he depicts an Angel of History trying to stop it. See McNulty, 1996.) Tomova-Stankova rendered this near literally as: "Скоро историята дълбоко ще се пропука. Милениумът наближав," changing only "wide open" to "deeply open." Does this original phrase mean anything literally? Will history stop, go back, turn around, reveal itself? Will there be an apocalypse? Or are we facing an "end of history" at the millennium? In context, Rosenberg seems to be telling Cohn that history has been going your way (e.g., Republicans are in power), but that it is about to change abruptly. In any case, some critics find this language poetic; others merely pretentious.

For Tomova-Stankova the language issue was not so much about capturing the poetry, but the more mundane task of conveying the sense of the American colloquialisms and slang. For the Yiddish term of endearment, "bubbulah" ("little boy," Kushner, 1993:25), she used the Bulgarian "buba" ("буба"), which is a shortening of "буболечка", which means a small bug. It is often used as an endearing term for loved ones, so works well in an equivalent. She had no such equivalent for the Yiddish "shtetl," a Jewish village in

Czarist Russia. Similarly she could find no apt Bulgarian words for the many slang versions of the words used for gays (e.g., "butch" and "queen"), Jews, and even semen, though by now "gay" has entered the Bulgarian language in a non-pejorative sense. The convenient meaning of the name Pryor as "before" (prior) when his ancestors take the stage, was also impossible to convey. Tomova-Stankova also could not translate Kushner's clever choice of Joe Pitt's asexual nickname for his wife, Harper: "buddy" (Kushner, 1993:23). Joe's "buddy kiss" with his wife (Kushner, 1993:27) did not work at all in literal Bulgarian ("приятелска целувка"), so she had to drop it.

Shpatova and her team, particularly her stage designer, Venelin Shuralov, had more tools at hand to realize Kushner's wish to both dazzle the audience with illusion but yet expose the joints of the play's mechanics:

> When I wrote [*Angels*], I was having fun asking directors and designers to do things that I felt the theater had surrendered to the movies because we don't do illusion as well as the movies do—which I felt was a misunderstanding of the nature and purpose of theatrical illusion. It's not intended to be 'effective': It's intended to be witty or clever or surprising or poetic, but it's always sort of transparently fake. (Kushner quoted in Feldman, 2010:online)

The unstated goal here is that the stage create not an illusion of reality but an illusion of "fantasia." Kushner shows you the set exposed like he shows you men as women and vice versa, so you can see the theatricality, which some would call the alienation effect. Several Bulgarian reviewers complained about this, but John Lahr, among other American reviewers, praises this in the 2010 Broadway revival: "The journey that Kushner's characters take is an epic one, and the transformations are as incredible to watch as they are to enact. (They're made even more exciting by…the Brechtian handling of the sets and props, and Wendall K. Harrington's clever projection design)" (Lahr, 2010:online).

Also on the subject of interpreting *Angels* as epic theatre in Brecht's sense, a theatre scholar wrote about a production in San Francisco that the

> material and scope of the set—industrial urban, explicitly theatrical—continually place the domestic scenes within the context of the social, economic, and political structure of our nation at century's end…the setting enhances or completes the play in this regard, strengthening the epic qualities and mitigating the tendency for the playscript to slip into bourgeois individualism. (Janelle Reinelt in Geis, 1997:239)

From my conversations with the National Theatre's creative team, I had no sense that they deliberately chose this sort of epic theatre setting, though Tomova-Stankova told me that the large scale of the stage caused practical issues, for example, that the Angel could not crash through the ceiling, per Kushner's directions, because it would be dangerous with the high ceiling.

Apart from these technical considerations of adaptation, there are meatier considerations regarding the politics, epic or otherwise, which were naturally derived from Kushner's personal politics. The left-wing political community, of which Kushner was a part, hated President Reagan, his policies, and his era. Their agenda of protest was not confined to the gay liberation theme, but to a raft of issues of domestic priorities, military spending, the environment, and social policies. The leftist academic community, which we heard from in chapter two, made common cause with this movement. To some extent, leftists even accepted a conspiratorial argument that Washington deliberately refused to fight AIDS out of hostility to homosexuals, and what was sometimes called their "lifestyle disease." E.g., one academic cited, "the top-down pressures of egocentric deceit and escapist denial that have taken over America as Reagan's Washington allows the epidemic to happen" (James Miller in Geis, 1997:69).

In this cosmology, for example, Roy Cohn is an epochal villain and Ethel Rosenberg is a hero, as indeed they are portrayed in *Angels in America,* though neither mainstream America nor historical consensus accepts this. Such a political agenda is part-and-parcel of Kushner's dramatic project, as he himself explains in his discussion of Brecht in the afterword to the play, with its approval of "a theatre of political analysis and engagement" and the "marriage of art and politics" (Kushner, 1992:153).

Put more bluntly, "Kushner's main objective is to raise awareness about moral authority in an age of AIDS" (Krasner, 2006:163) and his play "is a political call to arms for the age of AIDS" (Rich, 5.5.1993:15).

Kushner's politics suggest two apparent results: that liberal reviewers and critics seem to be much more sympathetic to his play, and for purposes of this study, as stated in my methodology, that one evaluating his success should ask whether Kushner has succeeded in influencing the political views of his audience. I examine these issues in the next two sub-chapters.

The Critical Reactions

A review of the critical reaction to *Angels in America*'s Broadway premier shows us that, even though the play had wind in its sails from the runs in San Francisco and London, and carried off a raft of major awards, several important American critics stood ground and either condemned the play or the production, while others sought to deflate what they thought were the overblown claims on its behalf.

As stated above, I cannot help noticing an ideological trend driving the critical reaction. In the climate of the early 1909s, when the Democrat Presidential candidate Bill Clinton had recently removed the Republicans from the White House after twelve years, political polarization had not diminished a bit from the Reagan years. In fact, a militant conservative lawyer, Kenneth Starr, conducted an impeachment investigation against President Clinton that went way beyond its original mandate. Kushner's play was part of the ideological liberal progressive ferment of these years.

There is no question that the bi-coastal media celebrated *Angels in America*, itself a product of San Francisco, Los Angeles, and New

York City. In addition to the major dramatic awards granted by the cultural Brahmins, fourteen reviewers or critics in major newspapers or magazines gave it a thumbs-up, by my count (see the spreadsheet of New York City reviews in appendix A.3). More importantly, almost all the major New York-based media liked it, and the real opinion-leading critics heralded the play as a milestone, including *The New York Times*, *Newsweek*, and the *Village Voice*. The language in many of these reviews was indeed hyperbolic: Frank Rich of the *Times* called it the "most thrilling American plays in years, astonishing, epic, intimate" (1993:15) and *Newsweek* called it the "broadest, deepest, most searching American play of our time" (quoted in Olson, 1994:71-72). The West Coast and New York critical reception surely generated similar high praise in regional and local newspapers, and to some degree in smaller magazines and journals.

Only one reviewer from a major liberal, intellectual magazine scorned Kushner's play, but this was ten years later and in reaction to the HBO movie. Lee Siegel in *The New Republic* (the same magazine's chief critic, Robert Brustein, warmly approved it) called it an "overwrought, coarse, posturing, formulaic mess" (2003:26-8). Siegel would agree with what David Mamet has called the "victim play," in which "such and such a group are oppressed, and well-meaning people must learn to overcome their prejudices and come to their aid" (Mamet, 2010:56). As Siegel tells it:

> Centering a work of art on the experience of marginality and suffering is like waterproofing your shoes. It repels criticism. You make the work

> seamless with its subject, so that anyone who criticizes the work seems callous about the subject…And once you join in the praise of a protected work such as Angels in America, you reap the benefit of demonstrating your own virtue by celebrating the play. (2003:26)

The conservative critics, on the other hand, had their knives out, and attacked the play for its political themes as crude agitprop. *The National Review* called it "a political tract," and also "rambling, garrulous, incoherent, and inchoate" (Grenier, 1993:55). Alisa Solomon wrote in "Wrestling with Angels: A Jewish Fantasia,": "*Angels* was reviled by right-wing critics…spewing about the play's leftist vision" (in Geis, 1997:121). Solomon cites the conservative Jewish monthly, *Commentary*, but its erudite critic, Terry Teachout, actually wrote a mixed appraisal some years after the premier. He called Kushner a prolix, flawed writer with a problematic style, but also wrote that *Angels*'s strongest scenes "are both emotionally powerful and theatrically effective." He also cited the "hectoring shrillness" and the "political diatribe" which "demonize conservatives" (2011:81-82).

The political tendentiousness has been a consistent theme among conservative commentators. For example, Leo Berani hit many of the same notes in his study, *Homos*:

> The enormous success of this muddled and pretentious play is a sign, if we need still another one, of how ready and anxious America is to see and hear about gays—provided we reassure America how familiar, how morally sincere, and particularly in the

case of Kushner's work, how innocuously full of significance we can be (1995:69).

Finishing with these rather scathing reactions in the U.S. can prepare us for some of the sharp criticism that the National Theatre's production of *Angels in America* provoked in Sofia. But overall there was understanding for this deliberately provocative work, and even remarks that it is dated and hardly scandalous anymore. Overall, twelve reviewers gave it a positive review or qualified praise. (These reviews have checks in both the "positive" and "neutral" on my spreadsheet.) Ten critics wrote mixed reviews, and only four wrote mostly negative notices. These figures include one preview and several appraisals written several weeks after the premier.

Several of the critics, interestingly, focused on the nature of the adaptation, and not only on the usual subjects of the acting and production values such as lighting and sets. Violeta Decheva, for example, writes in *Kultura* that *Angels in America* is really about America, not Bulgaria, which seems to me a way of saying that the production has failed or, as she writes, it is "a token in the Bulgarian theatre" (2010:2). The anonymous reviewer on lifestyle.iblox.bg is sure that the Bulgarian viewer will have trouble understanding the context of the play, so provides its history and the social context (2010:online). In *Novinar*, Liliyana Karadjova writes that it is hard for Bulgarians to understand and to get a full impression because the topic is not a problem of the present day, but that the play's chaotic structure is also part of the difficulty (2010:21). Two other reviewers also note that the theme and the passing of time makes the play difficult for Bulgarians to understand, but one does this in the context of an approving review, while the other is critical overall (Vasileva, 4/10.2010:15; and Konstantinov, 25.11.2010:13, respectively). This raises the further question whether it is a genuine basis for criticism to say that a play is difficult to understand, and whether it is the responsibility of the director, and especially the adapters reviving a foreign work, to make the changes necessary for easy assimilation.

Apart from the "heavy" themes several reviewers cited, there is the frequent reference to the play's being twenty years old, and dated, with the Cold War having passed. For some such as Peneva in *Kapital Light*, this did not pose a problem (2010:28), and for Slavina Ilieva-Syu in Stand.bg, the "Angel" is timeless (2010:online). For Yana Doneva in Vsekiden.bg, however, "the shock of the themes has worn off" (2010:online). Still, the loss of shock value did not necessarily lessen the dramatic impact for Doneva, who faulted more the play's length, over two hours, in a generally mixed review. The length of the production without an intermission for audiences that have been called impatient, was also a problem for Karadjova (2010:21). For Elena Peneva, however, the themes of AIDS and the Cold War may be dated for some playgoers, but not for her because the play held her attention throughout (2010:29).

The length of *Angels in America*, or even just the first half did cause concern among the creative team, as duration was a concern also to Morfov and his team. This was cited by many American critics too, including appreciative reviewers, who recognized that Kushner goes on too long: "Kushner's play survives, its vibrant high points and natteringly wordy weak spots intact" (Feingold, 1993:219). This is an example of even a left-wing critic who believed that the play is too talky. Even Albee, in my interview with him, said that all that Kushner writes is overwritten: two-thirds is wonderful, and one third is unnecessary, he said (phone interview, 4 October 2011). As for the Bulgarian version, Tomova-Stankova was aware of this, and also said that the problem with duration was compounded by the translation, since the English language has more short words.

Some of the Bulgarian critics took a swipe at stage designer Venelin Shuralov's creative choices. (See p. 155.) Mariana Tsvetkova wrote that the production is ugly and plain, with "almost no stage décor" (2010:24). I note, however, that this is what Kushner explicitly called for: "a pared-down style of presentation, with minimal scenery" (1993:5). In this case, the misunderstanding is on the part of the critic, not the creative team.

A more justified criticism, which goes to the heart of the adapters' choices, is how far they should go to help the audience understand a play, in this case, an admittedly challenging one. To some degree, many of the critics acknowledge the difficulty and remoteness (in time and space), but do not have answers about how to bring the drama to the Bulgarian audience while keeping true to Kushner's themes and spirit. Dilyana Dimitrova in *Trud* perhaps comes closest to the problem when she writes that the National

Theatre adaptation makes bold political arguments, fulfilling Kushner's didactic goal, but that it has "too little tenderness" (29.10.2010:22). This was echoed by Mariana Tsvetkova, who wrote that Shpatova lacked compassion and warmth toward the personal drama of the gay people in the play (2010:24), and by New Bulgaria University Professor of Acting Eva Volitzer, who said (personal interview, 11 May 2012) that the production not only lacks warmth and sensitivity, but "there is no love in its characters." The Kushner characters, she said, are "delicate; they would not proclaim in a public square." Her example is the somewhat bizarre hospital nurse, who, she says, treats Prior cruelly. Dilyana Dimitrova agreed when she wrote in her review that, "There is too little tenderness exchanged between the gays at the National Theatre" (29.10.2010:22). For her part, Tomova-Stankova was aware of this criticism, but argued that the gays will understand themselves in the play, but that more spectators will understand Harper and her family problems, and empathize with her (personal interview).

The best-argued view I've heard on this is from none other than Alexander Morfov, when I asked him why the show seems not to have succeeded to the same degree as his. "Desi Shpatova made a mistake," he said, "when she focused too much on the American problems in *Angels in America*. She didn't concentrate enough on the human problems." He elaborated that the adaptation had too much of politics, Jews, homosexuals, the Cold War, and taboos. Bulgarians didn't know the terminology, he said. Shpatova could have focused on other things, such as the relationships of parents and children, suffering, and love. "I feel I could have done it avoiding the typically American things that are not understandable for Bulgarian audiences."

This is truly insightful, I believe, but one must state: *Angels* is not *Cuckoo's Nest*. It is far more embedded in the American cultural context. How could Shpatova and her team have skirted these themes without violating Kushner's spirit and eviscerating his play?

The biggest thematic challenge for Shpatova was the homosexuality and the "indecency" attached to treating it, both vital to the play. They brought on what might have been the most unrestrained attack on it, from a freelance critic, Miroslava Kortenska, writing in a weekly tabloid. In her lengthy appraisal, she writes that many have asked her about the play because, "the text of Tony Kushnar is full of obscene remarks and candid confessions on homosexuality and AIDS." She expresses her revulsion at the play's language, such as "I want you to fuck me in the ass" ("Искам да ме чукаш отзад!," which is carried in highlighted text graphically in the newspaper) (2010:64-65). She writes that such "an abundance of hysteria, caricatures, political debates are played....the stage of our National Theatre becomes barbaric."

Yet Kortenska does not wish to appear anti-gay: she contrasts *Angels in America*, "the bible of the gay society today," with the film *Milk* and the plays of Marius Kurkinski, whose gay-themed work did not offend anyone. Indeed, she argues that the play contains primitivism, contortion, imitation, extremism, and is "a shallow and repellent production." The core problem for her, however, I believe, is that the characters are not adapted into a proper Bulgarian landscape. Mariya Kavardjikova, she notes, is forced to play an adult rabbi in addition to other male and female roles. These various shifts of plot are "completely unconvincing." Kortenska makes at least two conclusions: That mounting the play shows Bulgaria's inferiority complex toward foreign productions, and that such a production "can't move you ["не може да хване за гърлото"]... it only gives primitive signals to snobs and those seeking caresses in parks."

This article generated a controversy on television and then online, where Yana Doneva reported in *Vsekiden.bg* (9.11.2010) the televised remarks of *Angels in America* actor Vladimir Karamazov, who rebuts Kortenska for her factually untrue comments about the play, which he suspects she never even watched. Karamazov expresses his dismay at "the total lack of understanding" by the theatre critics [театроведите], and their criticism of the play's creative team.

Karamazov further claims that there is nothing scandalous in the production and that Bulgarian critics can write what they want, but that their articles are not read and they have no influence beyond a small circle of people.

In response, Kortenska is quoted saying in the same article that it is as unacceptable for actors to evaluate themselves as it is for the play to appear on the stage of the National Theatre. She also repeats her earlier concern: "I do not want our children to watch the gay parade on our biggest stage," and asks if *Angels in America* is the most appropriate play to represent American culture in Bulgaria. The answer is plainly that the play has won every major theatrical prize in the U.S., and has, as we've seen, been hailed as one of the greatest achievements of the American theatre in its era. Kortenska may not like highly acclaimed contemporary American theatre, but *Angels*'s stature is beyond doubt.

The Public Reception: Results of the Audience Questionnaires

The early closing of *Angels in America* after the first season at the National Theatre posed a bit of a problem for my audience survey. Although I received my initial survey results from playgoers immediately after attending the play, most of the responses were culled after the show closed. None of the questionnaires were actually collected in the theatre, and the final number of respondents was less than for the other two plays. Though I received responses from a handful of non-Bulgarians, none of them were American, and therefore not useful for this study.

Despite the many obvious difficulties of mounting a provocative and ground-breaking American play immersed in the history and politics of a generation ago, Desi Shpatova and her team did a respectable job with the Bulgarian audience, as she did with the Bulgarian critics. The results support this: of the 36 Bulgarian respondents, 24 said they enjoyed it very much or somewhat, of these an impressive 18 liked it very much.

Again, the raw data and comments are collated in the appendix, but other audience survey results are (numbers below keyed to questionnaires):

2. All but 3 of the playgoers said that they understood the play, and 19 of them said they understood it very much. One could argue, then, that Shpatova succeeded in making a difficult play understandable to a foreign audience, but another hypothesis emerges from a look at the next question, about the play's theme.

3. The responses to the thematic question were split almost evenly in thirds: A little over one third accepted my proposed political-social (callousness of political and other leaders toward gays) or sociological themes (humanity of the gay population), and almost another third offered a wide variety of themes of their own. Only four respondents took the bait of two obviously wrong themes. But the variety of ideas about the theme means, I believe, that Kushner's work permits disparate interpretations, all of them more or less reasonable. A complex work like this, operating on different levels, allows the audience to favor the political (McCarthyism and Reaganism), social (AIDS, alienation), or personal (betrayal, sickness and loneliness) themes, among others. The adaptation seems to have worked since parts of the audience understood them all.

4. Most Bulgarians, 26, thought the play's main characters seemed more American than Bulgarian, while only 3 thought they seemed more Bulgarian. With the urban quirks, language usage, irony and gay culture of New York, and a dollop of Salt Lake City Mormonism, it doesn't seem that this could be otherwise. Only one respondent said that despite this, the characters epitomized universal social tensions—in which particular area was unstated. The challenge for the Shpatova team was to make the lives of this very foreign cast of characters of importance or interest to Bulgarians.

5. Fifteen of the respondents, close to half, said that the actors portrayed possible or realistic Bulgarians. One respondent's telling comment, that the ailing Prior was the most realistic, indicates that the apparent universalism achieved is due not to the sexual lifestyle, ethnicity or other social category, but to their human appeal, something accessible to any Bulgarian or human being. This aspect of the play was cited by several critics above, as well as by Morfov, as the best way to widen its appeal.

6. Regarding the play's humor, the characters retain a sort of grim humor and irony that was clear from the laughter at the New York production I saw in 2010, despite the tragic subject matter. Some of the humor is situational, but most of it is verbal ("very Steven Spielberg" in reference to the Angel's appearance), so both the

translator and the actors get credit for conveying the original play's humor. Nineteen of the respondents found the play funny, while 13 were lukewarm or missed the jokes. This is not a triumphal result, but a moderate one.

7. The creative team did better in conveying the show's pathos. Twenty-four were moved by the characters' struggles and pain, and 12 were not. So although almost everyone claimed to have understood the play, about a third were unmoved, and close to half were not amused. They may have enjoyed it, but that would leave a cool, intellectual pleasure.

8. and 9. These questions tell us if the playgoers were aware that two characters, Roy Cohn and Ethel Rosenberg, are actual historical figures fictionalized by Kushner. Most answer correctly (17 and 20, respectively), and some of them probably because they read about the characters in the theatre's program brochure or in a review, or just know the background to the play or American history. This tracks with the educational level of the audience (per question 15, below), but about a quarter of the respondents (7 and 11, respectively) replied that they did not know who the characters really were.

10., 11., and 12. These questions ask the playgoers about their attitudes toward homosexuality, a central element of the play. Question 10, about whether homosexuality is a chosen lifestyle or the result of inheritance, did not provoke hostile responses such as that it is a sickness or a moral failing, and the 5 respondents who said it is "something else" did not identify what they thought it is. This tracks with their generally liberal and accepting view of homosexuality—counter to general Bulgarian public opinion described in chapter 3 above—identified in question 11. Here, 29 of the 36 respondents said that homosexuality is an acceptable or perfectly acceptable lifestyle. Clearly then, *Angels* played to a constituent audience of sympathetic viewers, at least on this social issue, if not on the radical politics. It is not surprising then, that in response to question 12 regarding whether the play changed their view of homosexuality, 22 said no or not at all. They already accepted Kushner's progressive, sympathetic view, and did not need consciousness-raising.

13., 14., and 15. These questions on the audience demographics showed that almost two-thirds of them were in the 20-35 age bracket, as expected for such a liberal group of people, and that 32 of them have college or advanced degrees, which also aligns with polls showing a more accepting attitude toward gays among the educated class. Interest in the theatre, however, was rather flat, and showed more serious or frequent theatre-goers, 20, compared to the rare playgoers, 6, or occasional spectators, 11. This particular play brought out about the same number of the rare playgoers, 17%, as the more mainstream *One Flew Over the Cuckoo's Nest*, (p. 82, above), 19%. As expected from the remarks of Lee Sankowich, *Cuckoo's Nest* drew a much greater proportion of youth (under 36 years of age), 68%, versus only 58% for *Angels in America*.

I will try to make sense of this empirical audience data and what I have learned about the American playgoers. The first phenomenon to analyze is the constituency audience (see 2.3, p. 33-5, above), that is, the narrow group of like-minded spectators in a political or social group who will uncritically approve of a play. Kushner conceivably has two such groups: the leftists or political radicals and the gay community.

To appeal to the former, *Angels in America* not only expresses this political stance, but makes, "crowd-pleasing swipes at conservatives, Republicans, and Mormons" (Olson, 1994:72). Kushner is fortunate in that New York and San Francisco, the venues for his early and later greatest triumphs, are arguably the most liberal cities in the U.S. But demonizing Ronald Reagan and glorifying putative Soviet spies has little traction in Sofia a generation after the fall of Communism. Kushner has described his religion as dialectical materialism, but it would be difficult to find many dialectical materialists in the National Theatre audience.

In New York, Kushner's financial backers depended on support from the gay community, and hoped for broader appeal. According to *Time* magazine, "the producers' main worry was keeping [*Millennium Approaches*] afloat long enough to get the second half, *Perestroika*, up and running. They feared *Millennium*'s gay outlook might limit audiences to homosexuals, sympathetic straights and the relative handful of theater mavens who see everything" (Henry, 1993:online).

The problem with relying on the gay community in Bulgaria is that, in a sense, it does not even exist. There is virtually no gay rights organization, according to Aksinia Gencheva, a former activist with Gemini, a defunct gay NGO (personal interview). Of course we can assume that there is the same number of individuals with a gay or lesbian orientation, but in Bulgaria they are not public about it, that is, they have not come out of the closet. This is true of *Angel*s's director, Desislava Shpatova, as it is for almost all others. What this means for her play is that few gay people will wish to attend to feel or show solidarity or support for the production, as was the case in the U.S.

In addition, the link between the politics of *Angels in America* and the Pride parade is not clear in Bulgaria. When I asked Boyko Krastanov, who plays Louis in the play, about this, he said that he hopes that the play changed the points of view of people in the audience. But when asked about Pride, he replied that he doesn't understand it. "Why do they have to be so out about their orientation?" he asked (personal interview, 17 June 2012). What this tells me is that gay Bulgarians might avoid attending the play, for reasons suggested above by Kortenska: it might also be perceived as too "out," too aggressive.

CHAPTER SIX: *The Goat, or Who is Sylvia?*: A Faithful Adaptation

History of the Play's Productions

Edward Albee, the octogenarian, eternally young provocateur of the American theatre, granted Broadway the gift of his *The Goat, or Who is Sylvia?*, which opened at the John Golden Theatre on 10 March 2002. The story of a mature, married, successful architect who falls in love with and has sexual relations with a goat, it puzzled the New York audience as well as the critics. Albee was coy as usual in his remarks to the press during rehearsals, and clearly intended to *épater la bourgeoisie*.

The outline of the story is as follows: Martin is the distinguished architect turning 50 years of age while also receiving the prestigious Pritzker Architecture Prize, a real-world honor granted by the Pritzker family of Chicago. The entire play takes place in his family's large and stylish living room. The set bespeaks affluence, good taste, and with the extensive art book collection, even erudition. Despite his high status and education, Martin appears in the first scene as an absent-minded, inattentive professional who doesn't have enough focus to give a coherent television interview to his "best friend," a TV journalist named Ross. After some prompting, Martin confides to Ross in showing him a photo of his love, Sylvia, who then promptly informs Martin's wife Stevie that her husband is having sex with a goat. The second scene depicts Stevie's and teenage son Billy's confrontation with Martin, in which Stevie tries desperately and increasingly violently to understand her husband.

Stevie departs while Billy raises his own questions about his father, and they also discuss Billy's homosexuality. In a striking denouement, just after the return of Ross, Stevie enters the living room with the bloodied carcass of Sylvia on her shoulders, shocking her family and Ross.

Albee added a subtitle to this play, "Notes Toward a Definition of Tragedy," and the climactic death of a "character" certainly has the air of tragedy. There is also a healthy brace of humor throughout the play until Stevie's return, so the play could better be called a tragicomedy like *Romeo and Juliet*. In this and many similar plays, Shakespeare provides the audience abundant laughter early on, which seems to throw the later tragic developments into sharper relief.

(I must also add that Albee's subtitle could easily be interpreted as a teasing reference to T. S. Eliot's famous little book, *Notes Toward a Definition of **Culture*** (emphasis added), published in 1948. In it, Eliot, a language purist like Albee, although a notable Christian conservative, explained in part why he is renouncing American culture and education in favor of the finer glories of the British tradition. Despite their political differences, Eliot and Albee share an identical scorn for what they consider America's debased popular culture.)

The first run of *The Goat* had a solid cast of Broadway veterans, including Mercedes Ruehl as the fierce, frustrated wife Stevie, and Bill Pullman as her sexually challenged husband, Martin. The original stars were succeeded by the equally distinguished pair of

Sally Field and Bill Irwin, and this personnel combined for a run of 309 performances. Box office receipts were good but not lavish, and the run was about average for a Broadway drama. There were some raised eyebrows when it won the Tony Award for Best Play since the critical reaction was not uniformly positive, and the word-of-mouth audience reaction was often bewilderment. It also won a Drama Desk Award for Best New Play in 2002, and earned a Pulitzer Prize for Drama nomination in 2003.

Although a close look at Albee's work reveals an examination of a series of sexual and other taboos, American theatre and film have taken other peeks at bestiality. A. R. Gurney poked fun at a married man a bit too smitten by his dog in a 1995 play titled, coincidentally, *Sylvia*, though Albee told me he was unfamiliar with the play (personal phone interview, 4 October 2011, and all unattributed quotes below are to this interview). (Yet the play is not obscure; I saw it performed at the commercial Studio Theatre in Washington, D.C., in March, 1997.) The couple also visit a sexually ambiguous psychiatrist to advise on their dog issues. In the end, Sylvia, played by a woman, is splayed, but not symbolically sacrificed, as in Albee's version. (See below how Albee has treated the theme of people's relations with animals in several of his plays.)

Since *The Goat* also has a homosexual son and winks at incest, S&M (sadism and masochism, when Stevie jokes that Martin is seeing a dominatrix –"садистична господарка" in the Bulgarian version--"who smells funny," Albee (2), 2008:545), and such kinky sex, it might not be inappropriate to mention Woody Allen's 1972 film, *Everything You Always Wanted to Know about Sex *(*But Were Afraid to Ask)*, a send-up of a best-selling sex manual of the era. The hit movie featured not only a TV game show, *What's My Perversion?*, but also Gene Wilder as a family doctor falling in love with a sheep named Daisy.

The Goat, in any case, has had moderate success in its short post-Broadway life. It opened at the Goodman Theatre in Chicago in 2003, and was produced at the Almeida Theatre in London in 2004, and then mounted at the Arena Stage in Washington in March of 2005. There was at least one critic who asked why producers risked bringing it to London, since it had economic difficulty in New York, despite winning the awards mentioned above (Wolf, 2004:41). *The Goat* also played at the Remy Bumppo Theatre Company in Chicago in the spring of 2011.

The Ivan Vazov National Theatre Production

The Goat, or Who is Sylvia? premiered at the National Theatre's basement chamber hall on 11 October 2009, with the literal title, *Kozata, ili, Koya e Silviya*? Albee himself had spent the previous two weeks in Sofia (his visit funded by the America for Bulgaria Foundation) working with the creative team on the production while also attending theatrical events and receiving an *Honoris causa* degree from the National Academy of Theatre and Film Arts. The play was and remains (June, 2012) a huge hit, at least for the chamber hall of 130 seats, and tickets were hard to come by even in the second season, with performances usually only three times per month.

The play was directed by the young (born in 1972) and acclaimed director, Yavor Gardev, who had previously directed two plays by Martin McDonagh, among many other plays by Shakespeare, Tracy Letts, Yasmina Reza, and Albert Camus in Sofia, Moscow, Caen, and Paris. He also directed Albee's *The Play about the Baby* (1998) in 2005. *The Goat* actors included a National Theatre star, the powerful Boyka Velkova as Stevie, but Gardev raised eyebrows when he chose Mihail Bilalov as Martin. Bilalov had not been active on the Bulgarian stage, but rather was living in Paris, where he was working, coincidentally, as a landscape architect. Albee approved the casting choices.

Albee has said that, "Yavor had good control over the production. He knew that I had directed the play so knew what was going on." He added that, "Yavor knew precisely what I wanted and he paid attention to what I said." Albee was well aware of what, to him, the threats to his vision were. He said that Gardev kept the Bulgarian excesses or additions, such as noise, music, and added lighting or color, to a minimum, "because I was around." Indeed, this *Goat* is not a flashy production. Most important, perhaps, Albee has said that Gardev, "showed that he understood everything I wanted to say with the piece" (*Zemya*, 2009:18).

Of course Albee spoke no Bulgarian, but he worked closely with the translator, Harry Anichkin, who had previously translated his *All Over* and *The Play about the Baby*, among many other plays and movies (for subtitles). Albee was strict about keeping to his original text, but allowed what he called "adjustments" when he said Anichkin convinced him to change a few phrases. In these cases, "We found good equivalencies, not distortions," Albee said. Throughout, he resisted "free adaptation" and got a "damned good" *Goat*, he said.

According to Bilalov, Albee did not interfere with or interrupt the rehearsals, except at what appeared to be what Albee thought were "sick" parts of the performance. He was present and attentive at the rehearsals, but spoke only for 5-10 minutes at the end of each rehearsal. Content with Bilalov's low-key style, Albee posed many questions instead to Yulian Vergov, who portrayed Ross, and challenged Velkova on her performance of the second scene, reportedly saying, "Stevie is not sick. She is a strong woman!" She certainly came across the floodlights that way in Sofia (as the same character did on Broadway). As any Albee fan knows, he very much likes strong women characters.

In the end, Bilalov says, Gardev learned a lot from Albee, who urged him to downplay, or not exaggerate the script, and helped ease the actors into the story. He also helped the actors understand the text's nuances or shadings, including its metaphorical ("inside" Bilalov said) meanings.

Of the three plays under examination here, *The Goat* may be the easiest to adapt. This is because it is the least embedded in America, with no local references, color, or dialect. Ralitsa Nenkova writes in her unpublished M.A. thesis, "Critics are unanimous that Albee's art is appropriated in completely different cultural contexts with an amazing ease due to its lack of rigid generic boundaries, multiplicity of themes and the universal philosophic and social messages, dominating his drama" (2002:2). For sure, Albee's frequent use of Everyman characters without names (e.g., "A," "B," and "C" in *Three Tall Women*, 1991; or "He" and "She" of *Counting the Ways*, 1977) suggests their universality, but some observers believe plays with vague "universal philosophic and social messages" may be the hardest to understand and therefore to adapt in foreign cultural contexts. This may simply be because they are already difficult to understand for their original domestic audience.

This group argues that, in terms of less exotic references, *The Goat* is relatively easy to adapt, but not in terms of its increasing abstraction. For example, Beckett's Everyman characters and Nowhere/Everywhere locations make his plays hard to get a hold of. He and Albee may like these purposely uncommon or inexperienced situations (such as one involving bestiality) and obscurity, which may be part of their plays' essence, but audiences may respond better to the local and specific more than to the abstract. Additionally, the local and specific works may be more difficult only on the verbal level, but not thematically, while creative teams could misunderstand or muddle the abstruse "universal" or absurdist message in an adaptation, and the public reception would suffer.

Let's look at one aspect of *The Goat*, which is its language. The witty, erudite, and polished dialogue of the highly educated upper middle class is typical of Albee's work, since, as he has said, it is the people he knows best. They happen to be Americans, and a casual playgoer might think they could be nationals of most Western European countries, or several affluent Asian ones.

But this is not so. Bilalov told me that the lead couple could not be Bulgarians because educated Bulgarians don't talk the way Martin and his wife Stevie do (personal interview, 31 October 2011). First of all, they swear like sailors, which such Bulgarian couples wouldn't do. The repeated use of the word "fuck" was a problem because the Bulgarian words ("чукаш," "шибана," and "заеби") are very strong, and are not used so often or so casually. In fact, Bilalov believes, it had not been heard on the Bulgarian stage, at least not by such educated characters—even though there has been plenty of nudity, for example. The contrast or irony of such high-class people speaking in this coarse way, another Albee device, was very noticeable and striking, he said.

American intellectuals, I would argue, do tend to talk in this coarse way, especially if they are angry or exasperated. This reflects, I believe, both a stronger urge to be "democratic," but also more comfort in their established career success and intellectual superiority than the *nouveau riche* post-Berlin Wall generation of Bulgarian elites.

In any case, in a translation decision apparently accepted by Albee, Anichkin says, there are 47 "derivatives and variations" of the f-word in the original text, but only 27 in his Bulgarian translation. Only two of those, he says, carry "the full and harsh meaning of executing the act—the drama calls for it. The rest are all emotional and de-semanticized meanings," for which he found other equivalents in the Bulgarian language. Finally, regarding the shock of the vulgar language, the English "bullshit" is translated several times as "глупости," which I understand has a range of meanings besides "nonsense" or "stupidities," but the original English is several degrees harsher than this Bulgarian rendering.

Another reason the couple doesn't seem Bulgarian, according to Bilalov, is that Martin and Stevie banter and play word games in the first scene in a well-known Albee style (at least since *Who's Afraid of Virginia Woolf?*), which Bilalov called very unusual in Bulgaria. As one New York reviewer nicely summed it up: there are "many flashes of wit and wordplay – the playwright finds humor, for example, in his upper-income, hyper-verbal New Yorkers lacing their sentences with the f-curse, like Mametian characters with graduate degrees" (Phillips, 2002:A16).

In this context, Pavis underlines how important speech and behavior are for an audience to identify a stage character's social class—but yet how difficult for it: "ambiguity arises out of unforeseeable modifications in the circumstances of reception—the temporal and cultural shift from utterance to reception...For example, it is difficult to ascertain a character's social milieu or group from his/her speech and behavior, and whether this speech conforms or not to the character's social origins" (1992:55). In this case, when Stevie and Martin speak with obscenities and in an ironic style unfamiliar to National Theatre audiences, the play's milieu must be especially difficult to identify.

Finally, many Bulgarians have said that Stevie is not recognizable as a Bulgarian wife because she is too strong for chauvinistic Bulgarian society, where men dominate and have affairs and women are patient and accepting. Of course, such a powerful female role is very typical for Albee. From Martha in *Who's Afraid of Virginia Woolf?* to the sadistic nurse in *The Death of Bessie Smith* (1960), the manipulative Mrs. Toothe in *Everything in the Garden* (1967), and to the virago Amelia in *The Ballad of the Sad Café* (1963), observers haven't failed to notice the dominant female women. This is explored also in the semi-autobiographical *Three Tall Women*.

But I would like to return to the absence of American references in the play. Despite this seeming universality, there is also the view touched on above that Albee and other plays in the absurdist tradition may be more difficult to adapt than more "localized" plays, at least in the sense that they pose greater burdens on the director to reach an audience. For example, Beckett's *Krapp's Last Tape* (1958) or the notoriously puzzling *Waiting for Godot* (1953) didn't take place in any particular country or city. Beckett was also famously bilingual, so the plays are not particularly anchored linguistically. This makes them as difficult to get across in any country because audiences have a hard time identifying with Krapp and Estragon. In the case of *One Flew Over the Cuckoo's Nest*, McMurphy may be an American anti-hero type, but he's also a type of charming rebel that many European societies identify with. So international audiences responded as well to Forman's film adaptation of the novel as did Americans. This localized story at least, it would follow, would reach audiences more easily than *The Goat,* though its story could occur in any modern society.

Albee made one other intervention in Sofia that reminds us of his intentions in the play. As noted above, the set reflects Martin and Stevie's social status and taste, which the latter systematically and symbolically destroys in the second act. I find this emotionally and dramatically appropriate. As she subconsciously feels that the bestiality belies the comfort and trust of their life together, she breaks its external symbols. The art objects are her targets, but Albee also oversaw the installation of the couple's library, which was not in all earlier productions, though this may have been on occasion due to budgetary restraints. Evidently, smashing pottery is more dramatic and kinetic than tearing up coffee-table books, but perhaps symbolically this makes sense in another way: the prestigious, showy, and public art is destroyed, but the knowledge inside the books remains with the couple. Albee has often attacked his characters' public pretensions or image, and here Stevie seems to do it for him. In any case, Albee insisted on the fancy art books, whose titles printed on covers and spines are in English, reminding us that Albee has said his characters are indeed Americans.

The Critical Reactions

Albee's provocative drama received many good notices at its Broadway premier, but the few critical voices were harsh in their fault-finding. Many both positive and negative were to some degree puzzled by what Albee meant to say in *The Goat*, and some of these critics still liked it. Overall, I found eleven positive reviews, three neutral, and two negative – actually very hostile – reviews or criticisms.

Interestingly, of the five American reviewers who called the play puzzling, tricky, or strange, all recommended it but one, who wrote a mixed review. The seriously critical reviews basically said there is no mystery to it: John Simon in *New York* magazine simply said that the play makes no sense (2002:133). Similarly, Howard Kissel in the *New York Daily News* called *The Goat* "an altogether specious play" without a theme in which "everything rings false," including the "arch, inelegant dialog" (2002:online).

Almost all of the positive reviews emphasized the play's humor, such as the praise in CurtainUp for the "wickedly funny" and "sly" wordplay in the script (2002:online). Among the other reviews of this sort, the critics called it funny and grim, while they seemed to struggle to sort out the comic and tragic elements. Lawrence Frascella in *Entertainment Weekly*, for example, noted the peals of laughter, but also cited the "excoriating tragedy" (2002:65). In one of the more insightful critiques, Robert Brustein wrote that *The Goat* is hard to classify, and that it "almost succeeds" in making a tragedy out of a dirty joke (2002:online).

Given that the play is both hard to classify as well as to evaluate, the American critics cited a range of themes and interpretations. Some just focused on the bestiality as transgression, or the irrationality of human emotions, and the more learned discussed these themes in the context of ancient Greek tragedy, such as its terror that affirms life, and the sacrifice of the goat on a metaphorical living room altar (Medoff, 2002:164-66). Those reviewers who seized on the social component of the story mentioned either Ross's betrayal or the upending of a sophisticated family by one of society's few remaining taboos (Levine, 2002:22).

Actually, though, this particular Albee drama is one of his least openly critical of American society or politics, but it may aim higher or broader. *Who's Afraid of Virginia Woolf*, which it resembles in many ways, skewers American academia, and its sham and hypocrisies. One apparent aim of subtitling *The Goat, Notes toward a Definition of Tragedy,* however, is that Albee is reaching beyond American social criticism to a tragedy that explores the universal human condition. And that human condition is the case in Sofia, Bulgaria, as much as it is in New York City or New England. Bulgarian society's reaction to bestiality, the architect Martin's "tragic" flaw that starts the play rolling, is equally abhorrent there as in the United States. Despite its unique history, the communist years and the struggles of transition, there is no social lag or conservative social attitudes, or even relative lack of wealth, that changes this public attitude.

The chief assault on Martin's "infidelity" is launched by Stevie, played apparently with equal force and conviction at the National Theatre by Boyka Velkova as by the formidable Mercedes Ruehl in the original Broadway production. Described as "a hurricane on stage" by one reviewer (Stoitcheva in *Slovoto*, 2009:online), her assault is the heart of the drama in that it contains both the robust humor, by turns caustic and outraged, and responds to the outrageous revelation in the first act that Martin loves a goat. Her onslaught seems to engender a similar audience reaction to that on Broadway or in the U.S., judging by reviews and YouTube postings of American productions that I've watched.

That is, the laughs are loudest when Martin somehow tries to explain the ordinariness of his actions, as when he recounts his visits to a therapy session for those having sex with animals: pigs, geese, etc. As if this is not ticklish enough, Stevie gives him a sort of resigned, dead look as she begins to destroy the room's pottery. She also has a strong series of Albee zingers for Martin, so the comic situation is built on several pillars: Martin's absurd narrative, Stevie's one-liners ("Goat-fuckers Anonymous" parodying Alcoholics Anonymous), and the slapstick of breaking pottery. So just at the moment when Martin begins to talk about bestiality, and make the international audience uncomfortable, he deploys both his witty verbal resources as well as some good old-fashioned knockabout comedy. Judging by the seemingly demonstrative laughter in the Sofia audience, it seemed that this was clearly laughter to relieve the tension, and Albee makes it easy for his viewers by piling the comedy on top of the perversion: At one point, even Stevie asks herself why she's laughing at bestiality (Albee, 2008:II,580).

The play's laughs themselves have been a matter of some concern in both New York and Sofia. For a sobering perspective, let's start with an observation by Arthur Miller, who wrote in the wake of Kennedy's death in 1963: "The only reliable recurring element in existence was the perverse, and the only sane reaction to it was bitter laughter, cousin to disgust." In this national climate, he wrote, laughter among the theatre audiences of the period did not mean that they are amused, but that the audience was "mortally bored, distracted" (1987:511).

In other words, Miller confirms that laughter is not always the result of amusement, but could have various explanations. In the case of *The Goat*, critics have noted the rather sharp turn from the howlers throughout the play to the putative tragic ending. As the playwright Steven Drukman wrote, "It is a play that seems to be one thing at the beginning but the chasm [between the beginning and the end] opens up as we go into it" (2002:110 and 181).

The question is really whether the turn is too sharp, and how that turn drives the play's effect on the audience. To quote the unhappy John Simon, who wrote about Albee's tendency to produce

> gales of laughter in the most inappropriate places. Especially irksome are three perennial Albee tics, here reaching their culmination. One is semantic one-upmanship, whereby characters continually and gratuitously correct one another's grammar and metaphors. Another is needless repetition of obvious things, because the hearer was preoccupied, deaf, or just thick. The third is relentless use of obscenity for cheap laughs. (2002:134)

Simon is an erudite but curmudgeonly critic, and no one could persuade him to like humor or "tics" that are not to his taste. But regarding the appropriateness of the audience's "gales of laughter," the fundamental issue turns on Albee's purpose, which he declares as tragedy. In a similarly performed play in Sofia at the National Theatre at the same time, the actors draw huge laughs from the audience, though the ending also turns serious, and then tragic. This is in the *avant garde* rendering of *Cyrano de Bergerac* by director Teddy Moskov. Moskov, however, told me pointedly (personal conversation, 20 March 2011) that he was very critical of his actors, who like to draw laughs, which drives them to overplay their roles. His concern is that the final emotional impact is diminished if the audience laughs too much en route to this finale. This is perhaps more challenging in Bulgaria, where actors are trained to bring out the audience's emotion or reaction, of which laughter is the most noticeable, and have a reputation for overacting.

Albee's view on this is that it is the director's responsibility to control the overacting, which can be hard to do. Directors must find the balance, he said. He added, in some self-defense, that he believes, "there is humor in everything, humor in tragedy and tragedy in humor." He also acknowledged that there is "not much" humor in the Greek classic plays (apart from Aristophanes)—and not much humor these days in Eastern European theatre.

Once the critics get beyond the belly laughs, they need to wrestle with what this strange play is all about, especially given the subtitle, *Notes Toward a Definition of Tragedy*. Starting with the American reviewers, there is, for example, the quandary of Barbara D. Phillips in *The Wall Street Journal* (2002:A16): "to take Martin's transgression seriously or to relish the patent absurdity...of the premise?...to see Stevie's rage as perfectly understandable or oddly excessive?... a fable about the power of the media...to expose secrets and destroy relatively innocent lives? A coded message about homosexuality and homophobia? A plea for the societal benefits of reticence? A rumination about the strange paths love and betrayal take?"

Several themes, however, seemed pretty clear to me. Many Albee experts have written that all of his plays are to some degree about loss (of innocence, of loved ones, of happiness), and this also seems to be true in *The Goat*, as Martin's family loses its formerly blithely happy cohesion. For Albee, the happy marriage has consistently been an illusion, that, per Hilton Als, "does nothing to dispel one's essential fear, anger, and loneliness" (2003:86). In *The Goat*, Martin and Stevie are undone by a familiar Albee device, an outside character posing as a "best friend," in this case Ross, who doesn't hesitate to destroy the domestic tranquility with his startling, sanctimonious betrayal. The ambiguous relationship of Martin and Ross really turns on what Michelle Robinson calls the play's theme, "Discovering what the intersection of the public and the private means" (2011:67). As in other Albee works, there is a deep personal shame—at least according to conventional society—that becomes public knowledge, with chaotic, unexpected consequences, both tragic and comic.

Albee, despite often vowing not to interpret or explain his plays, invites the audience in the Broadway theatre program notes to leave its prejudices in the cloakroom, and tells them that the play isn't about bestiality but tolerance, love and loss. He adds that he is pushing the boundaries in a way that playwrights should.

This is not the first time Albee has joked about bestiality in his work. In *Lolita* (1981), Humbert Humbert casually tells the Certain Gentleman that there "are usually perfectly rational relationships between people of the same sex, of different colors, and, now and again, with other animals…It is theoretically possible" (2008:I,1,15). In *The Man Who Had Three Arms* (1963), the woman host of the show introducing The Man reads a letter about a Doctor Tomlinson whose body was discovered with two photos in a locket, one of himself and the other of "a large pig" (2008:I,143). This revelation presumably generated the same guffaws in the audience at this earlier play, but Albee may not have been laughing with them. *The Man Who Had Three Arms* is very much an attack on both critics and theatre audiences for their bigotry, shallowness, and hypocrisy.

In both plays, as in *The Goat*, Albee is exploring the boundaries of the private and the public, of personal practices and public reputation, and the veneer of conventionality. This is particularly a fixation of the shallow Ross, who is most concerned with what the TV camera will show. The theme is perhaps most developed in Albee's *Everything in the Garden*, a pleasant tale of suburban tea parties and polite conversation, in which, in a twist on the 1975 movie *The Stepford Wives*, the elegant ladies turn out to be not robots, but prostitutes working part-time to pay the bills to support their showy, bourgeois lifestyle. This disconnect between private behavior and public acceptance is not always given this comic form, but Albee instead develops the poignant human emotions, which in many of his works also include human loneliness, given that private behavior is so at variance with public norms or proprieties that one feels excluded or ashamed.

The boundaries of acceptability are further clarified by Albee in an interview about *The Goat*, in which he said, "Every civilization sets quite arbitrary limits to its tolerances. The play is about a family which is deeply rocked by an unimaginable event and how they solve that problem." He clarifies this further when he states his hope that, "people will think afresh about whether or not all the values they hold are valid," and that, in his own case, "I tend to have ambivalences about all of our absolutisms" (Gussow, 2002:Section 2, online).

The ambiguous position of the "best friend," or Ross in this case, has been explored several times before in Albee's plays, a trope in which someone claiming this sort of intimate friendship, or sometimes a dubious family relationship (*The Ballad of the Sad Café*'s Cousin Lyman, and Elizabeth from *The Lady from Dubuque*) creates trouble or confusion for the main character. (This sort of comedy or confusion over identity has mainstream roots in absurdist drama reaching back to Luigi Pirandello's *So It Is (If You Think So)* (1917), in which neither the inhabitants of a small town nor even relatives can agree on who is the wife of their longtime neighbor,

Signor Ponza.) In *A Delicate Balance* (1966), for example, the "best friends" are Harry and Edna, a couple who are afraid to stay alone in their own home, and so inhabit the home of Tobias and Agnes, where, as their daughter Clair points out, they claim more right to stay there than she does. In *The Goat*, Ross says he is Martin's "oldest friend," and Martin asks if that gives him, "Rights, or something?" (I:556). Albee mocks this claim by making the purported friends hypocrites, frauds, and betrayers. In the closest parallel to *The Goat*, in *Everything in the Garden*, Albee similarly finds humor as the prostituted father Richard tells his son to "go to his room" while pontificating about "decency"—though his son is the only one hostile to the parents' racism. The repetition of this exchange in *The Goat*, when Martin tells Billy to go to his room, also carries a similar moral balance, since Billy is the innocent young homosexual, and his father engages in far more dubious sexual conduct.

In *The Goat*, of course, the entirely venal and clearly unfriendly Ross immediately betrays Martin in a sanctimonious letter to Stevie: "because I love you Stevie, as much as I love Martin," and closing with more stomach-turning syrup, "your own deeply devoted...," to which Martin can only blurt out, appropriately, "BULLSHIT!" (II:573).

The question of identity, not just about the "best friends" but also about the main character, arises here. Is Martin a poised, successful, and world-renowned architect, or better understood as a befuddled, sleazebag poseur who chases barnyard animals and can't give a coherent interview? The tension between the two is part of the texture of Albee's art.

Another Albee motif, limned above, is the primitive human beast beneath the veneer of polite society. (The theme goes back at least to Freud's theories of the id and ego in books such as *The Future of an Illusion*, with its tenet of "the renunciation of instinct" that civilization demands.) This theme emerged early in the explosion of violence at the end of A *Zoo Story* (1959), but Albee is actually closer in spirit to Yasmina Reza of *God of Carnage* (2006) than to Stanley Kubrick (in most of his films), for though his cosmopolitan Brahmins may yell and scream, they rarely commit violence, unless it's completely satiric in purpose (as in *Everything in the Garden*,). The only Bulgarian critic to cite this theme was Martina Panaiotova in Tialoto.bg, who wrote of the "the much greater savages in expensive clothes than in the time of the Greek heroes" ("доста по-големи диваци зад скъпите дрехи, отколкото във времето на древногръцките герои") (2009:online). For Albee, this uncivilized aggression and animal impulses get channeled into caustic wit.

Finally, Albee has had a consistent take on humankind's relations with animals, both pets and otherwise, since *The Zoo Story*. Here is an excellent explanation of this from Terry McCabe:

> The Goat also continues a recurrent minor theme in Albee's work: relationships between humans and animals. Ever since The Zoo Story, at the center of which is the long monologue about Jerry's complex relationship with his landlady's dog, Albee has held as a subspecialty the exploration of interspecies bonding.

> This is the central action of Seascape, one of his most hopeful plays, in which a middle-aged married couple sitting on the beach meets a pair of giant lizards, also apparently middle-aged and married, and they spend Act 2 finding out whether the four of them have a basis for a relationship. The play's last line is the male lizard's: "All right. Begin." And in A Delicate Balance, Tobias tells of the sense of betrayal he felt when he realized that the cat he had had for 15 years no longer liked him. In The Goat, the theme appears in cataclysmic form. (2002:B15)

What have the Bulgarian critics to say about these themes? Of the nine articles reviewing or analyzing the play, as noted earlier, since most of them are reviews, they discuss the acting and have less to say about the themes, or don't interpret the work at all. Some of what they do say is however in line with the American critics. For example, *Kapital Light* says the play is about a brave and honest man battling society's taboos. *Paraleli* says the play is not about bestiality, but about tolerance and what is humanly unacceptable. The most penetrating essays about the play are perhaps both in the arts magazine, *Kultura*. In one, Ave Ivanova writes that *The Goat* is a tragedy, because of a love denied by society (2009:online), and Violeta Decheva says that the play examines society's norms and its flexibility toward what is considered the abnormal (2009:online).

The Bulgarian reviews are all uniformly positive, even more so than in the case of Morfov's *Cuckoo's Nest*. All congratulate the actors. Indeed, the *Slovoto* reviewer writes about the "miraculous" cast and set (a superlative rarely heard in New York), but says nothing about the theme. Several of the reviews take note of the robust humor, but none address the question of balance of comedy and tragedy. Significantly, all of the literature, both reviews and criticism, is highly praiseworthy, with not a negative word about the text, the acting, the set, the lighting, or anything else. None of the Bulgarian critics echoes the American critics, who faulted Albee for obscurantism, tiresome jokes, or empty wordplay. Rather, as in the newspaper writing in advance of the premier, there seems to be almost a fawning respect for Albee and his gracious willingness to work at the Ivan Vazov National Theatre. Not just in *Slovoto*, mentioned above, but the *Paraleli* critic also calls the production "perfect." Ave Ivanova in *Kultura* merely calls it "great" four times. No one seems willing to criticize Albee's work.

Part of the praise for this play among the American critics was Albee's clever dialog, with its puns, double meanings and irony. Some American writers find this tiring (Simon, above), but most give Albee credit for it, such as his biographer Robert Brustein, who cites the "verbal dexterity, imaginative thrust, and technical dazzle of most of Albee's work" (1999:31). Several of the critics cite the same polish in the Bulgarian version, at least as manifest in the humor and irony (Decheva, 2009:online; and Konstantinov, 2009:13). But the translator Anichkin says he had to make "adjustments" in Albee's wordplay, so they are praising an alternative text.

A look at the original English and Bulgarian versions of the text will show how this is so. In several cases, Anichkin discussed the difficulties in the translation with Albee himself. The first case occurred early in the first act, when Stevie and Martin are bantering about Alzheimer's disease. Martin is teasing Stevie about his forgetfulness when she asks him, "Who am *I?*" Albee writes:

> MARTIN (*Acted*): You're the love of my life, the mother of my handsome and worrisome son, my playmate, my cook, my bottlewasher. Do you?
> STEVIE: What?
> MARTIN: Wash my bottles?
> STEVIE (*Puzzles it*): Not as a habit. I may have—washed one of your bottles. Do you have bottles?
> MARTIN: Everyone has bottles.
> STEVIE: Right. But what's my *name*? (2008:I,542)

Anichkin renders this simply as:

МАРТИН (*Ицзиграно*): Ти си любовта на живота ми, майката
на красивия ми и проблемен син, партньорката ми, готвачката ми...
СТИВИ: Точно така. Но как се *казвам*?

That is:

> MARTIN (Acting): You're the love of my life, the mother of my handsome and worrisome son, my partner, my cook...
> STEVIE: Exactly. But what's my *name*?

Anichkin made this elision with Albee's blessing when Anichkin said he could not render the dialog properly in Bulgarian. He could have simply translated it literally. This is what Sankowich said he had to do completely with *One Flew Over the Cuckoo's Nest* in Israel, where there were no equivalent Hebrew expressions for the slang or cusswords. Israelis just took everything literally, and still gave the play standing ovations. In the case of *The Goat*, a literal translation would mean the Bulgarian audience would have missed the allusion to an old English saying. Expressed usually as "chief cook and bottlewasher," it refers to the head chef, master of the kitchen, and the bottlewasher, the lowliest laborer. So for one to be both means to be everything in the kitchen. Martin is saying that Stevie is his everything.

The Bulgarian audience probably did not miss much, because this saying would not be familiar to most native Americans. Most would probably interpret it as typical Albee absurdist wordplay, as a riff on nothing. One naturally associates cooking with dishwashing, but he says "bottlewasher" instead, a close enough association, perhaps the best a person like Martin with mild Alzeimer's or dementia can manage. It's not a surprise to me that Albee let this exchange drop out without murmur.

More significant, I think are passages which are genuinely funny, clever, or provocative—and difficult to translate. The most obvious are Albee's puns. Two lost-in-translation examples are about homosexuality. Martin says his son Billy is "gay as the nineties," an idiomatic reference to prosperous 1890's America, and meaning Billy is happily or contently gay, which is neutrally translated as "gay, of course" ("гей, разбира се"), so Martin's glibness is not evident. Soon after, he tells Ross that Billy will "straighten out—to make a pun" (both I:551), meaning he will go from homo- to heterosexual, or "straight," in colloquial English, but this is rendered merely as, "Ще се върне в орбита. Така де, каламбур," or, "He will return to orbit. I'm making a pun." Yet the Bulgarian version contains no pun, or play on words in the sense of the original English.

Sometimes the changes cannot help but lesson the nuance about character. For example, Stevie refers to Martin's "prep school tie," translated as "first school tie" ("първата ми училищна връзка") (I:546). The added value of "prep school tie" versus merely "school tie" is that is tells us that Martin is the product of an elite boarding school for the privileged rich, with the connotation that he is weak and effete. Anichkin admits that this is the best he can do – even though Bulgarian pupils don't wear uniforms with ties!

Since I have already discussed the play's themes above, I would like to add only a few comments about the critical Bulgarian view of what *The Goat* says about sex and taboos, which the American critics have also broadly examined. I think most social critics would agree that though Bulgarians have roughly the same attitudes toward conventional sex and marriage (with Bulgarians perhaps less puritanical than rural or southern Americans), there is still much less open discussion of unconventional sex and "coming out" by gays, which is what made the public reception of *Angels in America* so rocky. This might be because Bulgarian society has retreated from its "extreme emphasis on sexuality" in the post-totalitarian period through the mid-1990s, which featured "exaggerated sexuality" on stage, cited by Ralitsa Nenkova (2002:54). Nevertheless, neither the critics nor the public had any trouble with *The Goat*, perhaps, I think, since there is no unconventional sex on stage, but merely talk about it, and most of that as part of the play's humor. One has to wonder, though, why the most audience members left the theatre, at least on Broadway, when Billy kisses his father on the mouth midway through the play (according to Albee, 2009:23): Is this because it is the only fleeting sexual moment, but one bordering on the universally prohibited kind known as incest (not to mention homosexuality)? Since Albee does nothing by accident, he seems to want us to address this question.

The Bulgarian critics, in any case, agree with their American counterparts that *The Goat* is about taboos, norms, and boundaries. Assen Terziev in *Kapital Light* (2009:32) calls the play a very brave, honest and thorough approach to one of the last remaining taboos. Violeta Decheva in *Kultura* (2009:online) writes that *The Goat* is about flexibility and norms, or the borders of the normal and abnormal.

In conclusion, I think it's fair to say that though there is analytical and knowledgeable theatre criticism in *Kultura* and similar magazines, the newspaper coverage was largely superficial and confined to abundant praise for Albee, Gardev, and the actors. None of them addressed the issues involved in the adaptation of an American play, or the directorial choices. The praise for the talented actors often lacked detail or examples. It has been said that Bulgarian reviewers do not see their role as providing a thumbs up or thumbs down, as in the U.S., but rather providing support or publicity for theatrical productions. In this view, this is a reflection in part of the smaller scale of the Bulgarian theatrical world, where the writers know all the theatre people personally, and don't wish to alienate them. In this situation, a hostile review might imperil one's access. So cold, objective judgments are sometimes precluded by friendships, intimacy and sympathy.

The Public Reception: Results of the Audience Questionnaires

As in the previous cases, *The Goat* questionnaires were collected over a period of about a year, but most were collected with the staff's assistance at a single performance at the National Theatre on 28 October 2011, about two years after the premiere. The others, as with the other productions, were collected via the Theatre's internet announcement, and through my network of theatre contacts. A total of 61 Bulgarians and 4 Americans playgoers responded, and third- and dual-nationality responses were not included.

The raw data and comments are collated in appendix A.16, but the general conclusions for the Bulgarian playgoers are listed here (numbers below keyed to questionnaires):

1. An overwhelming number of the Bulgarian respondents said that they enjoyed watching *The Goat*: 56 out of 62, or 90 percent, either liked it or liked it lot (with one double entry).
2. A similar great preponderance of Bulgarian respondents said that they think they understood the play: 55 out of 61. They clearly thought that they "got" the play, which is somewhat surprising given the bewilderment of the initial Broadway critics, noted above.
3. The Bulgarian respondents agree that the main theme of the play is either contemporary society's taboos and the limits of its tolerance of "deviant" behavior, 39, or the painfulness of

loss, 18. All the Bulgarians offered a theme, and 12 proposed different themes, almost all of them credible. Albee himself (in my interview with him), Albee experts, and the New York critics cite the sense of loss as the theme, as in the rest of the Albee oeuvre, most clearly loss of conjugal happiness in this case, answer "B." Many critics also cite "A," about taboos and deviant behavior in society, as the clearest theme of *The Goat*. Only one patron apparently misunderstood the play and chose a red herring response, "D."

4. When asked if the main characters seemed more like Bulgarian or American, almost half of the respondents, 26, said that they are about the same (or equal of both), and about half replied that the characters resembled Americans more or much more: 21 and 8, respectively.

5. In response to a similar question, the Bulgarian audience was more divided: One quarter or 15 said the family was realistically Bulgarian but 21 disagreed. Twenty-four straddled the fence with the "Somewhat" reply.

6. The first surprising result was that, despite my own perception of a rollicking house at each of the three performances I attended, 21 respondents, almost a third, said the play was not funny or not funny at all (13 and 8, respectively), a total of 24 found it funny or very funny, and 14 said "Somewhat." This suggests that even when it seems

the whole house is laughing, a sizable minority may be missing the jokes.

7. Seventy-three percent of respondents (44 of 60) thought the play was indeed a tragedy, and the rest were unsure or disagreed (though 90 percent thought they understood it, per question 2 above).

8. Forty-three respondents (of 57), or 75 percent, could make sense of the final scene with Stevie toting Sylvia's bloody carcass, while 7 admitted incomprehension. (Nine were not sure.)

9. Eighty-one percent or 48 respondents were moved by the play, and only 4 were not, with 7 unsure. From results so far, it appears that even if Bulgarians did not understand parts of the play, they were moved by it.

10. Very few Bulgarians replied that the play changed their ideas about sexuality, only 4 of 34 respondents.

12., 13. (I discuss question 11 about age later.) These questions confirmed general perceptions that the National Theatre attracts an audience of educated Bulgarian esthetes. Twenty-nine of 36 respondents, 81 percent, said that they attend the theatre once a month or more, and 31 of 33 respondents, 94 percent, have a Bachelor of Arts degree, an equivalent, or higher. I assume that the two respondents without degrees are students since the questionnaire was distributed among NATFA students.

The answers to questions 7, 8, and 9 tell us that the theatre-goers were not only entertained or amused, but affected on a deeper emotional level, which is obviously what Albee and the Sofia creative team was striving for. This certainly includes credit for the actors, who were praised not only by the critics, but were also singled out by several of the respondents. They seem to have managed to keep the drama from tipping over exclusively into comedy, or even farce, since about three-quarters of the respondents said they could make sense of the final traumatic scene despite the early humor. This tracks with the high percentage of respondents (73%) who think the play is a tragedy, by whatever definition they understand the term. (By their comments, many of them have a learned understanding of what it means.) This attests to an overall balanced and coherent adaptation that conveyed both the humor and emotional impact of the Broadway original to the Bulgarian audience.

The questionnaire results suggest five other conclusions:

1. Per (6) above, though one-third of respondents failed to see the humor of the play, only 10 percent of the total respondents did not enjoy it. This tells us that you did not need the humor to understand it or be moved by it, or that the drama or tragedy can succeed independently.

2. Less than 12 percent of spectator said that they learned something about human sexuality. I posed this question because Albee, like Kushner, was clearly pushing the envelope in the direction of trying to get playgoers to think

more broadly about "normal" sexual behavior, or to "raise their consciousness" about conventional ideas of sexuality. Either the audience already agreed with him when they entered the theatre, or they weren't buying the new creed.

3. It seems that the Sofia audience did in fact agree with Albee's progressive sexual politics, since almost all of them are frequent theatre-goers and have completed at least one degree of university, which seems consistent with his liberal views.

4. Regarding whether the National Theatre production appeared to feature American or Bulgarian characters (question 4), Gardev should be pleased to learn that only two respondents thought the characters appeared to be Bulgarian. He (personal interview, July 4, 2012) agreed with Albee that the actors are indeed trying to portray actual Americans, and that such plays in Bulgaria "require a suspension of disbelief for Americans portrayed on stage. We want to believe they are Americans though they speak Bulgarian. Emotionally it is not the same case as if they were real Americans." From the results, I think we can say that Gardev and his team succeeded on this score. The achievement is heightened if we consider that none of *The Goat* characters have obvious American traits like McMurphy or Kushner's New Yorkers.

5. On the related question about whether this is a realistic Bulgarian family (question 5), the audience was also about evenly divided. A strictly American family's troubles might

seem exotic, foreign, and hence difficult to understand, while a Bulgarian family's troubles might seem as familiar as that of the couple next door. Though conceptually risky to divide the two conclusions, one could tentatively say that the characters' language and mannerisms seemed American (e.g., the swearing noted above), but that their relationship or interpersonal dynamic could be Bulgarian, or at least more familiar. This is almost like finding the universal family drama in the particular American personalities. This was exactly Gardev's goal, and he told me that Bulgarian audiences "will watch any play and look for the human issues." The family "doesn't have to be American," but that Bulgarians "look for the universal themes." In any case, it is a credit to the creative team that the audience understood the drama in this case.

Looked at this another way, despite the difficulty of translating some of the language, discussed above, and the peculiarity of the way the American use language (per Anichkin and Bilalov), as well as Albee's conviction that the characters are essentially American, the universality of the themes of loss and social boundaries make perfect sense to Bulgarians when mounted in such a skillful way as at the National Theatre.

As with the earlier productions, my small control group of four Americans agreed with the Bulgarian audience. Almost all of them claimed that they enjoyed and understood the play. One wavered on the question of the humor, and they disagreed on whether the family seemed Bulgarian or not, but these few replies are probably not enough to draw conclusions. I should mention however that all the Americans have advanced college degrees, and tend to take both theatre-going and the questionnaires seriously. Like the American critics, they did not hesitate to criticize Albee or the production, and despite enjoying the play, three of the four were not willing to call the play a tragedy.

CHAPTER SEVEN: Conclusions

Audiences, Equivalences, and Free Adaptation

In order to draw conclusions or lessons about the three plays under study, and their reception by the National Theatre audience, I would like to return to one of Pavis's helpful generalizations about adaptations of plays from foreign countries:

> Every (especially linguistic) translation is an appropriation of the source culture by the target culture...by transforming and "rewriting" them on the stage for a western audience... the re-elaboration of gestural [sic] and choreographic materials within a new frame ...by a "stage auteur"...for members of an audience accustomed to stage discourse in which meaning is produced especially for them...the cultural and theatrical tradition of the source culture are transformed by the *needs of the target culture's theatrical and cultural traditions.* (emphasis added) (1992:161)

This excerpt is appealing for its telling and felicitous phrase, that "meaning is produced especially for them," i.e., the audience, and especially, *"needs of the target culture's theatrical and cultural traditions."* In other words, wherever a certain play may originate, the director's and creative team's job is to make it comprehensible and emotionally meaningful for the new target audience. This also reflects the definition of the verb "adapt," that is, to make something suitable to new requirements or conditions the new foreign audience), and to adjust or modify accordingly. This is what Pavis calls (in this case without the usual negative connotations) the "appropriation."

This was my hypothesis of adaptation based on my reading of Pavis and the definition of Dr. Nikolova, who describes "adaptations to specific target audiences, horizons of expectation, and modes of reception" (see p. 16). I call this the **Adaptation for the Needs of the Target Audience**. One example is Vitez's adaptation of *Electra* (see p. 20), about which it was claimed that the 1980s French audience could not understand it without the director's updating the story to contemporary Greece. This also conforms to Mamet's dictum regarding the purpose of drama (see p. 31).

My research of the three National Theatre adaptations seems to show a different goal of the creative teams, so that none of the plays fall into this category. Morfov did not really appropriate *Cuckoo's Nest* to produce meaning especially for his audience, though this is what he claimed in my interview with him, but rather for himself. That is, he had earlier interpreted plays according to his personal vision or philosophy of freedom, rebellion, and individualism, and conceivably even chose *Cuckoo's Nest* since it lends itself to these themes.

For the adaptation of his *Goat*, Albee kept a gimlet eye over the young Gardev to insure fealty to his vision without regard to the Bulgarian audience's needs; they would have to come, with some difficulty perhaps, to his original vision. That is why he says, significantly, that his characters are American; Gardev's team was not permitted to turn them into something quasi-Bulgarian, and the translator, Harry Anichkin, as we have seen, dropped any puns or idioms that could not be strictly rendered into Bulgarian. Gardev even acknowledged that Albee was co-director of the production (Momchilova, 28.5.2009:online).

In the case of *Angels in America*, Shpatova and her team struggled, I believe, to even understand herself the depths and complexities of the play, to speak nothing of unpacking them in any coherent way to the Bulgarian audience. Critic and playwright Ina Bozhidarova agrees that Shpatova did not seem to understand the original play (personal interview, 8 June 2012). In none of these cases then, and for different reasons, did the adapters fully strive to make the American plays comprehensible to their Bulgarian audiences. This is a strange and unexpected conclusion, given all that I have read in the academic literature about the goals of theatrical adaptation and appropriation.

This view of course rejects the universalists, in theatre and elsewhere, who go to Japan, India, and elsewhere in search of mythic and primitive rituals and emotions that all audiences everywhere can understand and appreciate without any translation or appropriation. In their view, creative teams do not need to strive to adapt and fit, but rather just to find the right fundamental material with universal appeal.

Apart from such rituals or emotions, though, plays also contain themes, and these too can be insular and nationalistic, or broader, even universal. One would expect plays with the latter to be easier to adapt. A look at the themes of the three plays seems to bear this out, though they have both common and unique themes. For example, all three plays are in some sense an attack on hypocrisy. In

Cuckoo's Nest, Nurse Ratched's smarmy solicitousness is matched by the sanctimonious letter of Ross in *The Goat* that exposes Martin's secret. Irina Vagalinska reasonably interprets this as the hypocrisy of a society that considers human betrayal that causes genuine pain more acceptable than bestiality (2009:53). The self-serving help offered to Joe by Roy in *Angels* was masked as selfless support, but at least it is not passive-aggressive like the hypocrisy in the other two plays. Bozhidarova agreed that one theme of this play is the political hypocrisy.

One common theme of the first two plays is their diametrically opposite views of American individualism. We saw above that Kesey celebrated the free living, free thinking, and independence of McMurphy. As Nikolova wrote in *Trud*, *Cuckoo's Nest* is a story of sensitive individualists yearning for freedom but crushed by fascist society (online:2010). And though one would think that the leftist Kushner would agree, almost all of his heroes (as opposed to his villains) are in pairs, not solitary romantics like McMurphy. The story is very much about their bonding and mutual support in a hostile public and political climate. Kushner made this ideological preference clear in the play's afterward, in emphasizing that even creating the play was an *ensemble* production. In developing this theme, he quickly becomes didactic: "We pay high prices for maintenance of the myth of the Individual: we have no system of universal health care, we don't educate our children, we can't pass sane gun control laws, we elect presidents like Reagan" (*Perestroika:*, 1992:150).

To return to Pavis, I would argue that plays produce meaning or themes in the form of movement (gestures and choreography), but also text, and these can be unique and specific to the source culture, or internationally understood and recognized. In our plays, the theme of American individualism in *Cuckoo's Nest* could be considered relatively unfamiliar to a country like Bulgaria with a recent history of socialism or collectivism. We have seen, however, that though seen as foreign and American, the play was warmly embraced as early as the 1980s. The hypocrisy attacked by all three plays would translate easily to Bulgaria, as it would to most societies. So too would the human condition of loss and alienation as depicted by Albee. This would leave the topical political and social themes of *Angels in America* the most specific, and requiring the most transformation, in Pavis's terms.

In terms of the categories of adaptation studies, given Albee's universal themes, and his presence during rehearsals, I would call Gardev's adaptation of *The Goat* the simplest of the three to categorize, being the **Faithful or Exotic Adaptation**, according to the terms in the academic literature. The adaptation of Mark Twain's *Huckleberry Finn* by Laura Eason (see p. 27) also falls in this category.

Morfov's *One Flew Over the Cuckoo's Nest* belongs in a new category, the **Free Adaptation of Personal Vision**. That is, he made changes based not on audience needs nor on something locally unintelligible that he discovered in the text, but based on compatibilities in the text with his personal philosophy or values.

Despite the difficulties of clearly articulating what is a political play (message play, problem play, etc.), I still find it useful to distinguish Morfov's work from the **Free Adaptation of Political Message**. What is different in these works, e.g., Aimé Césaire's *Une Tempête* (see p. 50) and Vitez's *Electra*, is that they are plainly didactic or polemical, even at the expense of the original playwrights' intentions or the works' artistic integrity. In this category, political urgency trumps art for art's sake.

Shpatova, as we have seen, did not impose her personal vision on *Angels*, but rather produced a play that was both faithful and political, that is, a **Faithful Adaptation of Political Message**. In other words, she was faithful to an at least partially politically themed play. This is the reason many critics, including even the politically liberal ones, criticized Kushner for wordiness, and said in effect that the political messages diminished his art. She was faithful to a difficult foreign play, and the National Theatre paid the price in diminished ticket sales.

For the adapters who take the opposite tack, they sometimes use the term "updating" when they change classic plays. For example, Peter Brook has said that trying to reconstruct Shakespeare's plays the way he did them would be "guess work and of only antiquarian interest" (Fortier, 1997:97). "The only way to recreate Shakespeare's magic is by contemporary theatrical means," he says. This makes me wonder then why they are called classics, since Brook's tone is somewhat harsh. Do classics require a creative director to rework them in order to appeal to a modern audience?

This quote is actually quite unrepresentative of Brook's thinking, since he provides insight into the problem of "free adaptation" raised by Albee and Miller in chapter two. The issue arises with adaptations like Morfov's, in which the director "proudly present[s] a very subjective version of the play without a glimmer of awareness that they might be diminishing the play." Such a director, Brook says, vainly believes "that this is the play and more," and that only he can make sense of a play even by Shakespeare. Brook concludes that "the virtue of having a feeling of love and enthusiasm has to be tempered by a cool sense that anybody's personal view of the play is bound to be less than the play itself" (Brook, 1987:77-8).

Since Morfov plainly added personal creative elements like the broom dance, it's appropriate to ask when it is fair to add such material. In Brook's experience, an actor suggested that the actors do an entire scene while skipping ropes. Brook decided that, "Only where you really feel confident that bits are badly written or boring does one have the freedom to invent skipping ropes and so forth…you can't do this with a masterpiece" (1987:87).

If asked if such material was "appropriate," and if this means advisable, then the answer seems to be yes, since Morfov's *Cuckoo's Nest* was a success—and not boring for most even over four hours. We have seen that the original play was a success in many ways, but not a masterpiece in Brook's sense of something like *King Lear*.

Let's return to the more modest goal of adapting not to express a personal vision, but to maintain the spirit or intention of the playwright, and convey it to a foreign audience. On this score, I have drawn another conclusion, somewhat at variance with Pavis, which seems to be the nub of the problem of adaptation. In this case, the translated original will suffer losses—of nuance, puns, topical references, and miscellaneous insider cultural material, etc., and so there will be a diminution of impact because the audience will not get the entire package. The question for the adapters is, then, whether they should take this lessened work as it is, or somehow try to compensate for the losses by adding equivalents. They would have to change the puns or jokes into similar jokes that the new audience would understand, and find topical references with equivalent impact.

As we saw with *The Goat*, for example, Anichkin just dropped the arcane joke about washing bottles, page 131, and the pun about the "gay nineties." This is clearly a loss. But, as indicated above, even most Americans do not get the joke about washing the bottles, and the American critics have lambasted Albee for just such coy, precious humor. Yet Albee has excellent company: From Marcel Proust and James Joyce to Pirandello and Beckett, Western literature is full of acclaimed masters who do not make it easy for mass audiences. So clearly loss of reception of meaning does not preclude success. In fact, many readers and theatre audiences enjoy the mystery, the puzzling out of plot, character, and theme. In Susanne K. Langer's philosophy of aesthetics, for example, she describes the pleasure of reading literature as the effort to find patterns or figure out the meaning, as in a detective story. So a negative answer to the questionnaire question about whether one understands the play does not necessarily mean that the production is flawed.

I should mention parenthetically that audiences fail to understand a play for the broadest and most mundane of reasons. Several playgoers said they could not understand actors in *Angels* because they talked too softly or too quickly. For this reason, many American theatres offer headsets with amplification to playgoers. Also, the Kabuki theatre on the Ginza in Tokyo rents headsets that provide the story's background or context, and updates the archaic language—for native Japanese speakers as well as foreigners. I do not think Kushner would accept this. He told me that his audience does not have to know and understand everything, just as in life, to get the point of the play. (I would add that some cineastes prefer to watch foreign films without subtitles, and just pick up what they can without the intrusion of a translation by someone outside the original creative team.) Also, he said he feels strongly that his play is a failure if the audience needs extra explanatory material, such as a program providing the historical background. You should just watch it and get the characters from context, he said. This, interestingly, is sharply in conflict with Brook, who has written that, "the primary virtue of a performance in the theatre is for it to be alive, and secondly, to be immediately understandable. Explanation and reflection can only come at a later time....if it is not good at the precise moment one drinks it [like wine], all is lost" (Brook, 1987:235).

My questions about whether the characters seem American or Bulgarian correspond to whether the adapters were content to let the characters and setting seem American and foreign, or whether they managed to achieve a more accessible domestic atmosphere, with target-culture jokes, references, or even gestures and body language. As one surveyed respondent wrote, if the struggles of the protagonists are universal, they could then be perceived as Bulgarian as well as American. But that would make the American references odd (New York City, basketball), and we would be more or less reminded along the way that the story really is about America. Bilalov's comment that *The Goat* characters' coarse language make them unrecognizable as Bulgarians is consistent with this, but there remains the core problem that Bulgarian actors are not Americans, so do not speak English, and that their trying to act like them may appear inauthentic to Americans, or to Bulgarians who know them well. This is what Pavis said about European actors trying to appear as Indians in Brook's *Indiade*, who "speak, think and dream like products of western humanism" (1992:202). Also, portraying strange American body language in a Bulgarian theatre may not convey the same emotional state to the foreign audience. It seems that at a certain point the only viable solution is to portray situations that are true, understandable, and meaningful for the local audience, however this is understood. This does not necessarily mean free adaptation because, despite Bilalov's concerns, the Albee dialogue worked in Sofia.

The other problem, or perhaps just a way to conceptualize the above problem, is that an adapted play cannot be both fully American and fully foreign. As Carlson says about the *Mahabharata* of Brook, it cannot retain the essence of *both* Indian and Western culture (Pavis, 1996:83-4). At each point in the adaptation process, the creative team has to make choices.

So, is the close, faithful adaptation better, or the free adaptation? Putting aside the legal and ethical issues raised by Albee and others, and considering just the artistic one, we have seen that Gardev had critical and commercial success with the former, and Morfov with the latter. Morfov would argue that his play needed free adaptation because the original is dated and has references unclear to Bulgarian audiences. Gardev could say the universal themes of Albee permit the faithful or exotic interpretation, which is not so exotic after all.

I think Brook, after his many years of experimenting and adapting in many countries, has this issue about right: In plays that are not masterpiece, he writes, "you can move words and scenes, but you have to do it in full recognition of how dangerous it is...this is really something for which there are no rules... One must trust one's judgment and take the consequences" (1987:95).

Similarly, I would conclude that directors should err on the side of respect and fidelity, but after due respect is taken to understand and flesh out the original, one should not be bound to adapt works slavishly. The director's goal remains, in either case, to capture the vision or truth of the playwright.

Audiences and Success

In the case of Shpatova and *Angels*, there was no commercial success, but to learn why I would like to discuss the different demographics of audiences in Sofia and in New York, and particularly at the National Theatre and on Broadway.

To begin, I wonder if Shpatova's creative team could agree with Albee's comment that serves as my epigraph in my introduction: "What the audience wants is so different from what a serious playwright wants." As I argued earlier, and the demographic data on the questionnaires show, the National Theatre attracts "serious" or highly educated audiences, and most of them liked Shpatova's production. By Albee's estimation, he would have nothing to complain about in Sofia. The lesson for Shpatova, though, it seems to me, is that there are not enough such people to fill the Theatre's large hall, nor of a constituent audience of Marxists or the openly gay, as there were for Kushner among the playgoers in New York. That is, she lacked a significant audience that both appreciated and understood the themes of Kushner's play. But the production, like Albee's *The Goat*, might have had a longer and therefore "successful" run in the small hall. Also, if the play were mounted in a small Bulgarian college playhouse, I would counsel keeping the exotic adaptation, not removing any of the original complexities, and letting the student audiences work out the play's mysteries.

This is, by the way, exactly what Brecht's chief American translator, Eric Bentley, cited approvingly about the German communist's plays. Brecht has no role to speak of in America's official Broadway theatre, and only a diluted presence Off-Broadway, he said. But Brecht's own preference for college performances "was probably a wise one." (Bentley, 1982:196).

On the other hand, young playgoers were an especially important element in the success of Morfov's *Cuckoo's Nest*, as Sankowich says they were for him in San Francisco. This is clear in this table:
Youth Attendance* at National Theatre Productions

Cuckoo's Nest	68%
Angels in America	58%
The Goat	71%

*35 years of age or under, based on demographic results in my questionnaires

Part of the problem of *Angels*, it seems, is its failure to attract as well this demographic, which the other two plays did. A study of National Theatre audiences by Ivan Evtimov and Ventsislav Djambasov at New Bulgarian University gives some support to this conclusion. It shows that theatre-goers in their thirties, along with those in their fifties, each at 23.9% of the audience, are the most active (Evtimov, 2004:Table 1, unpaged), and thus a key component of the potential audience.

Broadway producers are also deeply involved in trying to mount plays to appeal to younger audiences, with both special appeals and discounted tickets, though a recent study by The Broadway League showed that the average playgoer age is 44, even higher than the year before (2011:online).

Another comparative look at the National Theatre's audience demographics from my study shows how *The Goat* particularly appealed to college graduates:

College Graduates Attendance* at National Theatre Productions

Cuckoo's Nest	88%
Angels in America	89%
The Goat	94%

*Bachelor's degree or higher, based on demographic results in my questionnaires

My results are consistent with Evtimov's study. Although he did not pose questions about college degrees, his analysis of the theatre-goers' professions is instructive. The predominant professions, such as lawyers, engineers, and physicians, indicate higher education, and the single highest category of profession is student. He found that a typical National Theatre patron is either a male or female student, or a woman over forty years of age with advanced education and an intellectual profession. Those with little education seldom visited the National Theatre.

The finding about the predominance of female patrons may also be significant for the plays under study here. For Evtimov, women made up 61% of the audience, and men only about 24% (15% did not respond). This disproportion of women playgoers, I should add, is also a Broadway phenomenon. In the study of these theatre audiences by The Broadway League (ibid.), 65% of audience members were female. What this suggests is that casting an attractive male icon like Deyan Donkov was a cagy decision by

Alexander Morfov, since, as we have seen, he attracted a female audience. Though the decision to watch a play because of a particular star was not a significant factor according to Evtimov's poll (only 4.4% of the audience said so), 60.6% of his respondents said that they would recommend the National Theatre because of its actors, far more than for any other reason. Broadway producers have learned this lesson, and so almost always cast "bankable" Hollywood marquee actors as leads in major musicals.

Another key element that the Broadway and Evtimov polls indicate is the importance of the price of tickets, which all theatres seem to struggle with today. Still, Broadway theatres have a distinct advantage because 63% of tickets were purchased by presumably well-off out-of-town tourists (ibid.), who are primarily drawn to the musicals because they require little mastery of English. The National Theatre lacks this market. Equally significant, The Broadway League study showed an average annual household income among playgoers of $244,100, presumably adequate to cover even steep musical ticket prices. But when Evtimov asked Bulgarian respondents the reasons why they do not attend a show, 41.3% cited a lack of money, second only to a lack of time.

These several challenges clearly show that the National Theatre leadership must be especially mindful about appealing to all segments of its narrower potential audience vis-à-vis Broadway's market. As Evtimov concludes, the Theatre can rely on a "small but steady audience of theatre lovers."

One final barrier that Shpatova alone faced among my three directors was the lack of an established reputation or fan base. Evtimov's study showed both that 4.4% of theatre-goers regularly attended plays of certain directors. Among their favorites, Morfov was the most popular, at a substantial 43.5% of respondents, with Gardev in sixth place, at 8.7%. Shpatova did not appear in the rankings. This is I believe another reason to give credit to her for her achievement with *Angels*: The two other directors had a loyal following to drive spectators to their latest production. She had to generate public interest without this advantage, so had a steeper road to commercial success.

I should also mention a note of caution about my above questionnaire results on whether the theatre-goers liked the plays. In Evtimov's study, a great preponderance of respondents, 63%, also very much liked the National Theatre production they saw, and another 28.3% liked the production. Additionally, 95% liked the acting and 69.6% would recommend the show to acquaintances. Only 4.3% had mixed feelings and another 4.3% said that they disliked the production. So the high marks given by respondents to *Cuckoo's Nest*, *Angels*, and *The Goat* are not far from the Theatre's average.

If Shpatova's production failed to thrive on a commercial basis, we should nevertheless keep in mind that a Faithful Adaptation of Political Message has another measure of success. The play generated some fierce controversy over its graphic treatment of homosexuality. This was just Kushner's point, to push the discussion of gays in society, which Shpatova accepted. On those political terms, the play was a success.

A summary of the positive reviews and comparative success of the three plays at the National Theatre is summarized in two tables in the appendices, A.21 and A.22, respectively.

Mamet on Adaptation and Success

In closing, I would like to address what David Mamet's reductionist view that a play is essentially just a plot has for adaptation. If true, this would make the task of adaptation much easier. I am not alone in enjoying some plays for their ideas, though the more traditional audiences seeking entertainment may prefer pre-intermission cliffhangers or other plot-driven suspense. A play without ideas could be an adventure story or melodrama, but then less likely to become a classic. Do classic comedies have ideas? The best, such as Aristophanes, and Kaufman and Hart, mock human pretension, while Oscar Wilde elegantly pierces human foibles. For me, their poignancy or even piquancy depends on understanding the deeper themes, and not just on getting the jokes or following a plot. But this richness or depth is what Mamet rejects as "ideas." Rarely will I return to a play with no ideas. Thus I feel that Mamet's thesis could only apply to plays for the masses—who do not usually attend classic plays anyway. And as we have seen, all three playwrights under study want to write plays about ideas, and or at least get their audience to think differently at the end, while the masses, in theory anyway, want only entertainment.

One unlikely ally of Mamet is Vladimir Nabokov, who writes in a postscript to his 1955 novel, *Lolita*:

> I am neither a reader nor a writer of didactic fiction…*Lolita* has no moral in tow. For me a work of fiction exists only insofar as it affords me what I shall bluntly call aesthetic bliss, that is a sense of being somehow, somewhere, connected with other states of being where art (curiosity, tenderness, kindness, ecstasy) is the norm. All the rest is either topical trash or what some call the Literature of Ideas, which is very often topical trash. (1997:314-5)

The irony of course is that, if not exactly a novel of ideas, *Lolita*. like all of Nabokov's work, is hardly a work for the masses, but rather a refined artistic pleasure for the educated elite who can appreciate it.

In any case, it seems at least to me that a play with elaborate or creative costumes and sets—inessential in Mamet's thesis—provides a richer or fuller theatrical experience. Yet Mamet does have a point. Isn't adapting a bit like "colorizing" a movie from the black-and-white era? Modern audiences may prefer the richer look, but the black-and-white movies still resonate powerfully with us. Another example is the minimalist No theatre in Japan. It always has the exact same set, consisting of a stylized pine tree on an otherwise bare stage. The language of No is important, and some experts might argue essential, and not just its plot. Foreigners watch it in translation, and even native Japanese cannot understand much of the archaic language, but they relish the stark and simple formalism. One lesson seems to be that there are many paths to theatrical success, some via rich scenery and costumes, and others via language or plot. The other lesson seems to be that an adapter could probably leave out more of the original content, set, costume, idioms, etc., and still preserve adequate impact for commercial success, as Morfov and Gardev did to some degree in different ways.

A final variant on this theme is the play with ideas, but without plot or narrative. Chekhov's *Three Sisters* has often been cited as an example of this type, and examples of novels with scanty plot are Thomas Mann's *Death in Venice* and even Herman Melville's *Moby-Dick*, which provides hundreds of pages of whale lore before Ahab meets his nemesis.

In conclusion, I cannot completely agree with Kazan and Mamet that mass audiences are sovereign, or all that spell success. Good box office is great for theatre's continued commercial viability, but many classics cited above will never appeal to mass audiences, and the beauty of their language or the nuances of their characterization, even the novelty of their ideas, should not be discounted because most playgoers will not "get" them. This would be an unnecessary narrowing of theatrical experience, not to mention a rejection of vast amounts of dramatic literature.

Answering the Research Questions

To sum up my conclusion, I would like to answer my research questions introduced on page 6.

Question 1: As we see in the discussion above in chapter seven, the three Bulgarian creative teams took very different approaches in their adaptations, driven by personal vision, fidelity to the playwright's intention, or fidelity to the play's perceived political message. These approaches determined the team's decisions.

As for how the teams handled the "untranslatable" in the original plays, we have seen that Shpatova left in much (e.g., historical McCarthyism) that was not meaningful, while Gardev's translator simply dropped untranslatable idioms and puns (e.g., "gay nineties"). Morfov and his team were the only ones who liberally added scenes (e.g., the broom dance) to convey what he felt was the spirit of the original situations and the emotions of the characters.

Question 2: If I interpret my second question on the reaction of the Bulgarian public and critics to the adaptations, I can clearly conclude that the audiences appreciated both faithful and free adaptations. They were less accepting of a faithful adaptation based on a difficult and highly topical play set about a generation earlier. The critics were more appreciative of all three plays, though the unanimity of acclaim regarding Gardev's and Morfov's work tells us something also about the mutually supportive Bulgarian theatre world, and also about the reputations they brought to the adaptations. These observations suggest that though commercial success was easier for these directors, Shpatova's productions could still have met with popular success in a smaller, experimental, or academic theatre, where audiences, like Kushner himself (page 152), like to sort out a play's meanings after the curtain falls.

Question 3: The lesson from these particular adaptations about cultural adaptation in the theatre in general seems to be that there are several paths to success if we define that as either commercial box office receipts or critical acclaim. Working with very different plays, Morfov found success with a free adaptation and Gardev succeeded with a faithful adaptation supervised by the playwright. That both free or faithful adaptations could succeed is really not noteworthy since there are many prior examples. What is more interesting is that audiences liked what was added, which heightened the entertainment value as well as perhaps the characterizations, and that they did not seem to miss what was dropped from the original texts. This study does indicate that an exotic adaptation of a difficult play will not appeal to many playgoers without a constituent audience like in New York. The best advice I would give an adapter is to target your audience if you want commercial success, and fulfill your personal creative vision with the original play as your vehicle, like Kazin and Morfov, if the box office is a secondary consideration.

The literature of adaptation and audience reception diverges from these conclusions in that it entertains issues other than commercial or critical success. As we have seen, regarding adaptation, Pavis struggled with questions of how to bring Eastern stories and plays to a Western audience without betraying the rich cultural traditions a director may not fully understand. I could not say this about Gardev or Morfov in their adaptations, though it was said by two experts about Shpatova's production given the complexity of the original. Pavis also argues that faithfulness to an original text is meaningless because *mise en scene* is precisely the creative teams' role, not that of repeating what the text has already clearly stated (see p. 50). But a text is no more a complete artistic vision than a blueprint is a building. Also, whether a director chooses to follow a playwright's stage directions is not meaningless. Morfov's choice was in fact different from Gardev's.

Bennett's work is grounded in cultural studies that make assumptions about the receiving audiences' biases, which is her justification to support revolutionary or performance theatre. But the National Theatre productions show that the line between plays of communion and plays of rebellion is not clear, since all have social or political themes or messages (see pp. 11ff), yet they are not revolutionary manifestos. Rather, they aim to bring a broadening of understanding or feeling, along with a change of view on social issues. I believe that they do this in their modest way. The questionnaires show that only Morfov generated a significant change in spectators' views on his subject (question 11), since almost half (18 of 39) agreed. In the cases of *Angels* and *The Goat*, of 5 of 27 and 4 of 29, respectively, admitted to a different view after seeing the plays. (I eliminated those "not sure" in each case.) Even *Angels in America*, despite its limited success, provoked a public exchange about gays in Bulgarian theatre and society. This tells us that a proper theoretical understanding of these hybrid plays—between communion and rebellion—has not been reached.

Bibliography

Articles and Books

24 Chasa, (unsigned), "Desi Shpatova zabarkva vesela gei fantasiya," 20 September 2010, p. 26.

24 Chasa, (unsigned), "Svetiyat Sinod katerichno protiv gei-parada v Sofiya," 14 June 2012, p. 4.

168 Chasa (unsigned), "Gola na Tsenata," 12-18 November 2010, p. 34.

Aaltonon, Sirkku, "Time-sharing on Stage," *Topics in Translation* 17, 1980.

Agence France Presse (unsigned), "Amnesty Urges Bulgaria to Investigate Anti-gay Hate Crimes," 28 June 2012, <http://wires.univision.com/english/article/2012-06-28/amnesty-urges-bulgaria-to-investigate>, accessed on 16 September 2012.

Albee, Edward, "Shto za hora sme, ako ne obichame?" *Standart*, 12 October 2009, p. 23.

Albee, Edward, *The Collected Plays of Edward Albee, 1958-1965*. New York, Overlook Duckworth, 2007.

Albee, Edward (1), *The Collected Plays of Edward Albee, 1966-1977*. New York, Overlook Duckworth, 2008.

Albee, Edward (2), *The Collected Plays of Edward Albee, 1978-2003*. New York, Overlook Duckworth, 2008.

Albee, Edward, *Stretching My Mind,* New York, Carroll & Graf, 2005.

Als, Hilton, "He Said, She Said: One-acts by Edward Albee and Samuel Beckett," *The New Yorker*, 20 October 2003, pp. 86-7.

Als, Hilton, "Shadow and Act: Shakespeare without Words," *The New Yorker*, 2 May 2011, pp. 86-7.

Apostolova, Keva, "Pavel Vasev: Direktor na Naroden Teatar Ivan Vazov" [an interview], *Teatar*, April-June, 2011, pp. 15-19.

Atansova, Albena, "Boyko Krastanov Vliza v Narodniiya," *Standart*, 2 September 2010, p. 23.

Bennett Susan, *Theatre Audiences—A Theory of Production and Reception*, London, Routledge, 1990.

Bentley, Eric, *The Brecht Commentaries, 1943-1980*, New York, Grove Press, 1981.

Berend, Ivan T., *History Derailed: Central and Eastern Europe in the Long Nineteenth Century*, Berkeley, CA, University of California Press, 2003.

Bersani, Leo, *Homos,* Cambridge, MA, Harvard Univ. Press, 1995.

Bharucha, Rustom, "A Collision of Cultures: Some Western Interpretations of the Indian Theatre," *Asian Theatre Journal*, Vol. 1, No. 1, Spring, 1984, pp. 1-20.

Bigsby, C.W. E., *Critical Introduction to Twentieth-Century American Drama*, Volume Two, Cambridge, MA, Cambridge University Press, 1984. Revised 1989.

Bozhidarova, Ina, *Dramaturgichnata Adaptatsiya (Драматугичната адаптация)*, Sofia, Valenti Trayanov, 2009.

Brando, Marlon; Lindsey, Robert, *Brando: Songs My Mother Taught Me*, New York, Random House, 1994.

Brantley, Ben, "This Time, the Angel Is in the Details," *The New York Times*, 29 October 2010, page C1.

Brietzke, Zander, *American Drama in the Age of Film,* Tuscaloosa, University of Alabama Press, 2007.

Brook, Peter, *The Shifting Point: Forty Years of Theatrical Exploration, 1946-1987*, London, Methuen Drama, 1987.

Brustein, Robert, "Angels in America." *The New Republic*, 24 May 1993, pp. 29-31.

Brustein, Robert, "The Great Work Falters." *The New Republic*, 27 December 1993, pp. 25-27.

Brustein, Robert, *The Theatre of Revolt: An Approach to Modern Drama*, New York, Little, Brown, 1964.

Brustein, Robert, "A Question of Identity." *The New Republic*, 30 August 1999, pp. 29-31.

Campbell, Bob, "'Cuckoo's Nest': From Page to Stage," *The Star-Ledger* (Newark, New Jersey), 8 April 2001, Spotlight section, p. 7.

Canby, Vincent, "Two 'Angels,' Two Journeys, in London and New York," *The New York Times*, 30 January 1994, p. A.5.

Carlson, Marvin, *Theories of the Theatre: A Historical and Critical Survey, from the Greeks to the Present*, Ithica, NY, Cornell University Press, 1993.

Chicago Tribune (unsigned), "'Cuckoo' flies further," 11 June 2001, p. 6.

Cote, David, "Critical Juncture," *American Theatre*, November 2011, pp. 30-34, 80-82.

Cox, Gordon, "Noises Off." *Variety*, 23 January 2006, p. 41.

Crews, Chip, "Getting Edward Albee's 'Goat'," *The Washington Post*, 13 March 2005, p. N1.

Davenport, Ken, "The Demographics of the Broadway Audience 2010-11," TheProducersPerspective.com, 14 December 2011, <http://www.theproducersperspective.com/my_weblog/2011/12/the-demographics-of-the-broadway-audience-2010-11.html>, accessed 16 September 2012.

DeDanan, Mary, "Twice Over the Cuckoo's Nest," *American Theatre*, October 1995, Volume 12, Issue 8, pp. 12-13.

Dimitrov, Georgi P., "Donkov stresna Narodnia teatar," *Telegraf*, 3 December 2010, p. 23.

Dimitrova, Dilyana, "Opasen Tants na Gardev s Kozata," *Trud*, 13 October 2009, p. 24.

Dimitrova, Dilyana, "Rezhisyorat Aleksandar Morfov: Tova ne e Moyat Premier," *Trud*, 26 November 2010, p. 22.

Dnes.bg, "I aplodismentite sa za ‚Kozata, ili Koya e Silviya," 14 January 2010, <http://www.dnes.bg/teatar/2010/01/14/uspehi-za-kozata-ili-koia-e-silviia.84156>, accessed 23 June 2012.

Doneva, Yana, "Vlado Karamazov: Slava Bogu, U Nas Teatralnata Kritika Nyama Vliyanie. Miraslava Kortenska: Naprotif— Poslednata Duma Imame Nie," *Vsekiden.bg*, 9 November 2010, <http://www.vsekiden.com/80749>, accessed 8 April 2012.

Dnevnik (unsigned), "[Morfov:] Da si Realist dnes ne e nikak Priyatno," 29 November 2010, p. 7.

Dorbian, Iris, "The Spin Doctor is In," *Stage Directions*, April, 2007, 20,4, Arts Module, p. 39-41.

Drukman, Steven, "Interview: Edward Albee by Steven Drukman," *New York*, March, 2002, Vol. 32, Issue. 2, pp. 108-110, 181.

Dutton, Denis, "Umberto Eco on Interpretation," Philosophy and Literature 16, 1992, pp. 432-37, and

<http://www.denisdutton.com/eco_review.htm>, accessed 29 September 2012.

Eason, Laura, "'Written by ____, Adapted from ____': Adaptation and the Voice of the Playwright," *TriQuarterly*, Summer, 2009, pp. 142-181.

Eco, Umberto, *Six Walks in the Fictional Woods*, Cambridge, Massachusetts, Harvard University Press, 1994.

Eliot, T. S., *Notes Toward a Definition of Culture*, New York, Harcourt, 1948.

Eno, Will, "It's Going to be Dangerous Out: An Interview with the Playwright," *American Theatre*, December 2010, pp. 60-61.

Esslin, Martin, *Mediations: Essays on Brecht, Beckett, and the Media*, New York, Grove Press, 1982.

Esslin, Martin, *The Theatre of the Absurd*, New York, Vintage Books, 2004.

Evans, Everett, "Mixed Reviews Greet Albee's `The Goat'," *Houston Chronicle*, 17 March, 2002.

Evtimov, Ivan and Ventsislav Djambazov, "Naglasi u Predpochitaniya kam Teatara na Studentite ot Nov Balgarski Universitet," Unpublished study, Sofia, 2004.

Eyring, Teresa, "The Activist Impulse," *American Theatre*, April 1012, p. 8.

Feldman, Adam, "Q&A: Tony Kushner," *Time Out New York*, 1 September 2010, <http://www.timeout.com/newyork/theater/q-a-tony-kushner-off-broadway>, accessed 20 September 2012.

Fierstein, Harvey, *Torch Song Trilogy*, New York, The Gay Presses of New York, 1979.

Fortier, Mark, *Theory/Theatre: An Introduction*, London, Routledge 1997.

Gannon, Martin J., U*nderstanding Global Cultures: Metaphorical Journeys Through 17 Countries*, Thousand Oaks, CA, Sage Publications, 1994.

Geis Deborah R., and Steven F. Kruger, eds., *Approaching the Millennium: Essays on "Angels in America,"* Ann Arbor, MI, The University of Michigan Press, 1997.

Ginova, Irina, "Deyan Donkov vs. Reni Vrangova v Narodniya," *Novinar*, 23 November 2010, p. 21.

Green, Blake, "Gary Sinise Brings His Cocky 'Cuckoo's Nest,' Anti-hero to Broadway, But this Isn't Exactly the Drama Jack Nicholson Made Famous," *Newsday*, 8 April 2001, p. 1.

Grenier, Richard, "The Homosexual Millennium: Is It Here? Is It Approaching?" *National Review*, 7 June 1993, pp. 52-56.

Grunebaum, Dan, "Theater in the Wake of Disaster," *The International Herald Tribune*, 2 December 2011, p. 11.

Gussow, Mel, "Albee All Over, Or a Wealth of One," *The New York Times*, 17 February 2002, Section 2, <http://www.nytimes.com/2002/02/17/arts/theater-albee-all-over-or-a-wealth-of-one.html?pagewanted=all&src=pm>, accessed 15 September 2011.

Gussow, Mel, *Edward Albee: A Singular Journey*, New York, Applause, 2001.

Gussow, Mel, "Stage: Wooster Group," *The New York Times*, 31 October 1984, accessed 5 June 2012, no longer accessible on nytimes.com.

Henry III, William A., Simpson, Janice C., "The Gay White Way," *Time*, 17 May 1993, online.

Hirshman, Linda, "'Angels in America' Returns," *Newsweek*, 25 October 2010, pp. 66-67.

Hitchens, Christopher, "*Angels* over Broadway," *Vanity Fair*, March, 1993, pp. 71-76.

Hofler, Robert, "'Cuckoo' Clocks in Gotham," *Variety*, 16 April 2001, p. 9.

Hofler, Robert, "'Flew' Will Fly Away on July 29," *Variety*, 22 June 2001, p. 2.

Horwitz, Simi, "It's All Propaganda," *Back Stage*, 6 April 2001, p. 21.

Igov, Svetlozar, *Istoriya na Bulgarskata literature 1878-1989* [*The History of Bulgarian Literature 1878-1989*], Sofia, Ciela, 2001, 2010.

Jenkins, Speight, "The Operatic Overtones of 'Angels in America.'" *The New York Times*, 27 June 1993, p. H25.

Kaiser, Michael, *Leading Roles: 50 Questions Every Arts Board Should Ask*, Waltham, MA, Brandeis University Press, 2010.

Kaufman, Daniel, "Theatre: Love! Valour! Compassion!" *The Nation*, 19 December 1994, pp. 774-776.

Kazan, Elia, *A Life*, New York, Alfred A. Knopf, 1988.

Keller Julia, "Psychological Drama `Cuckoo's Nest' is Dated – But is it Dangerous?" *Chicao Tribune*, 12 May 2000, <http://articles.chicagotribune.com/2000-05-12/features/0005120022_1_mental-illness-psychiatric-problems-numbing/2>, accessed on September 25, 2012.

Kelly, Kevin, "Kushner is soaring with his `Angels,'" *Boston Globe*, 14 April 1993,

<http://pqasb.pqarchiver.com/boston/access/61755628.html>, accessed 7 October 2012.

Kesey, Ken, Letter to the Editor, *The New York Times*, 7 January 1964, in LettersofNote.com, <http://www.lettersofnote.com/search/label/kenkesey>, accessed 25 May 2011.

Kesey, Ken, *One Flew Over the Cuckoo's Nest*, New York, The Viking Press, 1962.

Kirkpatrick, David D., "Ken Kesey, Checking In on His Famous Nest," *The New York Times*, 10 May 2001, p. E1.

Kortenska, Miroslava, *The Cultural Vertical*, Plovdiv, Pygmalion Press, 2000.

Krasner, David, *American Drama 1945-2000: An Introduction*. Malden, MA, Blackwell Publishing, 2006.

Krasner, David, *A Companion to Twentieth Century American Drama*, Malden, MA, Blackwell Publishing, 2005.

Kushner, Tony, *Angels in America: A Gay Fantasia on National Themes. Part One: Millennium Approaches*, New York, Theatre Communications Group, 1993.

Kushner, Tony, *Angels in America: A Gay Fantasia on National Themes. Part Two: Perestroika*, New York, Theatre Communications Group, 1994.

Kushner, Tony, "Fighting the Art Bullies," *The Nation*, 29 November 1999, pp. 41-42.

Lahr, John, "Angels on Broadway," *The New Yorker*, 31 May 1993, p. 137.

Lahr, John, "Curtain Raiser," *The New Yorker*, 23 April 2012, pp. 32-37.

Lahr, John, "Dancing with Death," *The New Yorker*, 19 March 2012, pp. 86-87.

Lahr, John, "High Marx: Tony Kushner's Socialist Spectacular," *The New Yorker*, 16 May 2011, pp. 130-1.

Langer, Susanne K., *Feeling and Form: A Theory of Art*, Upper Saddle River, N.J., Prentice Hall, 1953.

Lehmann-Haupt, Christopher, "Ken Kesey, Author of 'Cuckoo's Nest,' Who Defined the Psychedelic Era, Dies at 66," *The New York Times,* 11 November 2001, p. 47.

Lord, Sterling, "When Kerouac Met Kesey," *The American Scholar*, Autumn, 2011, <http://theamericanscholar.org/when-kerouac-met-kesey>, accessed 25 September 2012.

Mamet, David, *Theatre*, New York, Faber and Faber, 2011.

McCabe, Terry, "Edward Albee Finds a New Audience, or It Finds Him," *Chronicle of Higher Education*, 22 March 2002, Vol. 48, Issue 28, pp. B14-B15.

McLellan, Dennis, "Dale Wasserman, 94: Playwright Created 'Man of La Mancha'," *Los Angeles Times*, printed in *The Washington Post*, 29 December 2008, <http://www.latimes.com/news/obituaries/la-me-wasserman27-2008dec27,0,1226953.story>, accessed on 25 September 2012.

McNulty, Charles, "Angels in America: Tony Kushner's Theses on the Philosophy of History," *Modern Drama*, Toronto, Spring, 1996, Vol. 39, pp. 84-101.

Medoff, Richard Brad, "The Goat, or Who is Sylvia?" *Theatre Journal*, Volume 55, Number 1, March 2003, pp. 164-166.

Milanova, Rumyana, "Gaiove Prevzeha Narodniya Teatar," *Telegraf*, 12 November 2010, pp. 34-35.

Miller, Arthur, *Timebends: A Life*, New York, Grove Press, 1987.

Mitova, Eliana, "Eduard Olbi: Seks s koza na Balkanite? Zvuchi interesno!" *Klasa*, 12 October 2009, p. 20.

Mitova, Eliana, "Direktorat na Narodniya Teatar Pavel Vasev: Shte Preborim Krisata c Po-dobri Spektakli," *Klasa*, 13 August 2010.

Momchilova, Penka, "Eduard Olbi: Proizvedenie na izkustvoto, koeto ne e opasno, e zaguba na vreme," BTA, 11 October 2009 (online).

Momchilova, Penka, "Eduard Olbi: Vinagi se iznenadvam, che xorata se shokirat kakto vidyat na tsenata ili ekrana neshta koito pravya vav vsekidnevito si," BTA, 28 May 2009 (online).

Momchilova, Penka, "Morfov Svi Kukuviche Gnesdo v Narodniya," *Zemya*, 24 November 2010, p. 18.

Montgomery, Benilde, "*Angels in America* as Medieval Mystery," *Modern Drama*, Winter, 1998, 41:4, p. 596-606.

Morfov, Alexander, "Polet nad Kukuviche Gnesdo," *24 Chasa*, 30 November 2010, p. 11.

Nabokov, Vladimir, *Lolita*, New York, Vintage Books, 1997.

Nenchev, Daniel, *"MakMorfov,"* *Kapital/Light*, 10-17 December 2010, pp. 11-17.
Nenkova, Ralitsa, "The Reception of Edward Albee on the Bulgarian Stage (1960s-1990s)," unpublished MA Thesis, Sofia, University of Sofia St. Kliment Ohridski, Fac. N 23778, 2002.

Nikolova, Iskra, "British Literature in the Context of Stage and Screen Arts Higher Education," in *English Studies on This Side: Post-2007 Reckonings,* Suman Gupta and Milena Katarska, eds., Plovdiv, Plovdiv University Press, 2009.

Nikolova, Iskra, "Interculturality and the Theatre Text", in "Intercultural Theatre" (Conference Proceedings), ed. Jelena Luzina, Edition Theatralica 07, Skopje, Faculty of Dramatic Arts, 2005

Nikolova, Iskra, *Tekstove v Dvijhenie: Problemi na Prevodi I Adaptatsiyata*, Sofia, Petko Benedikov, 2005.

Novinite (unsigned), "European Gay Couples Drawn to Bulgaria Property Market," 18 April 2011
<http://www.novinite.com/view_news.php?id=127433>, accessed 7 October 2012.

Novinite (unsigned), "LGBT Pride Parade Participant Assaulted in Sofia," 1 July 2012
<http://www.novinite.com/view_news.php?id=140850>, accessed 7 October 2012.

Orenstein, Ellen, "Discovering Delta: A Conversation with Bulgarian Director Petar Todorov," *TheatreForum*, Winter/Spring, 2008, pp. 102-106.

Orlando Sentinel (unsigned), "College In Texas: Show About Gays Will Go On," 15 October 1999, p. A16.

Orlando Sentinel (unsigned), "Outcry Spurs Ticket Sales for Gay Play in East Texas," 16 October 1999, p. A20.

Orwell, George, *The Road to Wigan Pier*, London, Penguin Books, 1962.

O'Toole, John, *The Process of Drama: Negotiating Art and Meaning*, London, Routledge, 1992.

Parvanova, Mariana, "Teatralna Reforma Kukna nad Tsenichnoto Gnezdo," *Politika*, 24-30 December 2010, p. 33.

Pavis, Patrice, ed., *The Intercultural Performance Reader*. London, Routledge, 1996,

Pavis, Patrice; Loren Kruger, translator, *Theatre at the Crossroads of Culture*. London, Routledge, 1992.

Peithman, Stephen, "Laughter -- Dark & Light," *Stage Directions*, September 2003, Vol. 16 Issue 9, p. 62.

Petrov, Plamen V., "Ot Stadoto se Pravi Kaima, no za Natsiya ne Stava," *24 Chasa*, 2 December 1010, p. 21.

Pogrebin, Robin, "Unwound and Ready for Some Cuckoo Time," *The New York Times*, 5 April 2001, p. E1.

Robinson, Michelle, "Impossible Representation: Edward Albee and the End of Liberal Tragedy," *Modern Drama*, 54:1, Spring, 2011, pp. 62-77.

Rorty, Richard, *Contingency, Irony, and Solidarity*, Cambridge, UK, Cambridge University Press, 1989.

Roudane, Matthew, *Understanding Edward Albee*, Colombia, SC, University of South Carolina Press, 1988.

Sawyer, Rick, "Review: 'Endgame' at American Repertory Theatre," Bostonist.com, 19 February 2009 <http://bostonist.com/2009/02/19/endgame-american-repertory-theatre.php>, accessed 7 October 2012.

Scolnikov, H. & Holland, P., eds., *The Play Out of Context: Translating Plays from Culture to Culture*, Cambridge, Cambridge University Press, 1989.

Slavova, Kornelia, *The Traumatic Re/Turn of History in Postmodern American Drama at the Turn of the 21st Century*, Sofia, St. Clement Ohridski University Press, 2009.

Slavova, Kornelia. "What's in a Name? The Functioning of the Label 'Bulgarian' in American Imagi/Nation", in *America Imagined, Selected Conference Papers*, Blagoevgrad, AUBG, Vernon Pedersen, eds., et al., 2002, pp. 73-80. [Merdjanska, Kornelia. "Difference Versus Indifference: Western Drama on the Bulgarian Stage".]

Solomon, Rakesh H., *Albee in Performance*, Bloomington, Indiana University Press, 2010.

Sontag, Susan, *Against Interpretation*, New York, Picador, 1961.

Staikov, Dimitar, "Kozata na Olbi e preparirana" *24 Chasa*, 12 October 2009, p. 40.

Stamboliyska, Sonya, "Darszhavata ni Zaprilicha na Kukuviche Gnezdo; Vseki ima Diagnoza," *Klasa*, 11-12 December 2010, p. 20.

Suettno.bg, (unsigned), "Edno Porasnalo Momche," 11 April 2009 <http://suetno.bg/index.php?page=bez_grim>, accessed 17 January 2012.

Teachout, Terry, "Tony Kushner's Characters Should Stop Talking Now," *Commentary*, July/August 2011, pp. 80-83.

Trud (unsigned), "Navalitsa za 'Kukuvicheto Gnezdo' v Narodniya," 21 January 2011, p. 20.

Trud (unsigned), "Poritsaha Pop Zaradi Geiovete," 28 June 2012, p. 7.

Tsaneva, Milena Georgieva, *Patriarkhut: etiudi vurkhu tvorchestvoto na Ivan Vazov* [*The Patriarch: Etudes on the Work of Ivan Vazov*], Sofia, 2000.

Turan, Kenneth and Joseph Papp, *Free for All: Joe Papp, the Public, and the Greatest Theater Story Ever Told*, New York, Anchor Books, 2009.

Vacheva, Mila, "Narodniat Teatar Stava Kukuviche Gnesdo," *24 Chasa*, 20 September 2010.

Vassileva, Sabina, "Za Zhivotnite s Lyubov v Naroden Teatar," *Sega*, 15 October 2009, p. 15.

Vesti.bg (unsigned), "'Polet nad Kukuviche Gnesdo' na Aleksandar Morfov," 5 December 2010 <http://www.vesti.bg/index.phtml?tid=40&oid=3453991>, accessed 7 October 2012.

Vesti.bg (unsigned), "Senzatsionnna postanovka v Narodniaya teatar," 15 October 2009 <http://www.vesti.bg/index.phtml?tid=40&oid=2508011>, accessed 7 October 2012.

Vsekiden.bg (unsigned), "Desi Shpatova Postavi 'Angeli v Amerika' Premierata e tazi Vecher v Narodniya Teatar,", 26 October 2010, <http://www.vsekiden.com/79667>, accessed 20 September 2012.

Vsekiden.bg (unsigned), "Morfov na Finalnata Prava s 'Polet nad Kukuviche Gnesdo'," 19 November 2010 <http://www.vsekiden.com/81572>, accessed 7 October 2012.

Wasserman, Dale, *One Flew Over the Cuckoo's Nest*, New York, Samuel French, Inc., 1970 (first edition, 1963).

Who Goes to Broadway? The Demographics of the Broadway Audience, 2010-2011 Season, New York, The Broadway League, November, 2011,
 <http://www.broadwayleague.com/index.php?url_identifier=the-demographics-of-the-broadway-audience>, accessed 16 September 2012.

Willett, John, ed. and trans., *Brecht on Theatre: The Development of an Aesthetic*, New York, Hill and Wang, 1957.

Wilmer, S.E., *Theatre, Society and the Nation: Staging American Identities*. Cambridge, Cambridge University Press, 2002.

Wilson, Garff B., *Three Hundred Years of American Drama and Theatre*. Englewood Cliffs, NJ, Prentice Hall, Second Edition, 1982.

Zatlin, Phyllis, *Theatrical Translation and Film Adaptation: A Practitioner's View,* Bristol, UK, Multilingual Matters, 22 February 2006.

Zemya (unsigned), "Edward Olbi Ostana Dovolen ot Spektakal na Yavor Gardev," 13 October 2009, p. 18.

Zuber, O., *The Language of Theatre*, Elmsford, NY, Pergamon Press, 1980.

Reviews

24 Chasa (unsigned), "Spin i Rok na Tsenata na Narodniya," 28 October 2010, p. 21.

Abarbanel, Jonathan, "Song for the 'Cuckoo'," *Back Stage*, 28 April 2000, p. 15.

Als, Hilton, "Shadow and Act: Shakespeare Without Words," *The New Yorker*, 2 May 2011, pp. 86-7.

Atanasova, Albena, "Deyan I Ivan Podludiha Naroda," *Standart*, 3 December 2010, p. 37.

Atanasova, Albena, "Boika Velkova Troshi Grantsi v Narodniya," *Standart*, 12 October 2009, p. 23.

Baichev, Raiko, "Morfov Kani v Narodniya," *Standart*, 30 December 2010, p. 23.

Bennett Ray, "The Goat, or Who is Sylvia?" *The Hollywood Reporter—International Edition*, 20 April 2004, pp. 21-89.

Bracken, Michael, "'Cuckoo' Flies Back to the '60s," *Newsday*, 4 April 2003, p. B22.

Brantley, Ben, "A Secret Paramour Who Nibbles Tin Cans," *The New York Times*, 11 March 2002 <http://www.nytimes.com/2002/03/11/theater/theater-review-a-secret-paramour-who-nibbles-tin-cans.html>, accessed 8 October 2012.

Brantley, Ben, "This Time, the Angel Is in the Details," *The New York Times*, Oct. 29, 2010, p. C1.

Brantley, Ben, "You're a Bad, Bad Boy and Nurse Is Going to Punish You," *The New York Times*, 9 April 2001, p. E1.

Brown, Scott, "The Spectacularly Overstuffed 'Angels in America'," *New York*, 29 October 2010 <http://www.vulture.com/2010/10/theater_review_1.html>, accessed 8 October 2012.

Brustein, Robert, "Angels in America," *The New Republic*, 24 May 1993, pp. 29-31.

Brustein, Robert, "The Audience, or Who Is the Goat?" *The New Republic*, 15 April 2002 <http://www.tnr.com/article/the-audience-or-who-the-goat>, accessed 8 October 2012.

Brustein, Robert, "The Great Work Falters," *The New Republic*, 27 December 1993, pp. 25-27.

Brustein, Robert, "A Question of Identity," *The New Republic*, 30 August 1999, pp. 29-31.

Burke, Thomas, "One Flew Over the Cuckoo's Nest," *Talkin' Broadway*, 9 April 2001 <http://www.talkinbroadway.com/world/CuckoosNest.html>, accessed 8 October 2012.

Canby, Vincent, "Two 'Angels,' Two Journeys, In London and New York," *The New York Times*, 30 January 1994, p. A.5.

Cote, David, "Review: Angels in America," *Time Out New York*, 29 October 2010, <http://www.timeout.com/newyork/theater/review-angels-in-america-off-broadway>, accessed 8 October 2012.

Cox, Gordon, "Noises Off," *Variety*, 23 January 2006, p. 41.

Decheva, Violeta, "Mezhdu Seriala i Shouto," *Kultura*, 19 November 2010, p. 2.

Decheva, Violeta, "Normata ili Kade Minava Granitsata," *Kultura*, 23 October 2009, p. 3.

Dimitrov, Georgi P., "Donkov Stresna Narodnia Teatar," *Telegraf*, 3 December 2010, p. 23.

Dimitrova, Dilyana, "Geiove, Izgybeni v Narodniya," *Trud*, 29 October 2010, p. 22.

Dimitrova, Dilyana, "Opasen Tants na Gardev s Kozata," *Trud*, 13 October 2009, p. 24.

Doneva, Yana, "Nyama Angeli v Amerika: Publika Razdvoena okolo Poztanovkata na Desi Shpatova," *Vsekiden.bg*, 28 November 2010 <http://www.vsekiden.com/79840>, accessed 8 October 2012.

Duma (unsigned), "Bunt v Ludnitsata," 4 December 2010, p. 26.

Duma (unsigned), "Prez Noviya Vek Vsichki shte Sme Lydi," 30 October 2010, p. 26.

Evans, Everett, "Mixed Reviews Greet Albee's 'The Goat'," *Houston Chronicle*, 17 March 2002 <http://www.chron.com/entertainment/article/Mixed-reviews-greet-Albee-s-The-Goat-2093369.php>, accessed 8 October 2012.

Feingold, Michael, "Building the Monolith: *Angels in America, Part One: Millennium*," *Village Voice*, 18 May 1993, pp. 218-9.

Feingold, Michael, "The Millennium Recedes: Looking Back at *Angels in America,*" *Village Voice*, 13 November 2010 <http://www.villagevoice.com/2010-11-03/theater/the-millennium-recedes-looking-back-at-angels-in-america/>, accessed 8 October 2012.

Frascella, Lawrence, "The Goat, or Who is Sylvia?," *Entertainment Weekly,* 29 March 2002, p. 65.

Gamerman, Amy, "Lovable Loons -- Mr. Sinise Brings Electric Energy To a 'Cuckoo's Nest' Revival; Mr. Sondheim's Faded 'Follies'," *The Wall Street Journal*, 11 April 2001, p. A16.

Gardner, Elysa, "A Perverse Albee Gloats in 'Goat'." *USA Today*, 11 March 2002, Life, p. 3d.

Gigova, Irina, "Mechtata, ili Koya e Silviya," *Novinar*, 12 October 2009, p. 8.

Grenier, Richard, "The Homosexual Millennium: Is It Here?" *National Review*, 7 June 1993, p. 55.

Henning, Joel, "This 'Cuckoo' Just Won't Fly," *The Wall Street Journal*, 15 May 2000, p. A46.

Henry III, William A., and Janice C. Simpson, "The Gay White Way," *Time*, 17 May 1993 <http://www.time.com/time/magazine/article/0,9171,978536,00.html>, accessed 8 October 2012.

Hirshman, Linda, "'Angels in America' Returns." *Newsweek*, 25 October 2010, pp. 66-67.

Hofler, Robert, "'Cuckoo' Clocks in Gotham," *Variety*, 16 April 2001, p. 9.

Ilieva-Syu, Slavina, "Arhidtektura na Svobodat -- Polet nad Kukuviche Gnezdo," Stand.bg, 3 December 2010 <http://stand.bg>, accessed 8 October 2012.

Ilieva-Syu, Slavina, "Trudni Choveshki Vaprosi, 'Angeli' Otgovori," Stand.bg, 2 November 2010
<http://stand.bg>, accessed 8 October 2012.

Isherwood, Charles, "One Flew Over the Cuckoo's Nest," *Variety*, 16 April 2001, p. 37.

Ivanova, Ave, "Prezhivyavaneto *Kozata* ili Otlozhenata Silviya" *Kultura,* 16 October 2009, p 4.

Jones, Chris, "One Flew Over the Cuckoo's Nest," *Variety*, 24 April 2000, p. 38.

Karadjova, Liliyana, "Homoseksualen Apokalipsis Zavldayava Narodniya." *Novinar*, 11 November 2010, p. 21.

Kelly, Kevin, "Kushner's Landmark Epic Kicks Off a Brilliant, Searing Look at Homophobia," *The Boston Globe*, 5 May 1993 <http://pqasb.pqarchiver.com/boston/access/61762661.html>, accessed 8 October 2012.

Kissel, Howard, "Albee's Latest a Tragedy? He's Got to be Kidding!" *New York Daily News*, 11 March 2002 <http://www.nydailynews.com/archives/nydn-features/albee-latest-a-tragedy-kidding-article-1.492487>, accessed 8 October 2012.

Konstantinov, Asen, "Predposlednoto Tabu," *Paraleli*, 29 October - 4 November 2009, p. 13.

Konstantinov, Asen, "Okolo Nulata," *Paraleli*, 25 November - 1 December 2010, p. 13.

Kortenska, Miroslava, "Gei Parad v Narodniya Teatar," *Uikend*, 6-12 November 2010, pp. 64-65.

Jones, Chris, "One Flew Over the Cuckoo's Nest." *Variety*, 24 April 2000, pp. 38-39.

Lahr, John, "Angels on Broadway," *The New Yorker*, 31 May 1993, p. 137.

Lahr, John, "Angels on the Verge," *The New Yorker*, 15 November 2010 <http://www.newyorker.com/arts/critics/theatre/2010/11/15/101115crth_theatre_lahr>, accessed 8 October 2012.

Levine, Eleanor, "The Goat, or Who is Sylvia," *New York Amsterdam News*, 9 May 2002, p. 22.

Momchilova, Penka, "Gostuvaneto na Albee i 'Vishneva Gradiina' na Azaryan sa Sabitiyata v Balgarskiya Teatar prez 2009 g. spored Eksperti," BTA, 19 December 2009, online (article no longer posted).

Murray, Mathew, "The Goat, or Who is Sylvia," *Talkin' Broadway*, 10 March 2002 <http://www.talkinbroadway.com/world/TheGoat.html>, accessed 8 October 2012.

Nenkova, Ralitsa, "The Reception of Edward Albee on the Bulgarian Stage (1960s-1990s)," unpublished MA Thesis, Sofia, University of Sofia St. Kliment Ohridski, 2002.

Nikolova, Patritsiya, "Brasnesht Polet nad Kukuviche Gnesdo," *Trud*, 7 December 2010 <http://www.trud.bg/Article.asp?ArticleId=70091>, accessed 7 October 2012.

Novinar (unsigned), "Uraganat Deyan Randal Donkov Makmarfi," 7 December 2010, p. 21.

Olson, Walter, "Winged Defeat," *National Review*, 24 January 1994, p. 71-3.

Panaiotova, Martina, "Yavor Gardev za Kozyata Pesen ili kak tozi Pat Nadmina i sebe si," Tialolo.bg, 12 October 2009 <http://www.tialoto.bg/art/2009/10/12> (article no longer posted).

Parvanova, Mariana, "Bunt v Matritsata na Morfov," *Monitor*, 4 December 2010, p. 37.

Parvanova, Mariana, "Gei Chypki v BG Teatara," *Monitor*, 29 December 2010, p. 24.

Parvanova, Mariana, "Kozya Tragediya," *Monitor*, 15 October 2009, p. 24.

Peneva, Elena, "Dyavolski Dobre" *Kapital/Light*, 6-12 November 2010, pp. 28-29.

Peneva, Elena, "Svoboda ili Smart" *Kapital/Light*, 10-17 December 2010, pp. 11-17.

Phillips, Barbara D., "Animal Passions -- A Man Falls for a Quadruped in an Edward Albee Play," *The Wall Street Journal*, 13 March 2002, p. A16.

Popov, Stefan, "Razhodka Pokrai Kukuvicheto Gnezdo," *Kultura*, 14 January 2010, p. 8.

Portillo, Michael, "Beastly Behavior," *New Statesman*, 16 February, 2004, Vol. 133 Issue 4675, p. 44.

Rizzo, Frank, "One Flew Over the Cuckoo's Nest," *Daily Variety*, 17 July 2007, p. 2.

Simon, John, "*Baa*, Humbug," *New York*, 25 March - 1 April 2002. Vol. 35, Issue 10, pp. 133-134.

Simon, John, "Hornet's Nest," *New York*, Apr. 23, 2001 <http://nymag.com/nymetro/arts/theater/reviews/4590/>, accessed 8 October 2012.

Sommer, Elyse, "One Flew Over the Cuckoo's Nest," CurtainUp.com, 12 April 2001,

<http://www.curtainup.com/oneflewoverthecuckoosnest.html>, accessed 8 October 2012.

Sommers, Michael, "Head games," *The Star-Ledger* (Newark, New Jersey), 9 April 2001, Today section, p. 27.

Staikov, Dimitar, "Deyan Donkov: Anarzhistat Sreshty Pravilata na Obsteshtvoto ," *24 Chasa,* 9 December 2010, pp. 20-21.

Staikov, Dimitar, "Kozata na Olbi ybita ot revnika" *24 Chasa,* 15 October 2009, p. 18.

Stoitcheva, Gergana, "Savarshenata Postanovka," *Slovoto,* 15 October 2009 < http://www.slovesa.net/archives/14994>, accessed 8 October 2012.

Stone, Robert, "The Prince of Possibility," *The New Yorker*, 14 June 2004, pp. 70-91.

Suetno.bg. (unsigned), "Histeriya ot Chustva i Edna Koza," 12 October 2009
<http://suetno.bg>, accessed 8 October 2012.

Terziev, Asen, "Piesata Sabitie," *Kapital/Light*, 23-30 October 2009, p. 32.

Tsvetkova, Mariana, "Gei Koswmari v Narodniya Teatar," *Monitor*, 2 November 2010, p. 24.

Vagalinska, Irina, "Golyamata Ludnitsa," *Tema*, 6-12 December 2010, p. 49.

Vagalinska, Irina, "Kozata, ili Kolko sme Liberalni," *Tema*, 19-25 October 2009, p. 53.
Valkova, Yuliya, "Petima Gaiove v Narodniya," *Sedmichen Trud*, 3 November 2010, p. 9.

Vasileva, Sabina, "Deyan Donkov c Glava v Stenata," *Sega*, 10 December 2010, p. 15.

Vasileva, Sabina, "Za Zhivotnite s Lyubov v Naroden Teatar," *Sega*, 15 October 2009, p. 15.

Vasileva, Sabina, "Strasti Evreiski i Gei Fantazii se Vihryat v Narodniy," *Sega*, 4 October 2010, p. 15.

Winer, Linda, "Pulitzer-Prize-Winning 'Angels' Emerges from the Wings," *New York Newsday*, 5 May 1993 (cited in Geis, 1997).

Wolf, Matt, "Getting Albee's 'Goat'," *Variety*, 1 March 2004, p. 41.

Wolf, Matt, "One Flew Over the Cuckoo's Nest," *Variety*, 4 October 2004, p. 122.

A.1 Table of Reviews of One Flew Over the Cuckoo's Nest in New York and Chicago

Cuckoo Reviews.US.Sinise.2000-01	Pos	Neu	Neg	Theme?	Misc. Humor? Mystery? Americana?
Back Stage. Abarbanel.Chicago.Sinise.28.4.2000	X			Something lost.	Handsome set, institution. Focused, deft ensemble. Morton and Sinise believable. Doesn't go overboard on audience. Elegiac. Good ol' boy Mac.
Back Stage.Horwitz.NY.6.4.2001 (mostly an interview)		X		Fun-loving eccentrics vs. authoritarian forces. "the individual vs. the world." Says Wasserman.	Dark yet, at moments, comic look
Curtain UP. NY.Sinise.Sommer.undated	X			Rebellion against Ratched's regime. Beting up of wives and mothers.	Somewhat updated adaptation, worth seeing, fresh and vigorous. More laid-back and playful, less maniacal and more vulnerable, Mac than Nicholson. Bromden monologues helpful.
New York.Simon.Sinise.23.4.2001			X	Madhouse world. Boy hero wages war of liberation against emasculating feminine. Child's rebellion against mother.	Too mired in its period. Best for those seeing it for first time. Mixed acting quality.
NYT.Brantley.Sinise.94.2001			X	Rebellion for adolescent boys. Simplistic good and bad guys.	Atavistic energy. Cute instead of confrontational. top-of-the-line production values. fablelike, schematic simplicity of script. Mac's "laugh is crucial" Disappointingly sane.
Star-Ledger.Sommers.Sinise.NYC.9.4.2001	X			Crazy people questioning their keeper's authority	Fiercely entertaining. enjoyably flashy acting. fairly obvious and rickety in some details, but the basic story remains potent. Mac a "howling coyote." Conclusion still packs a surprise…a few cartoon extremes…Effectively bringing out the comedy

Review				Theme/Plot	Evaluation
Newsday.Bracken.Bohemia.4.4.2003			X	Microcosm of society, Mac fights society's arbitrary rules.	Cliched characterizations. soggy sentimentality. Simplistic brand of antiestablishment idealism.
Talkin' Broadway.Burke.NY.Sinise.9.4.2001	X			A battle of giants (Mac and Ratched)	Entertaining lurid melodrama. Moments of greatness in the acting. Deserves Tony nomination for light and set. Faultless direction.
Variety.Jones.Chicago.Sinise.24.4.2000	X			Misogyny. Melodramatic, well-made. The insane are victims of repressive society's thought police.	Powerful. Sinise screams a lot. Very white set, very loud f/x. Accessible and gripping. Visceral theatrical thrills.
Variety.Isherwood.NY.Sinise.16.4.2001. (Similar Isherwood review in 9.4.2001 Variety)	X			Celebration of anarchy and rebelliousness suggesting that the natural response to American culture's warped values was a fine madness. psychological symbolism of Ratched. cheery anti-authoritarian message	emotional buttonpusher, wringing tears and cheers with mechanical precision. Expert ensemble, irresistible. heart-tugging pathos. May bring tears. Sinise is funny. Calibrated doses of laughter and tears. irresistible. Mac: happily extroverted showboater here, strutting and waddling about, slapping his belly for comic emphasis. energetic, funny and highly theatrical Some bathos.
WSJ.Henning.Chicago. Sinise.15.5.2000			X	Mocks 1960's women's lib and civil rights. Story of zany mental patients. Woman emasculating men.	Superficial period piece, like book. Sinise weak, so too characters. Precise, brisk directing, appropriately shrill rock music.
WSJ.Gamerman. New York.Sinise.11.4.2001	X			Misogyny, with castrating "witch." Institution is society in microcosm where acts of nonconformity and rebellion are mercilessly crushed. Power struggle of Ratched and McMurphy.	Sinise is "in your face." Full-bodied production. Good ensemble cast, especially Smapson. Play tends to trite and sentimental. Applause when inmate curses Ratched, laughs at her excessive conldness. Laughing at loonies.

A.2 Table of Reviews of *One Flew Over the Cuckoo's Nest* at the Ivan Vazov National Theatre

Cuckoo.Ivan Vazov.1.12.2010	Pos	Neu	Neg	Theme?	Misc. Humor? Mystery? Americana?
24 Chasa.Staykov.9.12.2010		X		Protest and rebellion, the anarchist against society. Uncertain message.	Will "make your head spin," a likable anarchist Mac. Great acting. Lacks excitement. Bulgarians don't like to follow rules.
Duma.4.12.2010	X			A fight to assert one's self.	Serious questions with cruel insight. Evokes feelings and appreciation of audience.
Eva.bg.Lily C.undated	X				All the acting very good, overall. Got main point of reversion of Bibbit. "Absolute hit of the season." Had to stand to applaud.
Kapital Light.Peneva.10.12.2010	X			Clash between the individual and the Establishment. desire for freedom and its price.	Secondary characters make bright and memorable roles.
Kultura.Popov.14.1.2010		X		Many themes, but a "list," not composed or shaped. Morfov allows viewer to interpret the play in a multitude of ways. Humanistic vision of power without feeling.	A milestone. Very close to the novel, literal gesture-by-gesture adaptation. Reverent, out-of-date, with just a few updates. Donev poor, physical, as in TV comedy. Party orgy also geared to TV viewers.
Monitor.Parvanova.4.12.2010	X			Contrast of shiny hospital setting and inhumane treatment.	Great acting. Vrangova's complex image that both repels and builds empathy.
Novinar.unsigned.7.12.2010	X			Is it worth it to be different? What do you lose if you break a law with your head? Mac and Ratchid "only opposites at first glance," both manipulative. Nut house as metaphor of society.	Donkov and Vrangova are perfect. Neither is all good or bad. Donkov's laughter will echo in viewers' consciousness long after the play. Plays asks important questions of fate and the cost of rebellion.
Sega.Vasileva.9.12.2010	X			Theatre spectators join the "group therapy." Powerful finale. Stage as model of the "cold, inharmonious world."	Donkov a strong rebel, makes a dent in the system. Obscenity adds nothing, may be too long.

Stand.bg Ilieva-sue.13.12.2011	X			Who is really mad? living tale of madness, diversity, freedom, resignation, fear, rebellion, conjuncture (?), and will. Counterculture escapes bondage.	Well-paced, well acted. Clever set. intense and brilliant game Dejan Donkov
Standart.Atanasova.3.12.2010	X			Ratched hates all who wish to love or be free. No doubt every system destroys the individual.	A triumph. Five minutes of applause at end. Vrangova is perfect, with white socks and black spirit. Screens are Big Brother. Wonderful metal, bars and glass set. Great ensemble acting. Much action, modern remarks, philosophy.
Standart.Baichev.30.12.2010	X			Anarchy machine destroys the perfect, disciplined world of Ratched.	Dazzling premier, epic and earth-shattering.. Pop culture: Metallica used. Ratched not a monster like in novel, but well-meaning. Comedy and seriousness.
Teatri.bg undated				Dictator nurse vs. freedom fighter.	Absolutely new, not from earlier versions. Not a review.
Telegraf.Dimitrov.3.12.2010	X				"hysteria is total" for a play with a "perfect" director, who has achieved, critics say, "total balance with no wavering into extravagance."
Tema. Vagalinska. 6-12.12.12.2010	X			Rebellion in a menta	Four hours
Rud. Nikolova. 7.12.2010	X				

A.3 Table of Reviews of *Angels in America* in New York City

Angels.NYC.1993	Pro	Neu	Neg	Theme?	Misc. Humor? Mystery?
America Magazine.Miracky.29.5.1993	X			Effects of AIDS and human relations. Personal identity has a political character.	First-rate acting. Strong treatment of human relations. Gripping crisis scenes. Hilarious, poignant. Tour de force acting. Effective sets, superb lighting. Extremely engaging though long and demanding. Often sharply comical relationships.
Boston Globe.Kelly.5.5.1993	X			A savage attack on homophobia	Steady booing infiltrated the standing ovation. It's steadily funny.
Commentary.Teachout.7.2011 (Teachout also in WSJ.29.10.2010 on a revival)		X		Tribulations of AIDS and political diatribe.	Flawed artist, problematic style. strongest scenes are both emotionally powerful and theatrically effective. Ambitious scale. Obvious scale, unconventional. Demonizes conservatives. Hectoring shrillness of politicized art. Strident, two halves too long.
Duke (Univ.) Chronicle 31.3.1994	X			Preciousness of life, human responsibility.	Utter virtuosity.
National Review.Grenier.1993			X	A political tract. Blaming Reagan for AIDS, without comfort from religion.	Rambling, garrulous, incoherent, inchoate. Not a complete play at all, with all loose ends. Bombastic and hollow.
National Review.Olson.24.1.1994		X		AIDS	Fine dir., virtuosic cast. a steady flow of funny lines and clever observations, defying the gravity of its subject, AIDS. Little plot, nonsense religious imagery. Shove toward polarization, not insight into common humanity.
New Republic. Brustein.24.5.1993	X			How people display, discover and affirm the fact that they are gay.	"Very literate play." Balanced historical sense and style. Authoritative achievement of radical new playwright". Flaw: no animating action in long play. Weak, over-literal set. Much of

Source					Theme	Review
						acting lacks depth.
New Republic.Seigel.29.12.2003			X			a "second-rate play written by a second-rate playwright" who happens to be gay, and because he has written a play about being gay, and about AIDS, no one will call it "the overwrought, coarse, posturing, formulaic mess that it is"
New York Newsday.Winer.5.5.1993 (in Geis)	X					Delightful, luscious, funny writer…political rage and scathing, unsanitized horror...hours zip by with the breezy enjoyment of a great page-turner.
NYT.Rich.5.5.1993	X				Call to arms in age of AIDS.	most thrilling American play in years, astonishing, epic, intimate, christalline directing,wicked sense of *humor*, timeless dramatic matters. *Reworked recently to reflect the future.*
NYT.Canby.30.1.1994 (reviews both NYC and London productions)	X				None mentioned.	funny, furious, dazzling (and occasionally overripe) Kushner text. Fireworks. occasionally uproarious, often brutal and sorrowful circus. A lot of glitz. Laughs popunded home. astonishing spectacle. Remarkable scope and magnitude.
New Yorker.Lahr 31.5.1993	X				"essentially about betrayal and how the heart learns or doesn't learn to live with loss." Director Wolfe, play is about "America, about justice, about decency, and about heart."	A "reductive set" (not a problem to achieve success. Wise heart, shrewd narrative, good talk, good humor, good story. Aud "rose en masse at the finale to give it a standing ovation." Not preachy.
Newsweek.Kroll (quoted also in National Review Olson review)	X				politics, sex and religion. AIDS, absconding of God.	Daring and dazzling. Ambitious epic. "Broadest, deepest, most searching American play of our time" quoted in Olson.
Orlando Sentinel.Maupin.5.5.1993	X				America. religion, history and the nature of love, nothing less than AIDS, Mormons, Roy Cohn and the ghost of Ethel Rosenberg.	Astonishing, ambitious. hype does not dampen one's enthusiasm.

Time.Henry.17.5.1993	X			Conventional drama about the intersections of three households in turmoil.	Visually ugly, far less magical than in L.A. Witty, energized and unpredictable script makes 3 1/2 hours fly by. Literary style.
Vanity Fair.Hitchens.3.1993	X			AIDS and illness, discontents.	A strike at the collective unconscious, a vigorous scrambling of the cerebral and the emotional. It bucks one up.
Variety	X				"Epic theatrical fever dream...a three-hour cliffhanger that leaves you wanting more."
Variety.Evans.9.5.1994	X			None mentioned.	Incredible cast, sharp today as on opening day. Mostly about cast and design.
Village Voice.Feingold.18.5.1993	X			Gayness and bigotry.	Vast, sprawling, and wordy. Includes everything. Best kind of political play. A few scenes heavily overdone, acting uneven. Need to see part two for message.

A.4 Table of Reviews of *Angels in America* Ivan Vazov National Theatre

Angels,Ivan Vazov 26.10.2010	Pos	Neu	Neg	Theme?	Misc. Humor? Mystery?
24 Chasa.20.9.2010	X			3 families interactions about AIDS and love. the three people talk about love, fear of death and other delicate family issues.	"Great feeling for humor" but otherwise just an announcement of the production. Funny gay fantasy, regarding national topics.
24 Chasa.28.9.2010	X			Homosexuality, family issues, politics, the plague of AIDS, loneliness and fear of rejection.	Excellent work of the director, nice lighting and scenography, powerful décor and actor performance.
24 Chasa.unsigned.28.10.2010	X			Freedom makes us slaves to responsibilities, and democracy is like three card monte. The lawyer Roy is equivalent to the sickness AIDS. Political themes are counterpoint to the heavy themes (illness). Democracy appears and disappears, "Freedom is the theft of responsibilities"? (license?).	Ambitious, immense Shpatova vision, a master. Good acting, lighting, sets. Knows cold war history, sees it in play as unobtrusive, light balance as humor to heavy AIDS theme. Good lighting and sets. Good acting by Karamazov as Joe.
Duma.unsigned.30.10.2010			X	Fear, rejection, loneliness, destruction of all values whatsoever. All of us will be crazy in the new century, in which all values are destroyed.	Expressive décor, dynamic music, direct messages. Actors mixed in a dynamic, strikingly strong cocktail of hallucinations, fantasies. Question to what degree suggestions/impressions of the play will find an audience.
Kapital LIght.Peneva.6-12.11.2010	X			Coming apocalypse, AIDS .	Play scandalized US. Though history of AIDS is out of date, 2-hour plays holds attention due to director's interpretation and terrific acting. Dated for some, but "an event." Black humor. Difficult to mount.
Kapital Light.Peneva.6-12.10. 2010.	X			Open discussion	Holds up after 20 years.

Source				Description	Analysis
				of sexuality, religion, fairness and justice, politics, social division, racism.	Special effects with Brechtian alienation. Grotesque theatrics plus intense drama. Minimalist and disco music mix. Eclectic style.
Kultura.Decheva.19.11.2010			X	About American issues, not Bulgarian.	A token in Bulgarian theatre, politically correct, abstractly aesthetic vision of AIDS and homosexuality, undisguised farce, really about America.
Lifestyle.ibox.bg 11.11.2010	X	X		Sadness of AIDS epidemic.	Viewer may have trouble understanding the US set. Describes play. Knows US history.
Monitor.4.10.2010	X			The most scandalous performance in the theater, like a textbook on life; a horrific story.	Says many things with few words—says actor in play, Vlado Karamazov.
Monitor.Parvanova. 29.12.2010		X	X	The director reveals the problems about the political homosexual lobby in the USA, the scourging threat of the AIDS, the betrayal.	It is a very brave attempt with many weaknesses (does not specify).
Novinar.Karadjova. 11.11.2010		X		Recreating the chaotic world and conflicts of American society during the mid.80s.	6 hours is too long. Because director has the task of creating the conflicted and chaotic world of AIDS in the 80s in US, the theme isn't current for Bulgaria, the chaotic structure makes the production hard to assimilate, one cannot get full-scale impression. brilliant actors performance. Hypnotic, moving, brilliant acting.. "A challenge both for the creative team and the spectators."
Novinar.net.Karadjova.10.11.2010 [fuller version of text review]		X		World of AIDS, chaos and difficulties.	Powerful dialog, great acting. Challenge for the creative team. No viewer will emerge unmoved. topic is not relevant to Bulgaria, the chaotic structure makes the play difficult to assimilate and fails to establish the overall

						impact. Chaotic structure, difficult task to recreate the conflict. Three families.
Paraleli.Konstantinov. 25.11.2010			X		Apocalyptic picture of the American society during the 80s, difficulties for the Bulgarian society to understand the reality of that time.	Awful scenography, poor acoustics, no connection between the scenes, lack of elaboration, overall mark-- zero.
Sega.Vasileva.4.10.2010	X				Not for everybody, but it is attractive and bold performance, it is difficult for the general public to get the idea, the theme about the policy of Reagan and the Mormonism are not super interesting for the average Bulgarian.	Excellent scenery-- the 6 levels of the scene,
Sedmichen Trud.Valkova.3.11.2010	X				Nightmare of a gay diagnosed with AIDS, fears and sacrifices people make, justice and tolerance towards the different, fighting your inner daemons, the play aims to prove that USA is not country of freedom, but just a melting pot for assimilation.	The stage is almost with no decor, which gives sense of loneliness and helplessness, and implies the powerful message of confusion.
Theatri.bg.Ilieva-Syu.12.11.2010	X				Self-awareness; Man in search of himself, fleeing lies.	Very complicated structure. The distant time of play doesn't seem to be a problem; angel is timeless.
Standart.Atanasova. 28.10.2010	X				Homosexuality, hypocrisy, AIDS, Mormons, Democrats, Republicans, Hollywood, lawyers, wars, pseudo passion between husband and wife.	Very convincing and influential performance, the actors play successfully many parts (it outlines the scene with the duo Batmen).
Telegraph. Dimitrov.27.10.2010	X	X			opportunity for the Bulgarian public to "count" the gay actors on the scene, starts many rumors regarding the homosexuality of Vlado Karamazov, the	Does not say anything about the performance.

					director Desi Shpatova.	
Trud.Dimitrova.29.10.2010		X			A dream of a suffering homosexual man. America not the land of freedom, justice and tolerance for gays.	Bold leap for alpha males of BG theatre to show gay sex. Less tolerance here for gays than in U.S. Too little tenderness but powerful political argument. Nice effort, not there yet. Actresses show too much testosterone.
Vesti.bg.undated	X				Actors say it is ironic, complex, about people facing their destiny (AIDS).	Only quotes actors on its importance, excellence.
Vsekiden.Doneva.28.10.2010		X			Problems of 1980s America: homosexuality and AIDS. Also: madness, hysteria, struggle with illusions, racism, vices, and our fears.	Dated: shock of the themes has worn off. Too long, no intermission. Heavy text but "bonus" for audiences is pop music. [Preview article 26.10.2010 said the play has brilliant dialog and beautifully drawn characters.]

A.5 Table of Reviews of *The Goat* in New York City

The Goat NYC 10.3.2002	Pos	Neu	Neg	Theme?	Misc. Humor? Mystery?
Advocate.Shewey.16.4.2002	X			Essay on nature of tragedy: the arrival of something unexpected that forces us to face the essential mystery of life and death.	Sly puzzle of a play. Corny jokes.
Amsterdam News.Levine.9.5.2002	X			Sophisticated society chokes itself on one of its few remaining taboos.	Hilarious. Ludicrous enough that it tickles our fancy. Review doesn't really take the play seriously.
Back Stage.Jacobs.22.3.2002	X			Bestiality, incest. Goat a metaphor for Martin's latent homosexuality or deviance. "Interpretive malleability."	You're exhausted and your imagination piqued. Exposition alienates. Not clearly moving.
Chronicle of Higher Ed.McCabe.22.3/2002	X			Crises of middle-aged married couples. Whether it is really possible to know the person you love. Relationships between humans and animals.	Quite good -- funny, grim, bracing, and ultimately devastating.
Curtain Up.online.2002	X			Tolerance of "sick" vs. normal.	Terrific performances, wickedly funny. Sly word play script and well-paced direction.
Entertainment Weekly.Frascella.29.3.2002	X			The ill fit between our emotional makeup and our morality.	Peals of laughter. An excoriating tragedy. A swift kick to our complacency.
Entertainment Weekly. unsigned.27.12.2002	X			Love or perversion? Infidelity or insanity?	Eminently worth puzzling over. Good acting, including after replacements.
New Criterion.Steyn.spring.2002		X		Bestiality and transgression.	Cunning staging. Audience decided this is a Neil Simon comedy.
New Republic.Brustein.15.4.2002	X			Justified the ways of "deviant" man to God, evokes pity and terror for Martin.	Tricky, hard to classify. Witty (but grows tedious). Attempt to subvert moral, aesthetic assumptions. Almost succeeds. to make tragedy of a dirty joke. Demands respect.
New York.Simon.25.3.2002			X	Simon says there is none: A metaphor, but for what?	Play makes no sense. Gales of laughter in inappropriate places. Obscenity for cheap laughs.
New York Daily News.Kissel.11.3.2002			X	It has none.	Altogether specious play. More boulevard comedy than tragedy, but still fails. Almost

						everything rings false. Arch, inelegant dialog. Set conveys architectural pretensions.
New York Times.Brantley.11.3.2002		X			The irrational, confounding and convention-thwarting nature of love. Good questions but with kid gloves.	Not uneasy startled laughs of Albee, but jolly laughs of Neil Simon. Sadly falls short of its high ambitions. Sitcom laugh track. Flippancy linked to savagery and anguish. Not emotionally credible. Characters give voice to universal conflicts. Semantic quibbles can seem juvenile.
Talkin' Broadway.Murray.10.3.2002	X				Murray doesn't say.	Strange theatrical experience. Fascinating. Unrelenting comedy, genuine or uncomfortable laughs. Till end, when laughter no longer enough. Dark tragic undercurrent. Good all-around acting. House looks like that of architect. Maintains dramatic intensity. Safe, dishonest ending. Provocative, thoroughly original.
Theatre Journal.Medoff.3.2002	X				Goat can be real goat or forbidden love, or sex appetite, or Dionysis-theatre. Love and betrayal. Multiple readings. Only thru terror of tragedy is life affirmed. Causes deliberate audience discomfort.	Stevie sacrifices the goat on a living room altar Greek-tragedy style.
WSJ.Philips.13.3.2002		X			To take Martin's transgression seriously or to relish the patent absurdity of the premise? To see Stevie's rage as perfectly understandable or oddly excessive? A fable about the power of the media to expose secrets and destroy relatively innocent lives? A coded message about homosexuality and homophobia? A plea for the societal benefits of reticence? A rumination about the strange paths love and betrayal take?	Puzzled, the theme a mystery. many flashes of wit and wordplay. The playwright finds humor, for example, in his upper-income, hyper-verbal New Yorkers lacing their sentences with the f-curse, like Mametian characters with graduate degrees
Variety.14.10.2002.Isherwood	X				A very funny but deeply	Good, but most credit goes to new actors Sally Field &

			serious exploration of the confounding complexities of love and sex, and the limits of human compassion, but it subtly softens its bleak vision.	Irwin. Stevie's final horror more forgiving.

A.6 Table of Reviews of *The Goat* Ivan Vazov National Theatre

The Goat.Ivan Vazov.11.9.2009	Pos	Neu	Neg	Theme?	Misc. Humor? Mystery?
24 Chasa.Staikov.15.10.2009	X			Gardev connects story to Greek tragedy, horror restored justice.	Stunning Velkova performance as Ancient Fury, smashes ancient pottery. Incredible Bilalov performance.
BTA.Momchilova.19.12.2009	X			Deep problems of man.	Powerful performances, no melodrama. Velkova performs between drama and tragedy.
Kapital Light.Terziev.23.10.2009	X			a very brave, honest and thorough approach to one of the last remaining taboos. Not about bestiality, but intimate human relations.	Literally a tragedy, "leading into horror."
Klasa.Mitova.12.10.2009					
Kultura.Ivanova.15.10.2009	X			Sylvia is tragedy, both denied by society. Is society or the family right to deny Martin's love? Civilization's commands are bizarre.	The indescribable is love and end of tragedy (?). Exact pitch of Gardev's score. Great play, production, experience, peak in theatre.
Kultura.Decheva.22.10.2009	X			Norms & flexibility, or the borders of the normal and abnormal. Martin's loneliness.	Masterpiece of irony, a tragedy. Philosophical. Directing with emotional profoundness and enthusiasm. Comedy ends when Martin's secret revealed.

					Stevie's defensive irony helps overcome her rage. Gardev's perfect rhythm and variable pace of the three acts.
Monitor.Parvanova.15.10.2009	X			Only talks about acting and directing.	Humor. Qualities of great drama, provocative.
Novinar.Gigova.12.10.2009	X			Many possible: identity crisis, middle age impulse, paucity of human relations in society, etc.	A heavy tragedy with catharsis. Velkova will get acting nominations.
Paraleli.Konstantinov.29.10.2009	X			Not about bestiality, but the humanly unacceptable.	Very Funny and very serious. Irony and eccentric humor. Challenges democratic societies' inhibitions and prejudices on individual freedom and tolerance of diversity. Gardev has constructed "perfect score."
Sega.Vassileva.15.10.2009	X			A catharsis of social therapy.	Subconscious fears, "magical." Brilliant directing.
Slovoto.Stoitcheva.15.10.2009	X			A shot of true art (No interpretation)	"Perfect" production. Exceeds all expectations. "Miracle" of acting, script, director. "true to the smallest detail" set. Brilliant play. A cocktail of questions.
Standart.Atansova.12.10.2009	X			Greek tragedy about honesty. Gardev understands that our primal instincts harbor demons below layers of culture.	Absolute hit for season of academics. No book in the vast library can explain Martin's love.
Tema.Vagalinska.19-25.10.2009	X			Indignation and shame. Whether what people say	Albee causes scandal by crossing borders of

				is more important than genuine pain.	liberalism. Betrayal with destructive consequences seem more acceptable to society than bestiality.
Tialoto.bg.Panaiotova.12.10.2009	X			Taboos. Ordinary, spontaneous, true love. Freedom in society. Savages in expensive clothes. True friendship.	Absolute hit of the theater season. Modern tragedy. Viewer forced to solve strange moral case. Wonderful direction.
Trud.Dimitrova.13.10.2009	X			Not discussed.	Sets a new standard for Bulgarian Broadway. Top-class acting.

A.7 Questionnaire for *One Flew Over the Cuckoo's Nest*

QUESTIONNAIRE

After viewing *One Flew Over the Cuckoo's Nest*, please circle the best responses to the following questions:

1. Did you enjoy the play?
   A. Yes, very much. B. Yes. C. Somewhat. D. No. E. No, not at all.

2. Do you think you understood the play?
   A. Yes, very much. B. Yes. C. Somewhat. D. No. E. No, not at all.

3. What do you think is generally the theme of this play?
   A. Society demands conformity and represses creative and energetic individuals.
   B. Nurse Ratched is a controlling monster, but Dr. Spivey represents a more humanitarian social elite.
   C. Chief Bromden is really sane, but racist American society has incarcerated him because of his insights.
   D. Billy's mother has been helping him adjust to society, but he still needs professional psychiatric care.
   E. I don't know
   F. The theme was:_____

4. Did the main characters seem more like Americans, or more like Bulgarians?
   A. Very much like Americans.
   B. More like Americans.
   C. About the same.
   D. More like Bulgarians.
   E. Very much like Bulgarians.

5. Is McMurphy a recognizable Bulgarian personality type?
   A. Yes. If yes, in any particular way?_____

B. No. If no, why not?_____
C. Hard to say.

6. How would you describe McMurphy's personality?
   A. Generally winning, attractive, natural. B. Mostly overbearing and obnoxious. C. Having good and bad points (e.g., energetic, but a little manipulative and calculating). D. Other:_____

7. Did you find the play funny?
   A. Yes—very funny. B. Yes, funny. C. Somewhat funny. D. No—not very funny. E. Not funny at all.

8. What do you think is the meaning of the title, *One Flew Over the Cuckoo's Nest*?
   A. It's based on an American children's verse, and suggests that McMurphy wants to visit the hospital, but not stay long.
   B. It's based on an American children's verse, and used because it refers to a hospital for the insane.
   C. The "cuckoo" bird is not very educated, like the characters in the play. (next page)
   D. I don't know
   E. Another meaning?_____

9. Why does Chief Bromden decide to break out of the hospital?
   A. McMurphy has given him back the confidence to live independently.
   B. McMurphy has given him back the confidence to fight the "Combine."
   C. Because he realizes he is "full size" so finally has the strength to break out.
   D. I don't know.
   E. My view:_____

10. What do you believe should be done about people like the "acutes" in this play?
    A. They can't fit in society and need treatment in medical facilities

B. Some of the acutes could probably do better without treatment
   C. Hospitals for insane people generally do a disservice to the patients
   D. I don't know.
   E. My view:_____

11. Did this play change your views about society's treatment of acute mental patients?
    A. Yes, very much. B. Yes. C. I don't know. D. No. E. No, not at all.

Please tell us a little about yourself:

12. My age:
    A. Under 20. B. 20-35. C. 36-49. D. 50 and above.

13. A. I attend the theater rarely. B. I attend occasionally (once or more every 6 weeks). C. I attend frequently (once per month or more). D. I attend frequently *and* enjoy avant garde, absurdist, or similarly challenging theatrical works.

14. My education:
    A. Secondary or below. B. Some college. C. Bachelor's degree or equivalent. D. Some or completed graduate school.

15. What is your nationality?
    A. Bulgarian. B. American. C. Other or dual (which?):_____

Other thoughts or comments?

Thank you!

A.8 Questionnaire for *One Flew Over the Cuckoo's Nest*, Bulgarian Language Version

ВЪПРОСНИК

След като гледахте постановката на *„Полет над кукувичето гнездо"*, моля да оградите с кръгче отговорите на въпросите, с които сте съгласни:

1. **Хареса ли ви пиесата?**
   А. Да, много. **Б.** Да. **В.** Донякъде. **Г.** Не. **Д.** Никак.

2. **Мислите ли, че разбрахте пиесата?**
   А. Да, напълно. **Б.** Да. **В.** Донякъде. **Г** .Не. **Д.** Никак.

3. **Каква е според вас в общи линии темата на пиесата?**
   А. Обществото изисква поведение на конформизъм и подтиска творческите и енергични индивиди.
   Б. Сестра Речид е властно чудовище, но д-р Спайви е представител на по-човечната елитна част на обществото.
   В. Началник Бромдън е всъщност нормален, но расисткото американско общество го е затворило заради неговите прозрения.
   Г. Майката на Били му помага да се адаптира към обществото, но той все пак има нужда от психиатър.
   Д. Не зная.
   Е. Темата беше: _____

4. **На кого приличат повече главните герои - на американци или на българи?**
   А. Много приличат на американци. **Б.** Повече приличат на американци. **В.** Няма разлика. **Г.** Повече приличат на българи. **Д.** Много приличат на българи.

5. **Познавате ли българин, който да прилича на Макмърфи?**
   А. Да. Ако отговорът е да, в какво отношение?..

    Б. Не. Ако отговорът е не, защо
    не? ....
    В. Трудно ми е да преценя.

6. **Как бихте описали образът на Макмърфи?**
    А. Обикновено побеждава, привлекателен, естествен.
    Б. В повечето случаи натрапчив и отблъскващ.
    В. Има и добри, и лоши страни (напр. енергичен, но манипулативен и меркантилен.
    Г. Друго..

7. **Мислите ли, че пиесата е забавна?**
    А. Да, много забавна.
    Б. Да, забавна е.
    В. Донякъде е забавна.
    Г. Не, не е забавна.
    Д. Никак не е забавна.

8. **Какво според вас е значението на заглавието „Полет над кукувичето гнездо"?**
    А. Заглавието е взето от американско стихче за деца и се предполаг, че Макмърфи иска да посети болницата, но не задълго.   (продължава)
    Б. Взето е от американско стихче за деца и се използва, защото става дума за лудница.
    В. Птицата "кукувица" не е особено интелигентна, също като героите в пиесата.
    Г. Не зная.
    Д. Друго значение? ....

9. **Защо началник Бромдън решава да избяга от болницата?**
    А. Макмърфи му възвръща вярата в независимия живот.
    Б. Макмърфи му възвръща вярата в борбата срещу „Машината".
    В. Защото осъзнава, че е пълноценен и в крайна сметка има сили да избяга.
    Г. Не зная.

Д. Моето
мнение: ....

10. Какво според вас трябва да се направи с „тежките случаи" в тази пиеса?
А. Те не могат да се адаптират към обществото и имат нужда от медицински грижи.
Б. Някои от „тежките случаи" могат вероятно да минат и без лечение.
В. Болниците за душевно болни обикновено са вредни за пациентите.
Г. Не зная.
Д. Моето
мнение: ....

11. Промени ли тази пиеса възгледите ви за лечението на сериозно душевно болни:
А. Да, много. Б. Да. В. Не знам. Г. Не. Д. Никак.

Моля, напишете ни нещо за себе си:
12. Вашата възраст:
А. Под 20. Б. Между 20 и 35. В. Между 36 и 49. Г. На 50 или повече.

13. Вашият интерес към театъра:
А. Рядко ходя на театър.
Б. Ходя на театър от време на време (веднъж на 6 седмици или по-често).
В. Често ходя на театър (веднъж месечно или по-често).
Г. Често ходя на театър и харесвам авангардистки, абсурдистки или подобни провокативни театрални творби.

14. Вашето образование:
А. Средно или по-ниско.
Б. Колеж.
В. Бакалавърска степен или нейният еквивалент.
Г. Някакво или завършено висше образование.

15. Каква е вашата националност?
   А. Българска.
   Б. Американска.
   В. Друга или двойна (каква?):_____.

Други мисли и коментари?

БЛАГОДАРИМ ВИ!

A.9 Table of Bulgarians' Results for *Cuckoo's Nest* (44)

One Flew Over the Cuckoo's Nest	A/А	B/Б	C/В	D/Г	E/Д
1 Enjoy the play?	32	4	7	1	0
2 Understand it?	20	20	3	0	0
3 Theme?	31	1	2	1	0
4 Main characters American? Bulgarian?	4	13	19	6	0
5 Is McMurphy a Bulgarian personality?	20	5	18	XXXX	XXXX
6 McMurphy's personality?	9	4	24	7	XXXX
7 Funny?	6	7	20	6	4
8 Meaning of the title?	14	15	0	5	9
9 Why does Bromden break out?	22	9	7	3	3
10 What to do with the "acutes"?	2	20	11	2	9
11 Play change your view of treatment of acute mental patients?	4	14	1	17	4
12 Your age?	3	27	6	8	XXXX
13 Attend the theater?	8	9	12	13	XXXX
14 Your education?	4	1	17	20	XXXX
15 Your nationality?	44	0	0	XXXX	XXXX

Comments:

[One or more respondents did not answer questions 3, 4, 5, 8, 9, 12, 13, and 14.]
[2. One of Morfov's stated goals (and Kazin's) is to make the play understandable.]
[4. Five of these marked as "B" on an early questionnaire that offered only three choices, that is, no "Very much like…"]
[9. Several respondents checked two boxes.]
[10. Several respondents checked two boxes.]

3. F. 1. The clinic as a repressive machine. 2. Craziness in the sense of Foucault. 3. The system and the absurdity: if you rebel, you have to accept it (Derrida). 4. Everyday problems of the U.S. in the 1960s-70s. 5. The relevance of democracy.
3. F. The way by which people in institutions for the psychologically ill fight treatments, don't help improvement of their conditions, and no one makes real effort to perceive them as equal human beings, to understand and love them, in order to help them to feel better.
3. F. The theme according to me is connected to the meaning that man should never forget who is he and what he wants to be, regardless of the situation in which he finds himself. The strength of spirit can topple mountains.
3. F. About human freedom. About his suppression and its removal. About the free human sprit, friendship and loyalty. I believe, that I cannot express myself exactly.
3. F. There are at least two sides to every story.
3. F. If you are different, you're labeled "insane."
3. F. This play is about voices. Ratched is the boss with big voice, but so does McMurphy. Billy and Bromden learn to speak, but they are shamed, silenced by family and society. Bromden was humiliated by his mother.
3. F. A lot of themes were presented, the central one was the strong are strong because they use fear to oppress the weak.
4. Can we seek the nationality of people in the 21st century?
5. A. Bai Ganyo and the city "wise guy" (терикат)
5. A. In the sense the he doesn't bow down and wants to change himself and the society in which he lives.
5. A. Character
5. A. I remember some of my acquaintance who, maybe not to the same degree, but showed the same energy, and unwillingness to conform to the limits invented by society, and instead of them followed their personal path because they believed in it.
5. A. At times he thinks he owns the world

5. B. In the past 60 years Bulgarians consistently lack energy, determination and passion and are forced, trained and "educated" to avoid them in life.
5. A. If the answer is yes, in what sense? In our daily milieu there are people who allow themselves to be suppressed and have a free loving spirit, loyalty, and honesty.
5. A. Undisciplined behavior
5. A. Nonchalant.
5. A. Although I don't know such personalities myself, just that McMurphy is a more intelligent and existential type than the Bulgarians rebel of his scale.
5. A. He likes swearing and is selfish.
5. A. He swears a lot and doesn't obey the rules.
5. A. The only character who has the courage to oppose the system; that makes him unique
6. D. Egotist (in performance)
6. C and D. Yes, really he could be manipulative but I think his positive sides are many more; I listed some of them in the previous question.
6. A and D. A, but he is also a freewheeling person, who rarely follows the rules.
6. D. Wonderful and inspiring person with tragic destiny.
6. D. Just different from the rest.
6. D. His primary charm is attractiveness, unbridled and difficult to place in any context.
6. D. Good and bad sides, that show that he's crazy, but still a human being.
7. E. This play is very tragic and the ending made me very sad.
7. I find it thought-provoking.
8. E. The "flight" assumes an external viewpoint from which you can see things which otherwise would remain unseen. The cuckoo's nest is an allusion for the insane asylum.
8. E. The title is a play on the very idea of the production. The cuckoo's nest is the insane asylum; wild geese fly over it. I didn't find where otherwise to write my opinion, so I will write here. I have seen almost all of the Bulgarian stage, but for the first time I have a total favorite, I saw this production of 4 full hours, completely already 3 times! Wonderful acting, unbelievably touching and at the same time full of small things from life!
8. The title of the Play is as complicated and profound as the Play itself because the cuckoo does not make its own nest and nests its eggs in other bird's nests; when the young cuckoo birds hatch, they eliminate all competition for themselves. The main character of the Play was definitely and tragically so misplaced. But this does not tie with the biological/ornithological reality. Probably, if I had known

the children's verse and the play it accompanies, I would have better understood the title and only the title of the Play.
8. E. It is similar to B. in a way, but takes on a bigger meaning about going too far in into the system., "flying over": the cuckoo's nest—reference to McMurphy.
8. E. the poem is from the Bromden's childhood.
8. E. The audience peeps [on] the people who are insane.
8. E. McMurphy vs. nurse Rached (different life philosophies)
8. E. Cuckoo's Nest can refer to an asylum, but the whole title refers to other things also—McMurphy being different and how he ends up, Chief escaping, Billy dying…
8. B. And the flying over refers to the free spirit and soul which have nothing to do with sanity or insanity… even the more insane the more free you are from the restriction of society.
8. E. It refers to the patients—those who leave and the rest (who stay).
8. E. The cuckoos do not have nests. It's some impossibility conveyed in the title.
9. E. Because according to me he recognizes his own impossibility of taking part in decisions regarding his hospital.
9. A. …after mercifully killing the lobotomized McMurphy, Bromden fulfills the latter's escape plan as he felt ready to face the outside world he was shunning by staying inside the cuckoo's nest.
9. E. Chief Bromden decides to break out of the hospital in order to fulfill McMurphy's wish.
10. E. Listen
10. E. They are people who do need psychiatric help but definitely not of the type depicted in the play.
10. E. They should get help from institutions and society so that they can fit in society and live normal lives. The society should get used to the fact that these people are one of us and shouldn't treat them like they are different.
10. B. the answer in real life is obviously a bit more complicated than that, but the way the play presented some of the characters, one gets the feeling that the system is just crushing the individuals it doesn't know how to deal with.
10. E. Isn't it true that there are acutes who are not appropriate in society?
10. E. They need to regain their sanity.
10. E. They should be loved and taken care of in various ways, but mostly loved.
10. E. They have problems which can be solved by a shrink, not a psychiatrist.
10. E. They need help but this help needs to be provided within society, not outside it.

A.10 Table of Americans' Results for *Cuckoo's Nest* (8)

One Flew Over the Cuckoo's Nest	A/А	B/Б	C/В	D/Г	E/Д
1 Enjoy the play?	1	1	6	0	0
2 Understand it? (one between A and B, and one between B and C)	2	5	2	1	0
3 Theme? (Write-in themes below in "Comments")	4	1	0	0	0
4 Main characters American? Bulgarian?	1	3	0	4	0
5 Is McMurphy a Bulgarian personality?	5	2	1	XXXX	XXXX
6 McMurphy's personality?	0	3	4	1	XXXX
7 Funny?	1	1	4	2	0
8 Meaning of the title? (multiple answers chosen)	5	3	0	1	1
9 Why does Bromden break out?	4	4	0	0	0
10 What to do with the "acutes"?	2	3	0	0	2
11 Play change your view of treatment of acute mental patients?	0	2	1	2	2
12 Your age?	0	2	4	2	XXXX
13 Attend the	0	6	1	1	XXXX

theater?					
14 Your education?	0	0	1	7	XXXX
15 Your nationality?		8		XXXX	XXXX

Comments:
3. F. An examination of **authority** and how it can be used to suppress those under its control.
3. F. At what price freedom? The conflicting expectations of society.
3. F. Sexual repression, independence vs. a tyrant.
5. A. He seems to exaggerate some qualities that are stereotypically "Bulgarian male"—smoking brash, macho, anti-authority, work-adverse.
5. A. It played into the idea that Bulgarians have about male gender roles in the worst way…
5. B. Have not seen the same level of confidence in a Bulgarian.
5. B. Bulgarians, especially with mental problems, are not the "can do" sort of people.
5. C. I saw the play so long ago, my memory fails me…
5. A. Like Bai Ganyo
5. A. Rebellious
5. A. Interestingly, some mannerisms and coordination appeared more Bulgarian; however, he did handle the basketball pretty well! ☺
6. D. Overbearing, manipulative, but also looked fake. Deyan only motivated by ego, stardom.
7. A. …of course he its depressing mood as we progressed to the climax of the play…
8. E. The rhyme is also about the bird who puts its egg in the wrong nest; McMurphy is the wrong bird for this nest.
10. A. But not in *this* hospital.
10. E. Depends on the level and quality of care, having never visited a hospital for the insane. I'm not sure how much is exaggerated by literary accounts. I'd imagine that there's smoke where there's fire, and that these sorts of institutions generally do a disservice to their patients. But there are probably some good facilities too.
10. E. Everyone is individual, with treatment required for the patient's condition.
10. B. At least it was portrayed that way for Billy!
11. E. This is a "problem play" with a social message.

Other thoughts or comments?

The one issue I had with the play is that you do not understand the conflict between Nurse Ratched and McMurpy [but marked 2.B.]

An American director working in Sofia:
Wow, they missed the boat on this one! As a director myself, I think the director has a responsibility to tell the story first and add his "vision" second. Our job is primarily interpretive, so the burden for what is seen, heard and done on stage rests with us. When you mistreat a script as egregiously as Sasha Morfov did with this FOUR HOUR (!) production of Cuckoo's Nest, I don't consider that good directing. As a director, you must be able to examine and cull from your impulses and I don't think a broom dream ballet to open Act II was perhaps the wisest choice. Yes, there is humor in the piece, but it is humor that arises from a combination of the situation and the characters being trapped in a "booby hatch"; the characters are still able to find moments of humor in their daily lives. If you want to create something humorous look to the text for support. And I can pretty much guarantee you there's nothing in the script about dancing with brooms.

Additionally, the director has at his disposal the space and resources of the National Theatre. He can do (and has done) virtually anything. Instead of creating an oppressive, suffocating world for the characters to inhabit, he seems to have encouraged his scenographer to create a sleek open world...completely antithetical to the intention of the script. Had he simply lowered the amazing ductwork by 6 feet, he could've succeded in that respect.
Then again, that's my interpretation and not his. Unfortunately, I'm not quite sure what Mr. Morfov was trying to say. Other than " Look at me!"

From student of student directing, long-time resident of Bulgaria:
Deyan: It's all about him onstage. A ham and a huge ego, so longer an ensemble production. More competitive than under the socialists. Girls love him. When he takes his shorts off, one said, "He's hot." He shouts too much.

Other directors could have done the play better. Morfov "didn't give a shit." Bulgarian critics won't insult people like Morfov. Everyone is "covering his back." Morfov missed some rehearsals. (I saw about 10 of them.) Morfov did not spend much time with the actors. He made a few sharp, critical remarks. [Teddy Moskov is similarly caustic of his actors.] Morfov had no interest in choreography of the dance. This doesn't show the imagination of his great work of the

1990s. A technical disaster with the lighting and images. In the tableau with Bromden, he is out of the spotlight, which is wrong. There is also no proper rhythm or build-up.

Good questionnaire and thoroughly enjoyed the performance. The acting was superb in my opinion. Thanks!

A.11 Questionnaire for *Angels in America*

QUESTIONNAIRE

After viewing *Angels in America*, could you answer these questions? Circle the answers you agree with most.

1. Did you enjoy the play?
A. Very much. B. Somewhat. C. Hard to say. D. Not so much. E. Not at all.

2. Do you think you understood the play?
A. Very much. B. Somewhat. C. Hard to say. D. Not so much. E. Not at all.

3. What do you think is the theme of this play?
G. The callousness of American society and political leaders toward AIDS victims
H. The variety and humanity of the gay population
I. Fighting AIDS is more worthy of public attention and resources than battling cancer or other diseases
J. Gay men cannot be integrated in mainstream society because of their offensive behavior
K. I don't know
L. None of the above. The theme was:_____

4. Did the main characters seem more like Americans, or more like Bulgarians?
F. Very much like Americans. B. More like Americans. C. About the same. D. More like Bulgarians. E. Very much like Bulgarians.

5. Do the characters seem like possible or realistic Bulgarians you know?
D. Yes, very much. B. Somewhat. C. Hard to say. D. Not really. E. Not at all.

6. Did you find the play funny?
B. Yes, very funny. B. Yes, somewhat funny. C. Hard to say. D. Not very funny. E. Not funny at all

7. Were you moved by the characters' struggles and pain?
E. Yes, a lot. B. Yes, a bit. C. Hard to say. D. Not very much. E. Not at all
Why or why not?_____

8. The character of Roy M. Cohn is:
A. A rightwing lawyer closely aligned with Joseph McCarthy, an anti-Communist Senator
B. A bullying and ambitious lawyer with no real political influence
C. A successful New York lawyer with political ambitions
D. I don't know

9. The character of Ethel Rosenberg is:
A. Based on a real character who was executed for treason
B. Based on a real character who was an old friend of Roy Cohn
C. A fictional character
D. I don't know

10. Do you believe that homosexuality is:
A. A personal lifestyle choice
B. A product of an individual's inheritance
C. Something else
D. I don't know

11. Do you think that homosexual activity is:
A. Something that should be illegal
B. Immoral
C. Not sure
D. An acceptable lifestyle
E. A perfectly acceptable lifestyle

12. Did this play change your understanding or feelings about homosexuality?

A. Yes, very much. B. Yes, somewhat. C. Not sure. D. Not really. E. Not at all.

Please tell us a little about yourself:
13. Your age: A. Under 20. B. 20-35. C. 36-49. D. 50 and above

14. Your theater interest: A. I attend the theater rarely. B. I attend occasionally (once or more every 6 weeks). C. I attend frequently (once per month or more). D. I attend frequently *and* enjoy *avant garde,* absurdist, or similarly challenging theatrical works

15. Your education: A. Secondary or below. B. Some college. C. Bachelor's degree or equivalent. D. Some graduate school.

16. What is your nationality? Bulgarian: _____; American: _____; Other or dual (which?):_____

Other thoughts or comments?
Thank you!

A.12 Questionnaire for *Angels in America*, Bulgarian Language Version

ВЪПРОСНИК

След като гледахте постановката на *„Ангели в Америка"*, бихте ли отговорили на следните въпроси? Оградете с кръгче отговорите, с които сте съгласни:

16. Хареса ли ви пиесата?
    А. Да, много. Б. Да. В. Донякъде. Г. Не. Д. Никак.

17. Мислите ли, че разбрахте пиесата?
    А. Да, напълно. Б. Да. В. Донякъде. Г .Не. Д. Никак.

18. Каква е според вас темата на пиесата?
    А. Коравосърдечието на американското общество и на политическите лидери към жертвите на СПИН.
    Б. Многообразието и човечността на гей общността.
    В. Борбата със СПИН заслужава по-голямо обществено внимание и подкрепа от битката с рака или с други болести
    Г. Гей лицата не могат да бъдат интегрирани в общоприетата структура на обществото заради обидното си поведение.
    Д. Не зная
    Е. Никоя от посочените. Темата беше:
    _____

19. На кого приличат повече главните герои - на американци или на българи?
    А. Много приличат на американци. Б. Повече приличат на американци. В. Няма разлика. Г. Повече приличат на българи. Д. Много приличат на българи.

20. Приличат ли героите на евентуални или действителни българи, които познавате?

А. Да, много. Б. Донякъде. В. Трудно ми е да преценя. Г. Не. Д. Изобщо не приличат.

21. Намирате ли пиесата за забавна?
А. Да, за много забавна. Б. Донякъде. В. Трудно ми е да преценя е. Г. Не особено. Д. Изобщо не е забавна.

22. Трогнаха ли ви страданията и болката на героите?
А. Да, много. Б. Да, донякъде. В. Трудно ми е да преценя. Г. Не особено. Д. Ни най-малко.
Защо се трогнахте или не се трогнахте
_____

23. Образът на Рой Кон е:
А. Адвокат с десни убеждения подобно на сенатора антикомунист Джоузеф Маккарти. Б. Безочлив и амбициозен адвокат без реално политическо влияние. В. Преуспяващ нюйоркски адвокат с политически амбиции. Г. Не зная.   (А още няколко въпроса на следващата страница)

24. Образът на Етъл Роузънбърг е:
А. Изграден въз основа на реална личност, екзекутирана за държавна измяна. Б. Основан на реална личност, стара приятелка на Рой Кон. В. Измислен образ. Г. Не зная.

25. Вярвате ли, че хомосексуалността е:
А. Личен избор на начин на живот. Б. Резултат от генетично наследство. В. Нещо друго. Г. Не зная.

26. Намирате ли, че хомосексуалността:
А. Трябва да се преследва от закона. Б. Не е морална. В. Не съм сигурен какво е. Г. Приемлив начин на живот. Д. Съвсем приемлив начин на живот.

12. Промени ли пиесата мнението за или отношението ви към хомосексуалността?
А. Да, много. Б. Да, донакъде. В. Не съм сигурен. Г. Не съвсем. Д. Изобщо не.

Моля, напишете ни нещо за себе си:
13.   **Вашата възраст:**
   А. Под 20. **Б.** Между 20 и 35. **В.** Между 36 и 49. **Г.** На 50 или повече.

14. **Вашият интерес към театъра:**
   А. Рядко ходя на театър. **Б.** Ходя на театър от време на време (веднъж на 6 седмици или по-често). **В.** Често ходя на театър (веднъж месечно или по-често). **Г.** Често ходя на театър и харесвам авангардистки, абсурдистки или подобни провокативни театрални творби.

15. **Вашето образование:**
   А. Средно образование или по-ниско. **Б.** Колеж. **В.** Бакалавърска степен или нейният еквивалент. **Г.** По-висока степен.

16.   **Каква е вашата националност?**
   А. Българска. **Б.** Американска. **В.** Друга или двойна (каква?):_____.

Други мисли и коментари?

A.13 Table of Bulgarians' Results for *Angels in America* (36)

Angels in America	A/А	B/Б	C/В	D/Г	E/Д
1 Enjoy the play?	18	6	0	7	3
2 Understand it?	19	11	2	1	0
3 Theme? (includes multiple responses)	15	13	2	2	E: 0 F: 11
4 Main characters American? Bulgarian? (one multiple response)	4	22	8	2	1
5 Characters realistically Bulgarian?	3	12	9	11	0
6 Funny?	5	14	4	6	7
7 Were you moved?	11	13	2	6	6
8 Roy Cohn is:	17	4	7	7	XXX
9 Ethel Rosenberg is:	20	1	3	11	XXX
10 Homosexuality is: (includes multiple responses)	15	12	5	5	XXX
11 Homosexual activity is:	1	1	1	20	9
12 Change your understanding of homosexuality?	1	4	5	13	9
13 Your age?	1	20	4	11	XXX
14 Your theater interest?	6	11	10	10	XXX
15 Your education?	1	3	12	20	XXX
16 Your nationality?	36	0	0	XXX	XXX

NOTES
Final replies June, 2012.
Some respondents did not respond to all questions.

Respondents' Comments:

3. F. Love, and Pain, all in the context of Homosexuality.
3. F. It is difficult to outline one theme but for me the strongest one which somehow embraces all the thematic and ideological scores is the incompatibility between the subtlety, the nuanced, fine sensibility of the human psyche and the pragmatic paradigm of the society (strongly emphasized in the American society with all its conservative attitudes based on the philosophy of utilitarianism, rationalism and pragmatism); the incompatibility of the soul with the economy of the pragmatism—everything subordinated to the idea of production in a material and metaphoric sense (gay people are the perfect emblematic figure of non-productivity).
3. F. Everybody wants to be free, to do what he wants, but can't, because the society has taboos.
3. F. Aspects of gay concerns and how AIDS changed perceptions and stereotypes.
3. F. People can't be what they want to be.
3. F. Panoramic view of American society at the end of the American century.
3. F. This is a quite complex play whose range of themes encompasses aspects of all the above-mentioned statements.
3. F. The multiplicity of American culture.
3. F. None of the above. The theme was: Gay life, political hypocrisy, tolerance, and difference.
4. B. The problem is that they seem like nothing…what I mean is that the director has missed to find the clue why and how to adapt the American realities to the Bulgarian context, to transmit some universal meanings, to make a very contextualized interpretation…why this play now in Bulgaria—I missed the answer…)
4. "A" in terms of culture. Otherwise "C" because they epitomize universal social tensions and problematic areas.
5. D, but playing like Americans
5. The sick character [Prior] is the most realistic.
6. A. Ironic, sarcastic.
6. B. The wife [Harper] was funny.
6. It made me think and discuss the topic.
7. D. The play is staged in a very decorative external way so it is hard to really feel something, you rather observe and rationally approach the piece.

7. E. Director's problem.
7. E. Because the performance was deeply unprofessional.
7. A. Joe, LGBT – common to Bulgarians, a struggle with oneself, to live with a double standard, its pressures.
7. A. Joe.
7. B. I could have been in their shoes.
8. D. Wacko! A beast!
8. D. Boring. Not a real lawyer.
10. B. I think it is biologically determined.

11. E. (if it is a lifestyle then it could be a problem. I think it should be simply a modification of the sexual preferences and not particularly accompanied with a peculiar or extravagant lifestyle; it is a different sensitivity [sensibility?])
16. One dual Bulgarian-German.

"Other thoughts or comments?"
I just remember I did not like the set design but found the production itself a bit un-spirited. I mean of course we are not in the 80s USA. But if you know the play and its importance it felt like it was just run through by the actors. And I am a big admirer of Bertold Brecht and the Verfremdungseffekt. That was just not used properly.

I mostly forgot the details of the play; it's been a year already.

One should split down [separate?] the play and the production.

Themes: Cross-section of (US) society (humanity) at a certain historical period. Themes: Politics, AIDS, homosexuality, immigration, displacement, adaptation, love, betrayal, faith, religion, God; fear, courage, death, survival (at what cost), truth, minority issues, tolerance; heritage; choices; escapism (Harper, Roy), spiritual journey (Joe), super-ego vs. ego; self-revelation, etc.

Milk was more moving; it opened minds.

There are two many associations [?] in *Angels in America* and that is why I cannot mark only A, B, C, or D. This is as much a play about AIDS as it is about what you are ready to do and how much you are prepared to sacrifice in the name of your career, also for family values, drugs, etc.

Very interesting piece, especially with a very interesting sense of humor, which I personally liked very much. The topic is current, and certainly shows a different side and neglected side of this problem, which is relevant for everyone, regardless of age, sexuality or nationality.

For me, this play shows freedom of thought and freedom of the spirit of the people of the National Theatre. I was absolutely ecstatic after I watched it. I think it is disappointing that it s no longer being mounted, because it is instructive. One must accept what is, in order to be honest with oneself and others around oneself and especially to be responsible for one's health.

A.14 Questionnaire for *The Goat*

QUESTIONNAIRE

After viewing *The Goat, or Who is Sylvia?*, please circle the best responses to the following questions:

17. Did you enjoy the play?
A. Yes, very much. B. Yes. C. Somewhat. D. No. E. No, not at all.

18. Do you think you understood the play?
A. Yes, very much. B. Yes. C. Somewhat. D. No. E. No, not at all.

19. What do you think is the theme of this play?
M. How far contemporary society will break taboos and accept "deviant" behavior
N. The painfulness of loss (of sense of purpose, love, etc.)
O. Architecture is a less worthwhile profession than journalism
P. Martin indulges in bestiality as a form of hostility toward his wife Stevie
Q. I don't know
R. The theme was:_____

_____

20. Did the main characters seem more like Americans, or more like Bulgarians?
A. Very much like Americans.
B. More like Americans.
C. About the same.
D. More like Bulgarians.
E. Very much like Bulgarians.

21. Does the family seem like a possible or realistic Bulgarian family?
A. Yes, very much. B. Yes. C. Somewhat. D. No. E. No, not at all.

22. Did you find the play funny?

C. Yes, very funny. B. Yes. C. Somewhat. D. No. E. Not funny at all.

23. Albee subtitled the play, *Notes Toward a Definition of Tragedy*. Do you consider *The Goat* a tragedy?
A. Yes, very much. B. Yes. C. Somewhat, or don't know. D. No. E. No, not at all.
Why or why not?_____

24. Did the final appearance of Stevie with the bloody goat make sense to you?
A. Yes, very much. B. Yes. C. Somewhat, or don't know. D. No. E. No, not at all.
Why or why not?_____

25. Were you moved by the play?
A. Yes, very much. B. Yes. C. Somewhat. D. No. E. No, not at all.

A few more questions on the next page...

26. Did this play change your understanding or feelings about human sexuality?
A. Yes, very much. B. Yes. C. Somewhat, or not sure. D. No. E. No, not at all.

Please tell us a little about yourself:

27. My age: A. Under 20. B. 20-35. C. 36-49. D. 50 and above

28. A. I attend the theater rarely. B. I attend occasionally (once or more every 6 weeks). C. I attend frequently (once per month or more). D. I attend frequently *and* enjoy *avant garde*, absurdist, or similar challenging theatrical works

29. My education:
A. Secondary or below. B. Some college. C. Bachelor's degree or equivalent. D. Some or completed graduate school.

30. What is your nationality?
A. Bulgarian. B. American. C. Other or dual (which?):_____

Other thoughts or comments?

Thank you!

A.15 Questionnaire for *The Goat*, Bulgarian Language Version

ВЪПРОСНИК

След като гледахте „*Козата,или коя е Силвия?*", моля, отбележете вашите отговори на въпросите по-долу:

1. Хареса ли ви пиесата?
А. Да, много. Б. Да. В. Донякъде. Г. Не. Д. Не, никак.

2. Мислите ли, че разбрахте пиесата?
А. Да, до голяма степен. Б. Да. В. Донякъде. Г. Не. Д. Не, изобщо.

3. Каква според вас е основната идея на тази пиеса?
А. Доколко съвременното общество е склонно да престъпи табутата и да приеме поведение „извън общоприетото".
Б. Болката и страданието от загубата (на цел, любов, т.н.).
В. Архитектурата не е толкова стойностна професия, колкото журналистиката.
Г. Мартин се отдава на бруталността, за да изрази враждебността си към своята съпруга Стиви
Д. Не зная.
Е. Идеята е:
_____

4. На кого приличат повече главните герои - на американци или на българи?
А. Много приличат на американци. Б. Повече приличат на американци. В. Няма разлика. Г. Повече приличат на българи. Д. Много приличат на българи.

5. Семейството напомня ли на хипотетично или реално българско семейство?
А Да, много. Б. Да. В. Донякъде. Г. Не. Д. Не, никак.

6. Намирате ли пиесата за забавна?
А. Да, много забавна. Б. Да, забавна. В. Донякъде. Г. Не, не много забавна. Д. Изобщо не е забавна.

7. Подзаглавието, дадено на пиесата от Олби е „Бележки към дефиницията за трагедия". Намирате ли „Козата" за трагедия?
А. Да, много. Б. Да. В. Донякъде или не зная. Г. Не. Д. Не, никак.
Защо или защо не? _____

8. Разбрахте ли смисъла в появата на Стиви с окървавената коза в края на спектакъла?
А. Да, много. Б. Да. В. Донякъде или не зная. Г. Не. Д. Не, никак.
Защо или защо не? _____

9. Успяхте ли развълнуван от играта?
А. Да, много. Б. Да. В. Донякъде. Г. Не. Д. Не, никак.
Защо или защо не? _____

10. Пиесата промени ли мнението или нагласата ви относно човешката сексуалност?
А. Да, много. Б. Да. В. Донякъде или не съм сигурен. Г. Не. Д. Не, никак.

Моля, разкажете ни накратко за себе си:

11. Вашата възраст:
А. Под 20. Б. Между 20 и 35. В. Между 36 и 49. Г. На 50 или повече.

12. Вашият интерес към театъра:
А. Рядко ходя на театър. Б. Ходя на театър от време на време (веднъж на 6 седмици или по-често). В. Често ходя на театър (веднъж месечно или по-често). Г. Често ходя на театър и харесвам авангардистки, абсурдистки или подобни провокативни театрални творби.

13. Вашето образование:
А. Средно или по-ниско. Б. Колеж. В. Бакалавърска степен или нейният еквивалент. Г. Някакво или завършено висше образование.

14. Каква е вашата националност?
А. Българска. Б. Американска. В. Друга или двойна каква?):_____

Други мисли и коментари?

A.16 Table of Bulgarians' Results for *The Goat* (61)

The Goat	A/А	B/Б	C/В	D/Г	E/Д
1 Enjoy the play?	39	17	4	1	1
2 Understand it?	35	20	6	0	0
3 Theme?	39	18	0	1	12*
4 Main characters American? Bulgarian?	8	21	26	1	1
5 Family realistically Bulgarian? 6	1	14	24	15	6
6 Funny?	7	17	14	13	8
7 A tragedy?	6	38	9	6	1
8 Final scene make sense?	10	33	10	2	2
9 Moved?	29	19	7	2	2
10 Feelings about human sexuality?	1	3	5	19	6
11 Your age?	0	25	5	5	XXX
12 Attend the theater?	0	7	17	12	XXX
13 Your education?	1	1	17	14	XXX
14 Your nationality?	61	0	0	0	0

Comments:
*This box represents F/E, "The theme is:" No one chose E/Д, "I don't know."
Some say not a tragedy, but Stevie makes sense and very moved.
May not understand what tragedy means (though all educated).
Theme A has first name on the ballot advantage (but belied by later responses)
I discarded one questionnaire that had "A" for all responses (inconsistent).
1. One double entry.

3. Several respondents provided multiple answers, including "F."
4. One wrote in "none."

Comments by respondents:
2. I suppose.
3. F. Egoism in all its dimensions (for and against).
3. F. Many-layered.
3. F. Everything which is love has meaning.
3. Does no one understand…
3. F. In my view, it is not to alienate other but to talk to each other.
3. F. Whether sleeping with a goat makes you a pervert.
3. A & F. In my view, Loneliness and misunderstanding, even when one is among those people who are closest.
3. F. The alienation of the members (wife, husband, children) of the modern family.
3. F. The craziness of human life and the paradox of human happiness.
3. A, B. as in the dynamic between husband and wife and party A, as well, how society treats those that are outside the norm.
3. F. Alienation. People are unable to relate to each other through their souls. Relationships are a mere façade, a display of happiness, an "add" of perfection in a pragmatic purposeful society orientated towards success and considering happiness an equivalent of social recognition, where everything is about appearance. The genuine deep demands of the soul remain unanswered and they take surprising, unacceptable (for the social environment) turns.
3. F. Some kind of a combination of unhappiness, alienation, and disorientation.
4. C. Except in their reactions.
4. None of the above. Seemingly and incredibly—Americans, but in fact, no; the characters transcend borders and stigmas.
5. B. No matter the nationality. It's a problem everywhere.
7. It is a skillfully balanced tragedy on the edge of humor, sarcasm and irony.
7. B. I think that Albee had in mind a tragedy in the classical Greek sense. In this sense, my answer is "Yes."
7. B. This is a contemporary tragedy, which, in contrast to the Aristotelian, occurs and survives with people, and has no consequences for society.
7. B. It's structured as a tragedy (and even the Greek word for tragedy has to do with goats).
7. B. Because the family as a basic unit of society has lost its significance.

7. B. The tragedy is because the architect didn't understand his basic problem. Because he has already devoted himself to his weakness and can't fix it at all.
7. D. I cannot find it a tragedy because despite everything the finale is "open." That is, one has the following opportunities to recreate oneself and give meaning to his relations with family and friends. Everything changes, so there is no final tragic note.
7. A. Tragedy is hidden somewhere in happiness.
7. B. A tragedy for the main character.
7. B. Because there is a classical structure, especially in the destiny of the protagonist.
7. B. Because most of the time was dedicated to underlying, subliminal messages which were or were not transmitted to reach the participants. And these messages always bore some sort of "tragic shadow," of something unsaid.
7. B. It is the tragedy of the contemporary society in terms of human relations.
7. C. It shows the limits of a person and the society.
7. B. Because it depicts a person who suffers from some kind of a combination of unhappiness, alienation, and disorientation.
7. D. It's a result, not a cause.
7. B. Despite that the subject of the play is considered to be what is weird and what is normal, the story of being in love with a goat seems to me a way to escape the reality, your own life, the [more] different the better.
7. B. Tragedy, according to the classical definition in dramatic arts.
8. [No answered chosen, just:] I suppose.
8. B. The reaction of society against pathology or sickness. The feeling of love is exclusive, and does not tolerate competition.
8. B. It is the natural end of her logic.
8. B. Because this is the only way an ideal marriage can end. ☺
8. It was an easy solution, much easier than the context suggested. Killing this instance of the problem would not remove the quintessential problem at all.
8. B. In my view, society is understood in all possible ways. [?]
8. B. Broken illusion. (2)
8. B. A hopeless attempt to erase what her husband did. (2)
8. A. The ending is unavoidable.
8. B. It fits.
8. B. Because in order to break free, you have to 'massacre' the remnants of the past—just like Stevie does with the 'intruder' Sylvia.
8. B. Because it is a display of a sweeping tragic experience which has its culmination in this apocalyptic gesture. And because this is a play which narrates through external spectacular signs and this is one of them. It comes naturally in the dramaturgical logic of the play –

as a chain of spectacular appearances (the perfection of the family, the striking goat motive, etc.)
8. C. I guess it shows how hurt she was after her husband's "affair" but it was a little bit too much for me.
8. D. I have no such recollection of the final scene (namely a bloody goat), but it was some time ago that I saw the play.
8. E. I didn't believe it.
8. B. Fantasy ends, bloody, cruel reality is back.
8. I can only guess.
9. B. Because of the very good actors. (2)
9. A. Catharsis! There is no other word.
9. The actors are appealing. The text is very good, and Yavor Gardev is one of the best Bulgarian theatrical directors.
9. Good actors.
9. A. Because it is a natural and naturalistic to a painful degree and because it is suspiciously close to reality.

General comments:
This is a difficult text to present to any audience, no doubt. But the excellent performance of the 2 major characters proved the critiques of the so-called conservative Bulgarian audience wrong. It was these two actors who hindered the easy stigmatizing response to the problem. It was all about the sense of loss (of the dearly loved one, of the connection and devotion) outside the normal context. Of course, it was a plot taken to absurdity but it was shown with so much humane emotion. One wouldn't think that Sylvia was less than a human before he described her nature as a goat, or would we?

Albee will remain for me as the author of *Who's Afraid of Virginia Woolf?* and *Three Tall Women*, which I consider as two of the greatest plays in the history of theater and humanity.

I saw the play 3 years ago on the premier date I think, so my memories are not so clear. The actors were great, the setting amazing. Yavor Gardev is very good director I respect very much and I was also very excited to see Albee in person.
Honestly the story didn't catch me that much, somehow [it] was something away from me. Maybe I am a liberate [liberal?] person and nothing considered as "scandal" impressed me that much. Yes, a lot of things we don't talk about do exist. Anyone the right o search for his happiness, there is just a simple rule – that [one] should not hurt the others. I am really curious to see the play again and see if I will discover new things.

The Goat is a more important play for Bulgarian society than for American society because Bulgaria has a problem with accepting differences (the other) and homosexuals for the most part. In Bulgaria to be gay=to be sick, to have an incurable disease! The play is important because it takes a step beyond that and talk about sodomy, thus "legitimizing" the rights of homosexuals. I think it is important, because it shows that there are worse "beasts."

A.17 Table of Americans' Results for *The Goat* (4)

The Goat	A/А	B/Б	C/В	D/Г	E/Д
1 Enjoy the play?	3	1	0	0	0
2 Understand it?	1	2	1	0	0
3 Theme?	2	3	0	0	0
4 Main characters American? Bulgarian?	1	2	1	0	0
5 Family realistically Bulgarian?	0	2	1	0	1
6 Funny?	1	2	1	0	0
7 A tragedy?	1	0	3	0	0
8 Final scene make sense?	1	3	0	0	0
9 Moved?	1	3	0	0	0
10 Feelings about human sexuality?	0	0	1	3	0
11 Your age?	0	0	2	2	XXX
12 Attend the theater?	1	0	2	1	XXX
13 Your education?	0	0	0	4	XXX
14 Your nationality? 4	0	3	1	0	XXX

Comments: Two Americans claim dual nationality (but the American understanding significant).
3. Two answers chosen.
7. C: It's a tragicomedy. C: Not exactly because the absurdity of the "crime" left a level of irony that made it not quite tragic.
8. B. It seems like one possible if unexpected reaction.
Great work of Yavor Gardev and Mihail Bilalov.
Excellently acted, extraordinarily important social questions.
The Goat is not your typical play. It is somewhat challenging.
12/30/11

A.18 List of Interviewees and Dates of Interviews

(All interviews are in person unless otherwise indicated)

Albee, Edward, author, *The Goat.* Telephone interview, 4 October 2011.
Anichkin, Haralampi, translator, *The Goat.* 11 November 2010, 17 December 2011.
Bilalov, Mihail, actor, National Theatre, *The Goat.* 31 October 2011.
Blush, Robert, American Theatre Director. 19 February 2011.
Bojidarova, Ina, Head of Theatre Department, Ministry of Culture, Bulgaria. 8 June 2012, 13 July 2012.
Campbell, Herb, psychiatrist. September, 2010.
Chanev, Rysi, actor, National Theatre, *One Flew Over the Cuckoo's Nest.* 16 January 2012.
Coigney, Martha, Director Emerita, International Theatre Institute of the U.S. 16 November 2010.
Delchev, Nedyalko, Professor of Theatre, American University of Bulgaria. 29 January 2012; 11 March 2012.
Demireva, Milena, Marketing Manager, National Theatre. Frequent consultations.
Evtimov, Ivan, Assistant Professor of Sociology (retired), New Bulgarian University. 7 July 2012.
Gardev, Javor, Director, National Theatre. *The Goat.* 5 July 2012.
Gencheva, Aksinia, Bulgarian gay rights activist. 10 February 2011.
Kaukov, Petar. Director, Nikolay Binev Youth Theatre. 4 December 2011.
Krastanov, Boyko, actor, National Theatre, *Angels in America.* 17 June 2012.
Kushner, Tony, playwright, *Angels in America.* Phone interview. May, 2012.
Landzhev, Ivan, TV scriptwriter and poet. 24 September 2011, 5 April 2012.
Morfov, Alexander, director, National Theatre, *One Flew Over the Cuckoo's Nest.* 16 January 2012.
Moskov, Stefan "Teddy", director, National Theatre. 20 March 2011.
Petrova, Lina, Dramaturge, Theatre Sofia. 8 June 2012.

Radachkova, Rosalia, Dramaturge, National Theatre, *Angels in America.* 22 May 2012.

Sankowich, Lee, Theatre Director, Zephyr Theater, Los Angeles, *One Flew Over the Cuckoo's Nest.* Telephone interview, 18 January 2012, and email exchanges.

Shpatova, Desi, Theatre Director, National Theatre, *Angels in America.* 29 October 2011.

Shurbanov, Alexander, translator, poet, literary critic, professor of literature, Sofia University (retired). December, 2010.

Slavova, Kornelia, Associate Professor, Dept. of English and American Studies, Sofia University. December, 2011, 13 July 2012.

Tabakova, Vyara, Actor, National Theatre, *One Flew Over the Cuckoo's Nest.* 16 March 2012.

Tancheva, Kornelia, Director, Two Humanities Libraries and Instructor in Drama, Cornell University. January 2011.

Tomova-Stankeva, Galina, Translator, *Angels in America.* 26 November 2011.

Turan, Kenneth, author and stage and screen critic, *The Los Angeles Times.* November, 2011.

Vandov, Nikola, Dramaturge, Satiric Theatre, Sofia. 18 May 2012.

Vasev, Pavel, Managing Director, National Theatre. June, 2011.

Volitzer, Eva, Professor of Acting, New Bulgarian University. 11 May 2012.

Volkoff, Andrew, Guest Theatre Director, Binev Youth Theatre. 4 December 2011

Zaharieva, Nadia S., Director, Programs for Art and Culture, America for Bulgaria. Foundation. Phone interview, October, 2011.

A.19 National Theatre Flyer for *The Goat*

A.20 Positive Reviews at National Theatre, Sofia

Cuckoo's Nest	86% (12/14)
Angels in America	56.5% (13/23)
The Goat	100% (14/14)

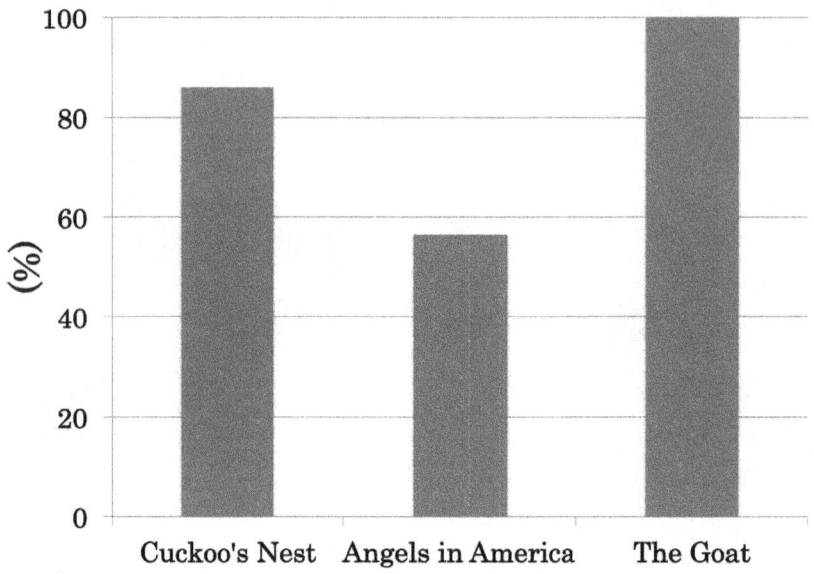

A.21 Comparative Success of the Plays in Sofia

	Enjoyed it?	Understood it?	Funny?	Characters are more Americans?
Cuckoo's Nest	98% (36/37)	100% (40/40)	56.5% (13/23)	74% (17/23)
Angels in America	70.5% (24/34)	97% (30/31)	59% (19/32)	89% (26/29)
The Goat	96.5% (56/58)	100% (55/55)	77% (24/31)	93.5% (29/31)

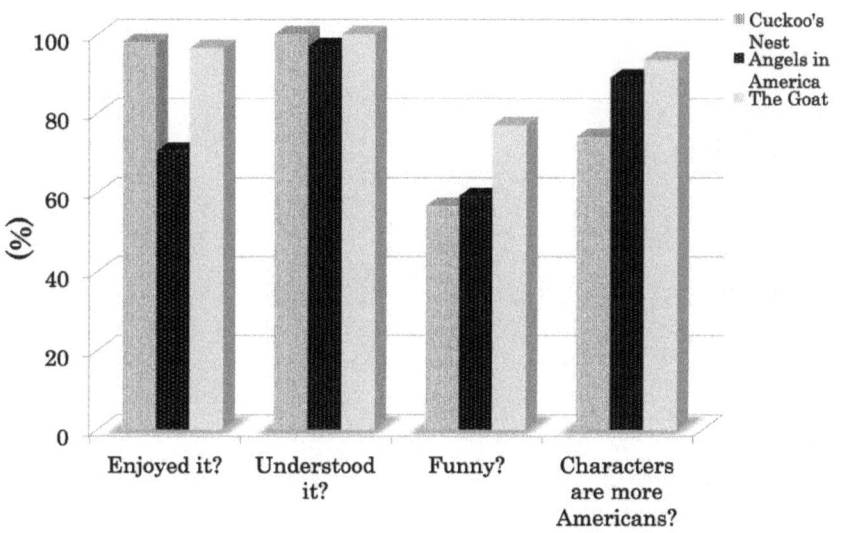

INDEX

adapter, 4, 21, 22, 27, 28, 29, 42, 217, 219
AIDS, 47, 63,75, 133-134, 147, 152, 155, 158
Albee, Edward, 1, 14, 21, 23, 26, 28, 30, 31,45, 46, 59, 60, 61, 64, 65, 66, 165-185, 181, 182, 183, 184, 185, 186, 187-189, 191, 193, 196, 198, 195, 197, 198, 199, 200, 201, 202, 203, 205-206, 208, 210, 211, 213, 216, 217, 218, 221-224
Allen, Woody, 167
Altman, Robert, 55
America for Bulgaria Foundation, 1, 13, 88, 136,138
American Repertory Theatre, 24
American Theatre, 59, 112
Angels in America, 1,14,19, 25,47,54-56,59-60,63-65, 67,72,75,76, 96,105,108, 131,164,201-202,210-212, 220, 252, 277,280,283
Anichkin, Haralampi, 66, 169-170, 172, 187-188, 190, 197, 200, 205
audience reception, 32, 36, 44, 49-50, 63, 68, 219

Bai Ganyo, 103, 123, 127
Bakalova, Ani, 88
Barker, Clive, 35
Beckett, Samuel, 24, 171, 174, 206
Benjamin, Walter, 56,144
Bennett, Susan, 33, 37-42, 44, 47, 49, 51, 97, 220
Bent, 75
Berani, Leo, 150
Berend, Ivan, 7-8, 10
Bharucha, Rastom, 36
Bilalov, Mihail, 169, 170, 172, 197, 208
Billy (character), 79, 82, 85, 165-166, 189
Boal, Augusto, 42
Boys in the Band, The, 74
Brantley, Ben, 100,108
Brecht, Bertolt, 37, 40-42, 43, 56, 59.97,131,146-147, 210-211
Broadway League, 211-212
Bromden (character) 77, 83, 92,103,107, 117,120,128
Brook, Peter,18, 34, 37, 42,4 4-45, 204-205, 208, 209
Brustein, Robert, 43, 131-132,143, 149, 176, 187

Cage, Nicholas, 87
Cage aux Folles, La, 75
Carlson, Marvin, 18, 22-23, 34, 44-46, 58, 209
Carriere, Jean-Claude, 21
Cats, 40
Césaire, Aimé, 20, 48, 53, 204

Chanev, Rusi, 93, 94, 99
Chekhov, Anton, 31-32, 137, 217
Clurman, Harold, 57
Cohn, Roy (character), 133-134, 143-144, 147, 160
Cote, David, 53, 112
creative adaptation, 20, 24, 26, 28-30
Crowley, Mark, 74
Crucible, The, 24, 39
cultural adaptation, 18, 42
Danailov, Stefan, 138
Death of a Salesman, 23, 26
Decheva, Violeta, 151, 186, 187, 191
DeDanan, Mary, 77, 82
Delchev, Nedyalko, 99
Devane, William, 84
Dimitrov, Simeon, 88
Dobchev, Ivan, 12
Donkey Show, The, 29, 40
Donkov, Deyan, 88-89, 101-102, 118-119, 125-128, 212
Douglas, Kirk, 77, 82, 84, 100
Drama Desk Award, 132, 167

Eason, Laura, 27-28, 48, 203
Eclipse, 89
Eco, Umberto, 39
Elefterov, Elefteri, 88
Elenov, Dimitar, 88
Eliot, T. S., 166
Evtimov, Ivan, 211-213
Eyring, Teresa, 59
faithful adaptation, 19, 22, 30, 128, 209, 218-219
Feral, Josette, 44
Fierstein, Harvey, 75
Fo, Dario, 38, 65-66

Forman, Milos, 81, 83, 85, 88, 99, 103, 107, 109, 112, 174
Fortier, Mark, 24, 34, 40, 43, 48, 204
free adaptation, 21-23, 77, 89, 122, 170, 205, 218-219
Freire, Paulo, 42

Gardev, Yavor, 45, 47, 169, 180, 182, 191, 196-197, 200, 203, 209, 214, 217-220
Gay (homosexual), 47, 55, 59, 63, 67-76, 131, 136 139, 142, 150, 151, 154-156, 158-159, 161, 163, 183-190, 215, 218, 220,
Geis, Deborah, R., 33, 54-55, 131, 146, 147, 150
Gencheva, Aksinia, 163
Goat, The, 1, 14, 28, 65-67, 42, 63, 105, 165-198, 200, 202-203, 206, 208, 210-212, 214, 220
Goethe, J. W., 20, 26
Gurney, A. R., 167

Hamilton, Linda, 75
Hamlet, 30, 128, 209, 218-219
Herman, Jerry, 78
Hitchens, Chris, 53, 131
Hollywood, 47, 87, 213
homosexual, 64, 68, 70-76, 92, 133-134, 138-139, 147, 154-155, 160-161, 143, 166-167, 181, 184, 189, 214
humor, 129, 159-160, 180, 187, 195, 197
hybrid, 22-23, 30, 220

identity-based theories, 33
Igov, Svetlozar, 9
Iser, Wolfgang, 33
Ivan Vazov National Theatre, 4, 7,9,10-13,21,27,46,50-51,55-56,87-89,92,94,101,113,115, 129,136-138,141,146,154-157, 162, 168-169, 173, 187, 194, 196-197, 199-200, 212-215, 220

Jauss, Hans Robert, 33

Kabuki, 207

Karamazov,Vladimir,156
Kaufmann, Moisés, 60
Kaukov, Peter, 111,114
Kazan, Elia,17,21-22, 29,57-58,90,217
Kerouac, Jack, 78
Kesey, Ken, 1,45,59,63, 81, 83-86, 89, 95-99, 103-109, 112-114, 120-122, 127, 129, 202
Kinney, Terry, 86-87, 90-91, 97, 110, 113
Kiss of the Spider Woman, 75

Kortenska, Miraslava 12, 141, 155-157
Kovacheva, Miroslava, 74
Kramer, Larry, 75
Kruger, Steven F., 33,54
Kurkinski, Marius, 155
Kushner, Tony, 1, 45.55, 60, 66-67, 75, 88, 131, 140, 142-151, 153-155, 158,160-163, 195-196

Lahr, John, 22, 146
Laramie Project,The, 62

Man of La Mancha, 80
McCarthy, Joseph, 39, 133
McCarthyism, 39,158,218
McMurphy (character), 47, 77,83-84,87-89,92-94,98,100-105,110,114-115,119-120,123-124,126-127,174,196,202
McNally, Terence, 75
Melville, Herman, 214
Meyerhold, Vsevolod, 136
Mihalkov, Georgi, 139,142
Miller, Arthur, 1, 22, 30-31, 39-40, 53, 57, 179, 205,
mise en scene, 30, 31
Misfits, The, 53

307

Mladenova, Margarita, 12
Mnouchkine, Ariane, 18, 34, 37, 44, 46
Morfov, Alexander, 81, 88-90, 92-93, 96-99, 102-103, 107, 111-112, 114, 116-117, 119, 121-122, 125-126, 129-130, 186
Moskov, Teddy, 22, 67, 180

Nabokov, Vladimir, 216
NATFA (National Academy of Theatre and Film Arts), 9, 168, 194
Nedelcheva, Mariana, 88-89
Nenchev, Daniel, 89
Nenkova, Ralitsa, 170, 190
Neuschaefer, Anne, 20, 26
Nichols, Mike, 55, 135
Nicholson, Jack, 17-18, 200
Nikolova, Iskra, 17-18, 200
Normal Heart, The, 75

obscenity, 66, 140-142, 155, 173
Odets, Clifford, 58
One Flew Over the Cuckoo's Nest, 1, 5, 14, 22, 46-47, 51, 59, 63-64, 68, 77-130, 135, 162, 174, 186, 200, 202-203, 211, 214
Outcasts, 87

Papp, Joseph, 95
Pavis, Patrice, 18, 20, 21,
Pirandello, Luigi, 183, 206
Poiret, Jean, 75
poll, 68-69, 121-123, 142
post-colonial theories, 34, 58
Pride Parade, 71-74, 163
Pulitzer Prize, 64, 111, 132, 167

questionnaire, 2, 5, 49-50, 56-58, 67, 115-130, 157-164, 192-198, 211-212

Ratched [character], 68, 77, 79-81, 87-88, 91-92, 100, 104-105, 109, 114-115, 117, 202
reader-response theory, 33
Reagan, Ronald, 49, 134, 147 160
Reza, Yasmina, 169, 185
Ritz, The, 75
Rodichkova, Rosalia, 136
Rosenberg, Ethel, 134, 144, 147, 160
Ruehl, Mercedes, 166, 177
Salza i Smyah, 13, 88, 138-139
Sankowich, Lee, 81-84, 87, 90, 96, 101-102, 106-108, 121, 211
Schiller, Friedrich, 20, 26
Shakespeare, William, 19, 20, 26, 28, 32, 38-39, 47, 49, 93-95, 140, 204-205
Sherman, Martin, 75

Shpatova, Desi, 96, 136-138, 141-143,145,154-155,157-158,201,204,214-215,218-219
Shuralov, Venelin, 145,153
Shurbanov, Alexander, 19,
Siegel, Lee, 149
Signature Theatre, 140
Simon, John, 77, 176, 179-180, 187
Sinise, Gary, 86, 91, 101, 105, 109
Sisters Rosensweig, The, 75
Slater, Christian, 87
Slavova, Kornelia, 56
Sontag, Susan, 38,124
Soviet Union, 25-26,35,98
Spasov, Krasimir, 88
Stanchev, Stancho, 88
Stefanov, Vasil, 12
Steppenwolf Theater, 86, 99, 108-109
Stoev, Galin, 12
Stonewall Inn, 60, 71
Sylvia, 167

Tabakova, Vyara, 104,118,129
Takayama, Akira, 41
target culture, 17, 18, 23, 35, 123,199-200,208,219
Tasca, Valeria, 65-66
theatre of protest, 43
Tomova-Stankova, Galina, 137, 141-144,146

Tony Award, 64-65,75,86,132,167
Torch Song Trilogy , 75, 86
translation, 18, 21-22, 31, 206-207,216
Tsaneva, Milena, 9
Turan, Kenneth, 96

untranslatable, 4, 218

Vandov, Nikola, 10, 12
Vasev, Pavel, 11, 136-137, 141
Vazrazhdane, 7
Velkova, Boyka, 69,170,177
Verne, Jules, 48
View from the Bridge, A , 25, 29-30
Vitez, Antoine, 8, 20, 26-27, 47,200,204
Vogel, Paula, 139
Volitzer, Eva, 154
Vrangova, Reni,115

Wasserman, Dale, 1, 61, 77-82, 84-85, 88-89, 91-92 100,103-108, 110-118, 121
Webber, Andrew Lloyd, 44
Werfel, Franz, 21
Who's Afraid of Virginia Woolf? 64, 177
Williams, Amb. Steve, 72

Yanov, Marin, 88

Zaharieva, Nadia S., 14, 138-139

www.ingramcontent.com/pod-product-compliance
Lightning Source LLC
Chambersburg PA
CBHW032034150426
43194CB00006B/270